2015 | THE LITTLE DATA BOOK ON FINANCIAL INCLUSION

WORLD BANK GROUP

Contents

Acknowledgments

The Little Data Book on Financial Inclusion 2015 was prepared by the Finance and Private Sector Development Team of the Development Research Group, by a team led by Leora Klapper under the supervision of Asli Demirguc-Kunt and comprising Saniya Ansar, Rafael Alonso Arenas, Dorothe Singer, and Peter Van Oudheusden. The work was carried out under the management of Kaushik Basu. The team is grateful to Douglas Randall for helping with the questionnaire design and to Massimo Cirasino, Mario Guadamillas, Jake Kendall, Douglas Pearce, Maria Soledad Martinez Peria, Peer Stein, Rodger Voorhies, and World Bank colleagues in the Development Economics Vice Presidency and the Financial Markets Global Practice as well as staff at the Bill & Melinda Gates Foundation, the Better than Cash Alliance, the Consultative Group to Assist the Poor, the GSM Association, and the Office of the United Nations Secretary-General's Special Advocate for Inclusive Finance for Development (UNSGSA) for providing substantive comments at different stages of the project. The team is also grateful for the excellent survey execution and related support provided by Gallup, Inc. under the direction of Jon Clifton.

The team is especially grateful to the Bill & Melinda Gates Foundation for providing financial support making the collection and dissemination of the data possible.

Production of this volume was managed by the Development Data Group, under the direction of Haishan Fu. Substantial contributions were made by Shelley Fu, Mohammed Omar Hadi, and William Prince, with additional support provided by Azita Amjadi, Leila Rafei, Jomo Tariku, and Sup Lee. The book's design was done by Jomo Tariku based on an original design by Communications Development Incorporated. Typesetting was done by Barton Matheson Willse & Worthington. Staff from the World Bank's Publishing and Knowledge division oversaw publication and dissemination of the book, and Alison Strong provided editorial assistance.

The reference citation for the 2014 Global Financial Inclusion (Global Findex) data provided in this book is as follows:

Demirguc-Kunt, Asli, Leora Klapper, Dorothe Singer, and Peter Van Oudheusden. 2015. "The Global Findex Database 2014: Measuring Financial Inclusion around the World." Policy Research Working Paper 7255, World Bank, Washington, DC.

Foreword

By Her Majesty Queen Máxima of the Netherlands
UN Secretary-General's Special Advocate for Inclusive Finance for Development
and Honorary Patron of the G20's Global Partnership for Financial Inclusion

Among those of us committed to advancing access to financial services for the poor, the release in 2012 of the Global Financial Inclusion Database—the Global Findex—represented the beginning of a new stage in our work. Before the Global Findex, we lacked reliable information about a number of vital questions, even the number of people we hoped to reach. Thanks to the collective efforts that resulted in that first Global Findex, a picture of financial inclusion emerged that transformed thinking, planning, and action. That first benchmark version provided high-quality data from 148 countries around the world on how adults were saving, borrowing, making payments, and managing risk.

Now, three years later, I am extremely pleased that a new, second edition of the Global Findex Database has been released, providing us with a wealth of data that look in even more depth at where financial inclusion stands and how far we have come. This landmark study allows policy makers, regulators, researchers, businesspeople, advocates, the development community, and others to see what is working, what isn't, and how we can focus our efforts most effectively to reach the goal of universal financial inclusion.

The main message embedded in the new Global Findex is tremendously encouraging. In a short time, financial inclusion has made great progress worldwide. The hard work being done around the globe is making a difference. Three years ago, 2.5 billion adults struggled to get by without formal financial services; that figure has dropped by 20 percent, to 2 billion. That means that 62 percent of adults now have an account at a financial institution or through a mobile device, up from 51 percent in 2011. This increase is being felt among the poorest populations in most regions, driven by mobile technology, digital payments, reforms that encourage correspondent banking, and relaxed customer identification.

This second edition of *The Little Data Book on Financial Inclusion* contains a wealth of detailed information from the Global Findex Database, with lessons for public- and private-sector stakeholders working in this field. Those countries that have established supportive and competitive environments, policies that encourage innovation, and national financial inclusion strategies are making great strides.

Thanks to the spread of mobile phones, mobile money is playing a crucial role in extending financial services to the underserved. In Sub-Saharan Africa, 12 percent of adults—64 million people—now use a mobile money account, helping to boost the number of financial account holders in the region to 34 percent, up from 24 percent in 2011.

Other regions are making progress in different ways. Digital banking and payrolls paid directly into bank accounts are exploding in Latin America

Foreword

and savings are growing in East Asia. Digital government payments made into accounts for pensions or cash transfers are driving a strong increase in financial inclusion globally—more than 400 million adults are part of such a system.

While the mere existence of bank accounts does not result in financial inclusion, this year's Global Findex delivers surprising and encouraging data showing widespread, high-quality account use. More than 65 percent of account users in East Asia, the Pacific, and Sub-Saharan Africa report using their accounts at least three times a month to send or receive money, pay bills, or save for the future.

Progress has been significant, but challenges remain. So far we have not seen a closing, or even a narrowing, of the gender gap. Account ownership has increased for both women and men, but an 8 to 10 percentage-point difference persists across income groups in developing economies. We must redouble our efforts to reach gender parity.

Global Findex findings point to several promising opportunities. One hundred million government employees around the world are still paid in cash; moving those payment programs into digital deposits represents a relatively straightforward step to increase financial inclusion. Strengthening market competition has been shown to drive demonstrable progress, as have supportive policies that encourage innovation. The success of these approaches underlines that governments are on the right track.

Over the past decade, financial inclusion has risen as a global priority. Extending affordable, effective, and client-centric financial services, especially to low-income populations and small businesses, creates countless opportunities—allowing individuals to put food on the table, afford better health care, start a business, or save for retirement. For governments, financial inclusion lays the foundation for stability and inclusive economic growth. For the global community, financial inclusion helps accelerate economic progress, reduce extreme poverty, and build shared prosperity.

Our current understanding of financial inclusion would not have been possible without the Global Findex Database. I am proud to have been involved in the discussions and decision making that led to the Findex, and I thank the World Bank Development Research Group, supported by the Bill & Melinda Gates Foundation, for its vital work on this groundbreaking initiative. I encourage governments, businesses, advocates, and others to study the data in this publication and put it to good use as we work together toward our shared goal of universal financial inclusion.

Introduction

The Little Data Book on Financial Inclusion 2015 is a pocket edition of the Global Financial Inclusion (Global Findex) database published in 2015. This data set represents a second round of data collection, following the initial round three years earlier. The database provides nationally representative, demand-side data on access to and use of accounts, credit, payments, and savings by adults age 15 and above in 143 economies. In addition, new indicators measure people's ability to manage risk. This book presents data for selected indicators by country, region, and income group. For some indicators the data are disaggregated by age, gender, income level, and rural residence.

This publication is part of the Global Findex suite of products, available both online and in hard copy. To learn more and to access the most recent version of the database, visit the Financial Inclusion topic page on the World Bank's Open Data Platform (http://datatopics.worldbank.org/financialinclusion) or the Global Findex web page (http://www.worldbank.org/globalfindex). The microdata files for each country are available in the World Bank's Microdata Catalog (http://microdata.worldbank.org).

Launched in 2011, the Global Findex database is housed in the World Bank's Development Research Group and funded by a 10-year grant from the Bill & Melinda Gates Foundation. It is the first public global database of demand-side indicators to track the financial lives of individuals over time. Covering a range of topics, the data can be used to create a more complete picture of how people save, borrow, manage risk, and send and receive money. The expanded 2014 Global Findex survey questionnaire included more nuanced questions on the use of mobile technology to pay bills, receive wages and government payments, and send money to and receive it from family living elsewhere. The data were collected by Gallup, Inc. over the 2014 calendar year alongside the Gallup World Poll survey. This book and the accompanying research have the potential to aid policy makers, the private sector, and the entire global community as together we shape an effective environment for shared prosperity.

Data notes

The data in this book are for 2014 unless otherwise noted in the tables or the glossary.

- Except for the regional grouping *High income: OECD*, regional aggregates include data for low- and middle-income economies only.

- Figures in italics are for years or periods other than those specified.

Symbols used:

    ..   indicates that data are not available or that aggregates cannot be calculated because of missing data.

0 or 0.0   indicates zero or a value small enough that it would round to zero at the number of decimal places displayed.

    $ indicates current U.S. dollars.

Data are shown for 143 economies. The term *country* (used interchangeably with *economy*) does not imply political independence or official recognition by the World Bank but refers to any economy for which the authorities report separate social or economic statistics.

Regional tables

The country composition of regions as used in this book is based on the World Bank's analytical regions and may differ from common geographic usage.

East Asia and Pacific

Cambodia, China, Indonesia, Lao People's Democratic Republic,[1] Malaysia, Mongolia, Myanmar,[2] Philippines, Thailand, Vietnam

Europe and Central Asia

Albania, Armenia, Azerbaijan, Belarus, Bosnia and Herzegovina, Bulgaria, Georgia, Hungary, Kazakhstan, Kosovo, Kyrgyz Republic, former Yugoslav Republic of Macedonia, Moldova, Montenegro, Romania, Serbia, Tajikistan, Turkey, Turkmenistan, Ukraine, Uzbekistan

High income: OECD

Australia, Austria, Belgium, Canada, Chile, Czech Republic, Denmark, Estonia, Finland, France, Germany, Greece, Ireland, Israel, Italy, Japan, Republic of Korea, Luxembourg, Netherlands, New Zealand, Norway,[2] Poland, Portugal, Slovak Republic, Slovenia, Spain, Sweden, Switzerland,[2] United Kingdom, United States

Latin America and the Caribbean

Argentina, Belize,[2] Bolivia, Brazil, Colombia, Costa Rica, Dominican Republic, Ecuador, El Salvador, Guatemala, Haiti, Honduras, Jamaica, Mexico, Nicaragua, Panama, Peru, República Bolivariana de Venezuela

Middle East

Djibouti,[1] Arab Republic of Egypt, Iraq, Jordan, Lebanon, West Bank and Gaza, Republic of Yemen

South Asia

Afghanistan, Bangladesh, Bhutan,[2] India, Nepal, Pakistan, Sri Lanka

Sub-Saharan Africa

Angola, Benin, Botswana, Burkina Faso, Burundi, Cameroon, Chad, Comoros,[1] Democratic Republic of Congo, Republic of Congo, Côte d'Ivoire,[2] Ethiopia,[2] Gabon, Ghana, Guinea, Kenya, Lesotho,[1] Liberia,[1] Madagascar,[2] Malawi, Mali, Mauritania, Mauritius, Namibia,[2] Niger, Nigeria, Rwanda, Senegal, Sierra Leone, Somalia,[2] South Africa, Sudan, Swaziland,[1] Tanzania, Togo, Uganda, Zambia, Zimbabwe

[1] Included in 2011 data only.
[2] Included in 2014 data only.

World

Population, age 15+ (millions)	**5,231.2**	GNI per capita ($)	**10,683**

Account (% age 15+)
All adults	61.5
Women	58.1
Adults belonging to the poorest 40%	54.0
Young adults (% ages 15-24)	46.3
Adults living in rural areas	56.7

Financial Institution Account (% age 15+)
All adults	60.7
All adults, 2011	50.6

Mobile Account (% age 15+)
All adults	2.0

Access to Financial Institution Account (% age 15+)
Has debit card	40.1
Has debit card, 2011	30.5
ATM is the main mode of withdrawal (% with an account)	..
ATM is the main mode of withdrawal (% with an account), 2011	48.3

Use of Account in the Past Year (% age 15+)
Used an account to receive wages	17.7
Used an account to receive government transfers	8.2
Used a financial institution account to pay utility bills	16.7

Other Digital Payments in the Past Year (% age 15+)
Used a debit card to make payments	23.2
Used a credit card to make payments	15.1
Used the Internet to pay bills or make purchases	16.6

Domestic Remittances in the Past Year (% age 15+)
Sent remittances	..
Sent remittances via a financial institution (% senders)	..
Sent remittances via a mobile phone (% senders)	..
Sent remittances via a money transfer operator (% senders)	..
Received remittances	..
Received remittances via a financial institution (% recipients)	..
Received remittances via a mobile phone (% recipients)	..
Received remittances via a money transfer operator (% recipients)	..

Savings in the Past Year (% age 15+)
Saved at a financial institution	27.4
Saved at a financial institution, 2011	22.6
Saved using a savings club or person outside the family	..
Saved any money	56.5
Saved for old age	23.9
Saved for a farm or business	13.8
Saved for education or school fees	22.3

Credit in the Past Year (% age 15+)
Borrowed from a financial institution	10.7
Borrowed from a financial institution, 2011	9.1
Borrowed from family or friends	26.2
Borrowed from a private informal lender	4.6
Borrowed any money	42.4
Borrowed for a farm or business	7.1
Borrowed for education or school fees	7.7
Outstanding mortgage at a financial institution	10.4

East Asia & Pacific

Population, age 15+ (millions)	**1,584.3**	GNI per capita ($)	**5,536**

Account (% age 15+)
All adults	69.0
Women	67.0
Adults belonging to the poorest 40%	60.9
Young adults (% ages 15–24)	60.7
Adults living in rural areas	64.5

Financial Institution Account (% age 15+)
All adults	68.8
All adults, 2011	55.1

Mobile Account (% age 15+)
All adults	0.4

Access to Financial Institution Account (% age 15+)
Has debit card	42.9
Has debit card, 2011	34.7
ATM is the main mode of withdrawal (% with an account)	53.3
ATM is the main mode of withdrawal (% with an account), 2011	37.0

Use of Account in the Past Year (% age 15+)
Used an account to receive wages	15.1
Used an account to receive government transfers	8.1
Used a financial institution account to pay utility bills	11.8

Other Digital Payments in the Past Year (% age 15+)
Used a debit card to make payments	14.8
Used a credit card to make payments	10.8
Used the Internet to pay bills or make purchases	15.6

Domestic Remittances in the Past Year (% age 15+)
Sent remittances	16.6
Sent remittances via a financial institution (% senders)	36.9
Sent remittances via a mobile phone (% senders)	8.7
Sent remittances via a money transfer operator (% senders)	18.5
Received remittances	20.6
Received remittances via a financial institution (% recipients)	29.0
Received remittances via a mobile phone (% recipients)	4.9
Received remittances via a money transfer operator (% recipients)	15.8

Savings in the Past Year (% age 15+)
Saved at a financial institution	36.5
Saved at a financial institution, 2011	28.5
Saved using a savings club or person outside the family	6.0
Saved any money	71.0
Saved for old age	36.5
Saved for a farm or business	21.3
Saved for education or school fees	30.7

Credit in the Past Year (% age 15+)
Borrowed from a financial institution	11.0
Borrowed from a financial institution, 2011	8.6
Borrowed from family or friends	28.3
Borrowed from a private informal lender	2.5
Borrowed any money	41.2
Borrowed for a farm or business	8.3
Borrowed for education or school fees	7.1
Outstanding mortgage at a financial institution	8.0

Europe & Central Asia

Population, age 15+ (millions)	**211.7**	GNI per capita ($)	**7,114**

Account (% age 15+)

All adults	51.4
Women	47.4
Adults belonging to the poorest 40%	44.2
Young adults (% ages 15–24)	35.6
Adults living in rural areas	45.7

Financial Institution Account (% age 15+)

All adults	51.4
All adults, 2011	43.3

Mobile Account (% age 15+)

All adults	0.3

Access to Financial Institution Account (% age 15+)

Has debit card	36.9
Has debit card, 2011	36.4
ATM is the main mode of withdrawal (% with an account)	66.7
ATM is the main mode of withdrawal (% with an account), 2011	72.5

Use of Account in the Past Year (% age 15+)

Used an account to receive wages	22.5
Used an account to receive government transfers	7.3
Used a financial institution account to pay utility bills	12.5

Other Digital Payments in the Past Year (% age 15+)

Used a debit card to make payments	22.9
Used a credit card to make payments	14.9
Used the Internet to pay bills or make purchases	11.9

Domestic Remittances in the Past Year (% age 15+)

Sent remittances	12.9
Sent remittances via a financial institution (% senders)	31.5
Sent remittances via a mobile phone (% senders)	2.5
Sent remittances via a money transfer operator (% senders)	11.8
Received remittances	15.5
Received remittances via a financial institution (% recipients)	22.1
Received remittances via a mobile phone (% recipients)	1.0
Received remittances via a money transfer operator (% recipients)	15.6

Savings in the Past Year (% age 15+)

Saved at a financial institution	8.4
Saved at a financial institution, 2011	4.9
Saved using a savings club or person outside the family	6.6
Saved any money	38.5
Saved for old age	11.8
Saved for a farm or business	5.1
Saved for education or school fees	12.1

Credit in the Past Year (% age 15+)

Borrowed from a financial institution	12.4
Borrowed from a financial institution, 2011	7.8
Borrowed from family or friends	23.6
Borrowed from a private informal lender	2.1
Borrowed any money	39.5
Borrowed for a farm or business	2.8
Borrowed for education or school fees	6.2
Outstanding mortgage at a financial institution	10.2

High income: OECD

Population, age 15+ (millions)	**877.7**	GNI per capita ($)	**44,479**

Account (% age 15+)
All adults	94.0
Women	93.8
Adults belonging to the poorest 40%	90.6
Young adults (% ages 15–24)	84.1
Adults living in rural areas	93.8

Financial Institution Account (% age 15+)
All adults	94.0
All adults, 2011	90.0

Mobile Account (% age 15+)
All adults	..

Access to Financial Institution Account (% age 15+)
Has debit card	79.7
Has debit card, 2011	61.9
ATM is the main mode of withdrawal (% with an account)	..
ATM is the main mode of withdrawal (% with an account), 2011	68.5

Use of Account in the Past Year (% age 15+)
Used an account to receive wages	44.3
Used an account to receive government transfers	17.2
Used a financial institution account to pay utility bills	61.1

Other Digital Payments in the Past Year (% age 15+)
Used a debit card to make payments	65.3
Used a credit card to make payments	46.7
Used the Internet to pay bills or make purchases	54.1

Domestic Remittances in the Past Year (% age 15+)
Sent remittances	..
Sent remittances via a financial institution (% senders)	..
Sent remittances via a mobile phone (% senders)	..
Sent remittances via a money transfer operator (% senders)	..
Received remittances	..
Received remittances via a financial institution (% recipients)	..
Received remittances via a mobile phone (% recipients)	..
Received remittances via a money transfer operator (% recipients)	..

Savings in the Past Year (% age 15+)
Saved at a financial institution	51.6
Saved at a financial institution, 2011	45.3
Saved using a savings club or person outside the family	..
Saved any money	70.8
Saved for old age	39.7
Saved for a farm or business	9.0
Saved for education or school fees	25.0

Credit in the Past Year (% age 15+)
Borrowed from a financial institution	18.4
Borrowed from a financial institution, 2011	14.2
Borrowed from family or friends	14.9
Borrowed from a private informal lender	0.9
Borrowed any money	39.8
Borrowed for a farm or business	2.6
Borrowed for education or school fees	5.6
Outstanding mortgage at a financial institution	26.1

Latin America & Caribbean

Population, age 15+ (millions)	**428.2**	GNI per capita ($)	**9,542**

Account (% age 15+)

All adults	51.4
Women	48.6
Adults belonging to the poorest 40%	41.2
Young adults (% ages 15–24)	37.4
Adults living in rural areas	46.0

Financial Institution Account (% age 15+)

All adults	51.1
All adults, 2011	39.3

Mobile Account (% age 15+)

All adults	1.7

Access to Financial Institution Account (% age 15+)

Has debit card	40.4
Has debit card, 2011	28.9
ATM is the main mode of withdrawal (% with an account)	71.1
ATM is the main mode of withdrawal (% with an account), 2011	57.0

Use of Account in the Past Year (% age 15+)

Used an account to receive wages	18.0
Used an account to receive government transfers	9.0
Used a financial institution account to pay utility bills	6.3

Other Digital Payments in the Past Year (% age 15+)

Used a debit card to make payments	27.7
Used a credit card to make payments	18.0
Used the Internet to pay bills or make purchases	6.9

Domestic Remittances in the Past Year (% age 15+)

Sent remittances	9.5
Sent remittances via a financial institution (% senders)	..
Sent remittances via a mobile phone (% senders)	..
Sent remittances via a money transfer operator (% senders)	..
Received remittances	11.3
Received remittances via a financial institution (% recipients)	34.2
Received remittances via a mobile phone (% recipients)	4.3
Received remittances via a money transfer operator (% recipients)	28.4

Savings in the Past Year (% age 15+)

Saved at a financial institution	13.5
Saved at a financial institution, 2011	9.6
Saved using a savings club or person outside the family	7.9
Saved any money	40.6
Saved for old age	10.6
Saved for a farm or business	10.6
Saved for education or school fees	17.2

Credit in the Past Year (% age 15+)

Borrowed from a financial institution	11.3
Borrowed from a financial institution, 2011	7.9
Borrowed from family or friends	13.5
Borrowed from a private informal lender	4.7
Borrowed any money	32.7
Borrowed for a farm or business	6.1
Borrowed for education or school fees	8.3
Outstanding mortgage at a financial institution	9.6

Middle East

Population, age 15+ (millions)	**102.0**	GNI per capita ($)	**3,894**

Account (% age 15+)
All adults	14.2
Women	9.2
Adults belonging to the poorest 40%	7.3
Young adults (% ages 15-24)	7.6
Adults living in rural areas	10.7

Financial Institution Account (% age 15+)
All adults	14.0
All adults, 2011	10.9

Mobile Account (% age 15+)
All adults	0.7

Access to Financial Institution Account (% age 15+)
Has debit card	8.5
Has debit card, 2011	5.5
ATM is the main mode of withdrawal (% with an account)	44.9
ATM is the main mode of withdrawal (% with an account), 2011	42.4

Use of Account in the Past Year (% age 15+)
Used an account to receive wages	3.3
Used an account to receive government transfers	0.9
Used a financial institution account to pay utility bills	0.2

Other Digital Payments in the Past Year (% age 15+)
Used a debit card to make payments	3.3
Used a credit card to make payments	1.5
Used the Internet to pay bills or make purchases	2.1

Domestic Remittances in the Past Year (% age 15+)
Sent remittances	9.3
Sent remittances via a financial institution (% senders)	..
Sent remittances via a mobile phone (% senders)	..
Sent remittances via a money transfer operator (% senders)	..
Received remittances	11.3
Received remittances via a financial institution (% recipients)	9.8
Received remittances via a mobile phone (% recipients)	0.2
Received remittances via a money transfer operator (% recipients)	15.6

Savings in the Past Year (% age 15+)
Saved at a financial institution	4.0
Saved at a financial institution, 2011	2.7
Saved using a savings club or person outside the family	11.5
Saved any money	30.5
Saved for old age	5.0
Saved for a farm or business	5.1
Saved for education or school fees	9.1

Credit in the Past Year (% age 15+)
Borrowed from a financial institution	5.6
Borrowed from a financial institution, 2011	4.4
Borrowed from family or friends	30.7
Borrowed from a private informal lender	7.9
Borrowed any money	45.7
Borrowed for a farm or business	4.2
Borrowed for education or school fees	8.2
Outstanding mortgage at a financial institution	6.2

South Asia

Population, age 15+ (millions)	**1,168.6**	GNI per capita ($)	**1,483**

Account (% age 15+)

All adults	46.4
Women	37.4
Adults belonging to the poorest 40%	38.1
Young adults (% ages 15–24)	36.7
Adults living in rural areas	43.5

Financial Institution Account (% age 15+)

All adults	45.5
All adults, 2011	32.3

Mobile Account (% age 15+)

All adults	2.6

Access to Financial Institution Account (% age 15+)

Has debit card	18.0
Has debit card, 2011	7.2
ATM is the main mode of withdrawal (% with an account)	31.1
ATM is the main mode of withdrawal (% with an account), 2011	16.9

Use of Account in the Past Year (% age 15+)

Used an account to receive wages	3.5
Used an account to receive government transfers	3.1
Used a financial institution account to pay utility bills	2.7

Other Digital Payments in the Past Year (% age 15+)

Used a debit card to make payments	8.5
Used a credit card to make payments	2.6
Used the Internet to pay bills or make purchases	1.2

Domestic Remittances in the Past Year (% age 15+)

Sent remittances	10.7
Sent remittances via a financial institution (% senders)	20.1
Sent remittances via a mobile phone (% senders)	7.7
Sent remittances via a money transfer operator (% senders)	13.7
Received remittances	12.2
Received remittances via a financial institution (% recipients)	15.8
Received remittances via a mobile phone (% recipients)	4.7
Received remittances via a money transfer operator (% recipients)	9.8

Savings in the Past Year (% age 15+)

Saved at a financial institution	12.7
Saved at a financial institution, 2011	11.1
Saved using a savings club or person outside the family	8.8
Saved any money	36.2
Saved for old age	9.1
Saved for a farm or business	7.3
Saved for education or school fees	14.6

Credit in the Past Year (% age 15+)

Borrowed from a financial institution	6.4
Borrowed from a financial institution, 2011	8.7
Borrowed from family or friends	31.4
Borrowed from a private informal lender	10.9
Borrowed any money	46.7
Borrowed for a farm or business	8.6
Borrowed for education or school fees	8.9
Outstanding mortgage at a financial institution	3.8

Sub-Saharan Africa

Population, age 15+ (millions)	**533.1**	GNI per capita ($)	**1,686**

Account (% age 15+)
All adults	34.2
Women	29.9
Adults belonging to the poorest 40%	24.6
Young adults (% ages 15–24)	25.9
Adults living in rural areas	29.2

Financial Institution Account (% age 15+)
All adults	28.9
All adults, 2011	23.9

Mobile Account (% age 15+)
All adults	11.5

Access to Financial Institution Account (% age 15+)
Has debit card	17.9
Has debit card, 2011	15.0
ATM is the main mode of withdrawal (% with an account)	53.8
ATM is the main mode of withdrawal (% with an account), 2011	51.7

Use of Account in the Past Year (% age 15+)
Used an account to receive wages	7.3
Used an account to receive government transfers	3.8
Used a financial institution account to pay utility bills	2.8

Other Digital Payments in the Past Year (% age 15+)
Used a debit card to make payments	8.7
Used a credit card to make payments	1.9
Used the Internet to pay bills or make purchases	2.4

Domestic Remittances in the Past Year (% age 15+)
Sent remittances	28.7
Sent remittances via a financial institution (% senders)	31.0
Sent remittances via a mobile phone (% senders)	30.8
Sent remittances via a money transfer operator (% senders)	21.0
Received remittances	37.2
Received remittances via a financial institution (% recipients)	26.6
Received remittances via a mobile phone (% recipients)	27.6
Received remittances via a money transfer operator (% recipients)	22.1

Savings in the Past Year (% age 15+)
Saved at a financial institution	15.9
Saved at a financial institution, 2011	14.3
Saved using a savings club or person outside the family	23.9
Saved any money	59.6
Saved for old age	9.8
Saved for a farm or business	22.7
Saved for education or school fees	22.9

Credit in the Past Year (% age 15+)
Borrowed from a financial institution	6.3
Borrowed from a financial institution, 2011	4.8
Borrowed from family or friends	41.9
Borrowed from a private informal lender	4.7
Borrowed any money	54.5
Borrowed for a farm or business	12.8
Borrowed for education or school fees	12.3
Outstanding mortgage at a financial institution	5.2

Income group tables

The World Bank's main criterion for classifying economies for operational and analytical purposes is gross national income (GNI) per capita. Each economy for which data are presented in this book is classified as low income, middle income, or high income based on its GNI per capita in 2013. Low- and middle-income economies are sometimes referred to as developing economies. The use of the term is convenient; it is not intended to imply that all economies in the group are experiencing similar development or that other economies have reached a preferred or final stage of development. Classification by income does not necessarily reflect development status. Income classifications of economies remain fixed over the course of the World Bank's fiscal year (ending on June 30) regardless of any revisions during the year to their income per capita data.

Low-income economies are those with a GNI per capita of $1,045 or less in 2013.

Middle-income economies are those with a GNI per capita of more than $1,045 but less than $12,746. Lower-middle-income and upper-middle-income economies are separated at a GNI per capita of $4,125.

High-income economies are those with a GNI per capita of $12,746 or more.

Euro area includes the member states of the Economic and Monetary Union of the European Union that had adopted the euro as their currency when the surveys took place: Austria, Belgium, Cyprus, Estonia, Finland, France, Germany, Greece, Ireland, Italy, Latvia, Luxembourg, Malta, the Netherlands, Portugal, Slovak Republic, Slovenia, and Spain.

Low income

Population, age 15+ (millions)	**516.2**	GNI per capita ($)	**728**

Account (% age 15+)

All adults	27.5
Women	23.9
Adults belonging to the poorest 40%	19.4
Young adults (% ages 15–24)	20.2
Adults living in rural areas	24.8

Financial Institution Account (% age 15+)

All adults	22.3
All adults, 2011	21.1

Mobile Account (% age 15+)

All adults	10.0

Access to Financial Institution Account (% age 15+)

Has debit card	6.6
Has debit card, 2011	6.3
ATM is the main mode of withdrawal (% with an account)	20.2
ATM is the main mode of withdrawal (% with an account), 2011	19.7

Use of Account in the Past Year (% age 15+)

Used an account to receive wages	3.2
Used an account to receive government transfers	1.0
Used a financial institution account to pay utility bills	0.9

Other Digital Payments in the Past Year (% age 15+)

Used a debit card to make payments	2.1
Used a credit card to make payments	0.6
Used the Internet to pay bills or make purchases	1.2

Domestic Remittances in the Past Year (% age 15+)

Sent remittances	18.3
Sent remittances via a financial institution (% senders)	15.4
Sent remittances via a mobile phone (% senders)	42.8
Sent remittances via a money transfer operator (% senders)	14.1
Received remittances	25.6
Received remittances via a financial institution (% recipients)	13.0
Received remittances via a mobile phone (% recipients)	33.8
Received remittances via a money transfer operator (% recipients)	14.8

Savings in the Past Year (% age 15+)

Saved at a financial institution	9.9
Saved at a financial institution, 2011	11.5
Saved using a savings club or person outside the family	16.3
Saved any money	46.5
Saved for old age	8.3
Saved for a farm or business	16.7
Saved for education or school fees	16.6

Credit in the Past Year (% age 15+)

Borrowed from a financial institution	8.6
Borrowed from a financial institution, 2011	11.7
Borrowed from family or friends	34.9
Borrowed from a private informal lender	6.5
Borrowed any money	52.5
Borrowed for a farm or business	12.2
Borrowed for education or school fees	10.9
Outstanding mortgage at a financial institution	4.1

Middle income

Population, age 15+ (millions)	**3,650.4**	GNI per capita ($)	**4,754**

Account (% age 15+)
All adults	57.6
Women	52.9
Adults belonging to the poorest 40%	49.1
Young adults (% ages 15–24)	44.9
Adults living in rural areas	53.8

Financial Institution Account (% age 15+)
All adults	57.1
All adults, 2011	43.3

Mobile Account (% age 15+)
All adults	1.5

Access to Financial Institution Account (% age 15+)
Has debit card	34.4
Has debit card, 2011	24.6
ATM is the main mode of withdrawal (% with an account)	51.2
ATM is the main mode of withdrawal (% with an account), 2011	38.1

Use of Account in the Past Year (% age 15+)
Used an account to receive wages	12.2
Used an account to receive government transfers	6.7
Used a financial institution account to pay utility bills	8.1

Other Digital Payments in the Past Year (% age 15+)
Used a debit card to make payments	15.1
Used a credit card to make payments	9.0
Used the Internet to pay bills or make purchases	9.4

Domestic Remittances in the Past Year (% age 15+)
Sent remittances	14.8
Sent remittances via a financial institution (% senders)	34.4
Sent remittances via a mobile phone (% senders)	8.3
Sent remittances via a money transfer operator (% senders)	19.0
Received remittances	17.8
Received remittances via a financial institution (% recipients)	28.0
Received remittances via a mobile phone (% recipients)	5.7
Received remittances via a money transfer operator (% recipients)	17.3

Savings in the Past Year (% age 15+)
Saved at a financial institution	24.1
Saved at a financial institution, 2011	18.2
Saved using a savings club or person outside the family	8.4
Saved any money	54.7
Saved for old age	22.2
Saved for a farm or business	14.9
Saved for education or school fees	22.9

Credit in the Past Year (% age 15+)
Borrowed from a financial institution	9.1
Borrowed from a financial institution, 2011	7.6
Borrowed from family or friends	28.3
Borrowed from a private informal lender	5.3
Borrowed any money	42.2
Borrowed for a farm or business	7.8
Borrowed for education or school fees	8.0
Outstanding mortgage at a financial institution	7.0

Lower middle income

Population, age 15+ (millions)	**1,759.1**	GNI per capita ($)	**2,074**

Account (% age 15+)
All adults	42.7
Women	36.3
Adults belonging to the poorest 40%	33.2
Young adults (% ages 15–24)	34.7
Adults living in rural areas	40.0

Financial Institution Account (% age 15+)
All adults	41.8
All adults, 2011	28.7

Mobile Account (% age 15+)
All adults	2.5

Access to Financial Institution Account (% age 15+)
Has debit card	21.2
Has debit card, 2011	10.1
ATM is the main mode of withdrawal (% with an account)	42.4
ATM is the main mode of withdrawal (% with an account), 2011	28.1

Use of Account in the Past Year (% age 15+)
Used an account to receive wages	5.6
Used an account to receive government transfers	3.3
Used a financial institution account to pay utility bills	3.1

Other Digital Payments in the Past Year (% age 15+)
Used a debit card to make payments	9.6
Used a credit card to make payments	2.8
Used the Internet to pay bills or make purchases	2.6

Domestic Remittances in the Past Year (% age 15+)
Sent remittances	14.2
Sent remittances via a financial institution (% senders)	30.9
Sent remittances via a mobile phone (% senders)	7.7
Sent remittances via a money transfer operator (% senders)	18.3
Received remittances	17.8
Received remittances via a financial institution (% recipients)	26.0
Received remittances via a mobile phone (% recipients)	5.7
Received remittances via a money transfer operator (% recipients)	16.6

Savings in the Past Year (% age 15+)
Saved at a financial institution	14.8
Saved at a financial institution, 2011	11.1
Saved using a savings club or person outside the family	12.4
Saved any money	45.6
Saved for old age	12.6
Saved for a farm or business	11.8
Saved for education or school fees	20.0

Credit in the Past Year (% age 15+)
Borrowed from a financial institution	7.5
Borrowed from a financial institution, 2011	7.3
Borrowed from family or friends	33.1
Borrowed from a private informal lender	8.5
Borrowed any money	47.4
Borrowed for a farm or business	9.2
Borrowed for education or school fees	10.1
Outstanding mortgage at a financial institution	4.7

Upper middle income

Population, age 15+ (millions)	**1,891.3**	GNI per capita ($)	**7,604**

Account (% age 15+)
All adults	70.5
Women	67.3
Adults belonging to the poorest 40%	62.7
Young adults (% ages 15-24)	58.1
Adults living in rural areas	68.8

Financial Institution Account (% age 15+)
All adults	70.4
All adults, 2011	57.4

Mobile Account (% age 15+)
All adults	0.7

Access to Financial Institution Account (% age 15+)
Has debit card	45.9
Has debit card, 2011	38.5
ATM is the main mode of withdrawal (% with an account)	55.7
ATM is the main mode of withdrawal (% with an account), 2011	42.8

Use of Account in the Past Year (% age 15+)
Used an account to receive wages	18.1
Used an account to receive government transfers	9.6
Used a financial institution account to pay utility bills	12.3

Other Digital Payments in the Past Year (% age 15+)
Used a debit card to make payments	19.9
Used a credit card to make payments	14.4
Used the Internet to pay bills or make purchases	15.3

Domestic Remittances in the Past Year (% age 15+)
Sent remittances	15.4
Sent remittances via a financial institution (% senders)	37.2
Sent remittances via a mobile phone (% senders)	8.8
Sent remittances via a money transfer operator (% senders)	19.7
Received remittances	17.8
Received remittances via a financial institution (% recipients)	29.8
Received remittances via a mobile phone (% recipients)	5.6
Received remittances via a money transfer operator (% recipients)	17.9

Savings in the Past Year (% age 15+)
Saved at a financial institution	32.2
Saved at a financial institution, 2011	25.1
Saved using a savings club or person outside the family	4.9
Saved any money	62.7
Saved for old age	30.6
Saved for a farm or business	17.6
Saved for education or school fees	25.4

Credit in the Past Year (% age 15+)
Borrowed from a financial institution	10.4
Borrowed from a financial institution, 2011	7.9
Borrowed from family or friends	24.0
Borrowed from a private informal lender	2.6
Borrowed any money	37.7
Borrowed for a farm or business	6.6
Borrowed for education or school fees	6.1
Outstanding mortgage at a financial institution	9.1

Low & middle income

Population, age 15+ (millions)	**4,166.6**	GNI per capita ($)	**4,168**

Account (% age 15+)
All adults	54.1
Women	49.6
Adults belonging to the poorest 40%	45.7
Young adults (% ages 15–24)	41.0
Adults living in rural areas	49.5

Financial Institution Account (% age 15+)
All adults	53.1
All adults, 2011	41.3

Mobile Account (% age 15+)
All adults	2.5

Access to Financial Institution Account (% age 15+)
Has debit card	31.2
Has debit card, 2011	22.9
ATM is the main mode of withdrawal (% with an account)	49.7
ATM is the main mode of withdrawal (% with an account), 2011	37.1

Use of Account in the Past Year (% age 15+)
Used an account to receive wages	11.2
Used an account to receive government transfers	6.0
Used a financial institution account to pay utility bills	7.2

Other Digital Payments in the Past Year (% age 15+)
Used a debit card to make payments	13.6
Used a credit card to make payments	8.1
Used the Internet to pay bills or make purchases	8.4

Domestic Remittances in the Past Year (% age 15+)
Sent remittances	15.2
Sent remittances via a financial institution (% senders)	31.8
Sent remittances via a mobile phone (% senders)	13.0
Sent remittances via a money transfer operator (% senders)	18.4
Received remittances	18.7
Received remittances via a financial institution (% recipients)	25.7
Received remittances via a mobile phone (% recipients)	10.1
Received remittances via a money transfer operator (% recipients)	16.9

Savings in the Past Year (% age 15+)
Saved at a financial institution	22.5
Saved at a financial institution, 2011	17.6
Saved using a savings club or person outside the family	9.3
Saved any money	53.8
Saved for old age	20.6
Saved for a farm or business	15.1
Saved for education or school fees	22.1

Credit in the Past Year (% age 15+)
Borrowed from a financial institution	9.0
Borrowed from a financial institution, 2011	8.0
Borrowed from family or friends	29.0
Borrowed from a private informal lender	5.5
Borrowed any money	43.4
Borrowed for a farm or business	8.3
Borrowed for education or school fees	8.3
Outstanding mortgage at a financial institution	6.7

High income

Population, age 15+ (millions)	**1,064.6**	GNI per capita ($)	**39,812**

Account (% age 15+)

All adults	90.6
Women	90.5
Adults belonging to the poorest 40%	86.9
Young adults (% ages 15–24)	79.7
Adults living in rural areas	90.2

Financial Institution Account (% age 15+)

All adults	90.6
All adults, 2011	84.8

Mobile Account (% age 15+)

All adults	..

Access to Financial Institution Account (% age 15+)

Has debit card	75.1
Has debit card, 2011	58.4
ATM is the main mode of withdrawal (% with an account)	..
ATM is the main mode of withdrawal (% with an account), 2011	68.5

Use of Account in the Past Year (% age 15+)

Used an account to receive wages	43.2
Used an account to receive government transfers	16.7
Used a financial institution account to pay utility bills	54.2

Other Digital Payments in the Past Year (% age 15+)

Used a debit card to make payments	61.1
Used a credit card to make payments	43.0
Used the Internet to pay bills or make purchases	48.9

Domestic Remittances in the Past Year (% age 15+)

Sent remittances	..
Sent remittances via a financial institution (% senders)	..
Sent remittances via a mobile phone (% senders)	..
Sent remittances via a money transfer operator (% senders)	..
Received remittances	..
Received remittances via a financial institution (% recipients)	..
Received remittances via a mobile phone (% recipients)	..
Received remittances via a money transfer operator (% recipients)	..

Savings in the Past Year (% age 15+)

Saved at a financial institution	46.7
Saved at a financial institution, 2011	40.9
Saved using a savings club or person outside the family	..
Saved any money	67.0
Saved for old age	36.7
Saved for a farm or business	8.5
Saved for education or school fees	23.1

Credit in the Past Year (% age 15+)

Borrowed from a financial institution	17.3
Borrowed from a financial institution, 2011	13.3
Borrowed from family or friends	15.0
Borrowed from a private informal lender	0.9
Borrowed any money	38.3
Borrowed for a farm or business	2.4
Borrowed for education or school fees	5.2
Outstanding mortgage at a financial institution	24.9

Euro area

Population, age 15+ (millions)	**285.6**	GNI per capita ($)	**39,350**

Account (% age 15+)
All adults	94.8
Women	94.0
Adults belonging to the poorest 40%	92.5
Young adults (% ages 15–24)	80.5
Adults living in rural areas	94.7

Financial Institution Account (% age 15+)
All adults	94.8
All adults, 2011	90.6

Mobile Account (% age 15+)
All adults	..

Access to Financial Institution Account (% age 15+)
Has debit card	81.1
Has debit card, 2011	68.5
ATM is the main mode of withdrawal (% with an account)	..
ATM is the main mode of withdrawal (% with an account), 2011	73.0

Use of Account in the Past Year (% age 15+)
Used an account to receive wages	43.5
Used an account to receive government transfers	16.4
Used a financial institution account to pay utility bills	61.3

Other Digital Payments in the Past Year (% age 15+)
Used a debit card to make payments	70.5
Used a credit card to make payments	34.5
Used the Internet to pay bills or make purchases	48.6

Domestic Remittances in the Past Year (% age 15+)
Sent remittances	..
Sent remittances via a financial institution (% senders)	..
Sent remittances via a mobile phone (% senders)	..
Sent remittances via a money transfer operator (% senders)	..
Received remittances	..
Received remittances via a financial institution (% recipients)	..
Received remittances via a mobile phone (% recipients)	..
Received remittances via a money transfer operator (% recipients)	..

Savings in the Past Year (% age 15+)
Saved at a financial institution	47.6
Saved at a financial institution, 2011	40.8
Saved using a savings club or person outside the family	..
Saved any money	67.2
Saved for old age	35.1
Saved for a farm or business	7.9
Saved for education or school fees	19.8

Credit in the Past Year (% age 15+)
Borrowed from a financial institution	15.8
Borrowed from a financial institution, 2011	11.8
Borrowed from family or friends	14.5
Borrowed from a private informal lender	0.4
Borrowed any money	35.4
Borrowed for a farm or business	2.8
Borrowed for education or school fees	4.0
Outstanding mortgage at a financial institution	23.5

Country tables

Afghanistan

Gender-matched sampling was used during the final stage of selection.

Algeria

Global Findex data exclude parts of the southern regions of the country.

Azerbaijan

Global Findex data exclude Nagorno-Karabakh and territories.

Bahrain

Global Findex data exclude residents unable to participate in the survey in Arabic or English.

Canada

Global Findex data exclude the Northwest Territories, Nunavut, and Yukon.

Chad

Global Findex data exclude selected regions.

China

Unless otherwise noted, data for China do not include data for Hong Kong SAR, China; Macao SAR, China; or Taiwan, China.

Cyprus

GNI per capita data refer to the area controlled by the government of Cyprus.

Democratic Republic of Congo

Global Findex data exclude North Kivu and South Kivu.

Georgia

GNI per capita, population, and Global Findex data exclude Abkhazia and South Ossetia.

India

Global Findex data exclude Northeast states, remote islands, and selected districts.

Israel

Global Findex data exclude East Jerusalem. This area is included in the sample for West Bank and Gaza.

Kuwait

Global Findex data include only Kuwaitis, Arab expatriates, and non-Arabs who were able to participate in the survey in Arabic or English.

Lebanon

Global Findex data exclude Baalbek, Bint Jbeil, and Hermel as well as the Beirut suburb of Dahiyeh.

Madagascar

Global Findex data exclude remote and inaccessible areas.

Country tables

Mali
> Global Findex data exclude the regions of Gao, Kidal, Mopti, and Tombouctou.

Moldova
> GNI per capita, population and Global Findex data exclude Transnistria (Prednestrovie).

Myanmar
> Global Findex data exclude the states of Chin, Kachin, and Kayah.

Nigeria
> Global Findex data exclude the states of Adamawa, Borno, and Yobe.

Pakistan
> Global Findex data exclude Azad Jammu and Kashmir and Gilgit-Baltistan. Gender-matched sampling was used during the final stage of selection.

Saudi Arabia
> Global Findex data include only Saudi nationals, Arab expatriates, and non-Arabs who were able to participate in the survey in Arabic or English.

Singapore
> Global Findex data exclude households in condominiums and bungalows.

Somalia
> Global Findex data exclude inaccessible regions.

Sudan
> Global Findex data exclude Blue Nile, Darfur (North, West, and South), and South Kurdufan.

Tanzania
> GNI per capita data refer to mainland Tanzania only.

Ukraine
> Global Findex data exclude selected regions in the East and, starting in 2014, exclude Crimea.

United Arab Emirates
> Global Findex data include only Emiratis, Arab expatriates, and non-Arabs who were able to participate in the survey in Arabic or English.

Vietnam
> Global Findex data exclude An Giang, Dak Lak, Ha Tinh, Kien Giang, Quang Binh, and Thanh Hoa.

West Bank and Gaza
> Global Findex data include East Jerusalem.

Republic of Yemen
> Gender-matched sampling was used during the final stage of selection.

Afghanistan

South Asia			Low income
Population, age 15+ (millions)	**16.3**	GNI per capita ($)	**690**

	Country data	South Asia	Low income
Account (% age 15+)			
All adults	10.0	46.4	27.5
Women	3.8	37.4	23.9
Adults belonging to the poorest 40%	6.6	38.1	19.4
Young adults (% ages 15–24)	7.4	36.7	20.2
Adults living in rural areas	9.2	43.5	24.8
Financial Institution Account (% age 15+)			
All adults	10.0	45.5	22.3
All adults, 2011	9.0	32.3	21.1
Mobile Account (% age 15+)			
All adults	0.3	2.6	10.0
Access to Financial Institution Account (% age 15+)			
Has debit card	1.7	18.0	6.6
Has debit card, 2011	4.7	7.2	6.3
ATM is the main mode of withdrawal (% with an account)	..	31.1	20.2
ATM is the main mode of withdrawal (% with an account), 2011	..	16.9	19.7
Use of Account in the Past Year (% age 15+)			
Used an account to receive wages	2.5	3.5	3.2
Used an account to receive government transfers	0.4	3.1	1.0
Used a financial institution account to pay utility bills	0.6	2.7	0.9
Other Digital Payments in the Past Year (% age 15+)			
Used a debit card to make payments	1.7	8.5	2.1
Used a credit card to make payments	1.1	2.6	0.6
Used the Internet to pay bills or make purchases	0.6	1.2	1.2
Domestic Remittances in the Past Year (% age 15+)			
Sent remittances	13.3	10.7	18.3
Sent remittances via a financial institution (% senders)	16.0	20.1	15.4
Sent remittances via a mobile phone (% senders)	0.0	7.7	42.8
Sent remittances via a money transfer operator (% senders)	6.0	13.7	14.1
Received remittances	17.2	12.2	25.6
Received remittances via a financial institution (% recipients)	13.1	15.8	13.0
Received remittances via a mobile phone (% recipients)	1.4	4.7	33.8
Received remittances via a money transfer operator (% recipients)	10.5	9.8	14.8
Savings in the Past Year (% age 15+)			
Saved at a financial institution	3.6	12.7	9.9
Saved at a financial institution, 2011	2.8	11.1	11.5
Saved using a savings club or person outside the family	8.0	8.8	16.3
Saved any money	25.8	36.2	46.5
Saved for old age	11.4	9.1	8.3
Saved for a farm or business	7.8	7.3	16.7
Saved for education or school fees	10.3	14.6	16.6
Credit in the Past Year (% age 15+)			
Borrowed from a financial institution	3.6	6.4	8.6
Borrowed from a financial institution, 2011	7.4	8.7	11.7
Borrowed from family or friends	22.3	31.4	34.9
Borrowed from a private informal lender	7.6	10.9	6.5
Borrowed any money	34.6	46.7	52.5
Borrowed for a farm or business	8.3	8.6	12.2
Borrowed for education or school fees	5.4	8.9	10.9
Outstanding mortgage at a financial institution	9.4	3.8	4.1

Albania

Population, age 15+ (millions)	**2.3**	GNI per capita ($)	**4,510**

	Country data	Europe & Central Asia	Upper middle income
Account (% age 15+)			
All adults	38.0	51.4	70.5
Women	33.6	47.4	67.3
Adults belonging to the poorest 40%	23.4	44.2	62.7
Young adults (% ages 15–24)	30.0	35.6	58.1
Adults living in rural areas	33.2	45.7	68.8
Financial Institution Account (% age 15+)			
All adults	38.0	51.4	70.4
All adults, 2011	28.3	43.3	57.4
Mobile Account (% age 15+)			
All adults	..	0.3	0.7
Access to Financial Institution Account (% age 15+)			
Has debit card	21.8	36.9	45.9
Has debit card, 2011	21.1	36.4	38.5
ATM is the main mode of withdrawal (% with an account)	51.4	66.7	55.7
ATM is the main mode of withdrawal (% with an account), 2011	64.7	72.5	42.8
Use of Account in the Past Year (% age 15+)			
Used an account to receive wages	10.8	22.5	18.1
Used an account to receive government transfers	3.5	7.3	9.6
Used a financial institution account to pay utility bills	2.6	12.5	12.3
Other Digital Payments in the Past Year (% age 15+)			
Used a debit card to make payments	4.0	22.9	19.9
Used a credit card to make payments	4.0	14.9	14.4
Used the Internet to pay bills or make purchases	3.3	11.9	15.3
Domestic Remittances in the Past Year (% age 15+)			
Sent remittances	19.5	12.9	15.4
Sent remittances via a financial institution (% senders)	16.5	31.5	37.2
Sent remittances via a mobile phone (% senders)	1.1	2.5	8.8
Sent remittances via a money transfer operator (% senders)	10.9	11.8	19.7
Received remittances	27.1	15.5	17.8
Received remittances via a financial institution (% recipients)	13.9	22.1	29.8
Received remittances via a mobile phone (% recipients)	1.4	1.0	5.6
Received remittances via a money transfer operator (% recipients)	12.1	15.6	17.9
Savings in the Past Year (% age 15+)			
Saved at a financial institution	7.5	8.4	32.2
Saved at a financial institution, 2011	8.6	4.9	25.1
Saved using a savings club or person outside the family	3.2	6.6	4.9
Saved any money	38.4	38.5	62.7
Saved for old age	8.8	11.8	30.6
Saved for a farm or business	8.3	5.1	17.6
Saved for education or school fees	20.0	12.1	25.4
Credit in the Past Year (% age 15+)			
Borrowed from a financial institution	10.2	12.4	10.4
Borrowed from a financial institution, 2011	7.5	7.8	7.9
Borrowed from family or friends	44.4	23.6	24.0
Borrowed from a private informal lender	2.2	2.1	2.6
Borrowed any money	55.5	39.5	37.7
Borrowed for a farm or business	3.9	2.8	6.6
Borrowed for education or school fees	11.6	6.2	6.1
Outstanding mortgage at a financial institution	8.7	10.2	9.1

Algeria

		Upper middle income	
Population, age 15+ (millions)	**28.3**	GNI per capita ($)	**5,330**

	Country data	Upper middle income
Account (% age 15+)		
All adults	50.5	70.5
Women	40.1	67.3
Adults belonging to the poorest 40%	36.7	62.7
Young adults (% ages 15-24)	38.5	58.1
Adults living in rural areas	42.3	68.8
Financial Institution Account (% age 15+)		
All adults	50.5	70.4
All adults, 2011	33.3	57.4
Mobile Account (% age 15+)		
All adults	..	0.7
Access to Financial Institution Account (% age 15+)		
Has debit card	21.6	45.9
Has debit card, 2011	13.5	38.5
ATM is the main mode of withdrawal (% with an account)	10.3	55.7
ATM is the main mode of withdrawal (% with an account), 2011	14.2	42.8
Use of Account in the Past Year (% age 15+)		
Used an account to receive wages	15.6	18.1
Used an account to receive government transfers	7.7	9.6
Used a financial institution account to pay utility bills	0.2	12.3
Other Digital Payments in the Past Year (% age 15+)		
Used a debit card to make payments	7.3	19.9
Used a credit card to make payments	4.7	14.4
Used the Internet to pay bills or make purchases	5.7	15.3
Domestic Remittances in the Past Year (% age 15+)		
Sent remittances	7.9	15.4
Sent remittances via a financial institution (% senders)	..	37.2
Sent remittances via a mobile phone (% senders)	..	8.8
Sent remittances via a money transfer operator (% senders)	..	19.7
Received remittances	12.6	17.8
Received remittances via a financial institution (% recipients)	12.4	29.8
Received remittances via a mobile phone (% recipients)	2.0	5.6
Received remittances via a money transfer operator (% recipients)	5.9	17.9
Savings in the Past Year (% age 15+)		
Saved at a financial institution	13.8	32.2
Saved at a financial institution, 2011	4.3	25.1
Saved using a savings club or person outside the family	3.4	4.9
Saved any money	45.3	62.7
Saved for old age	11.3	30.6
Saved for a farm or business	11.1	17.6
Saved for education or school fees	10.5	25.4
Credit in the Past Year (% age 15+)		
Borrowed from a financial institution	2.2	10.4
Borrowed from a financial institution, 2011	1.5	7.9
Borrowed from family or friends	13.2	24.0
Borrowed from a private informal lender	1.5	2.6
Borrowed any money	23.1	37.7
Borrowed for a farm or business	4.0	6.6
Borrowed for education or school fees	4.0	6.1
Outstanding mortgage at a financial institution	3.9	9.1

Angola

Sub-Saharan Africa			Upper middle income

Population, age 15+ (millions)	**11.3**	GNI per capita ($)	**5,170**

	Country data	Sub-Saharan Africa	Upper middle income
Account (% age 15+)			
All adults	29.3	34.2	70.5
Women	22.3	29.9	67.3
Adults belonging to the poorest 40%	12.9	24.6	62.7
Young adults (% ages 15–24)	14.9	25.9	58.1
Adults living in rural areas	18.8	29.2	68.8
Financial Institution Account (% age 15+)			
All adults	29.3	28.9	70.4
All adults, 2011	39.2	23.9	57.4
Mobile Account (% age 15+)			
All adults	..	11.5	0.7
Access to Financial Institution Account (% age 15+)			
Has debit card	21.4	17.9	45.9
Has debit card, 2011	29.8	15.0	38.5
ATM is the main mode of withdrawal (% with an account)	36.0	53.8	55.7
ATM is the main mode of withdrawal (% with an account), 2011	49.0	51.7	42.8
Use of Account in the Past Year (% age 15+)			
Used an account to receive wages	14.0	7.3	18.1
Used an account to receive government transfers	1.2	3.8	9.6
Used a financial institution account to pay utility bills	4.8	2.8	12.3
Other Digital Payments in the Past Year (% age 15+)			
Used a debit card to make payments	13.7	8.7	19.9
Used a credit card to make payments	3.5	1.9	14.4
Used the Internet to pay bills or make purchases	1.0	2.4	15.3
Domestic Remittances in the Past Year (% age 15+)			
Sent remittances	14.6	28.7	15.4
Sent remittances via a financial institution (% senders)	33.7	31.0	37.2
Sent remittances via a mobile phone (% senders)	0.0	30.8	8.8
Sent remittances via a money transfer operator (% senders)	17.1	21.0	19.7
Received remittances	20.3	37.2	17.8
Received remittances via a financial institution (% recipients)	21.1	26.6	29.8
Received remittances via a mobile phone (% recipients)	0.4	27.6	5.6
Received remittances via a money transfer operator (% recipients)	8.2	22.1	17.9
Savings in the Past Year (% age 15+)			
Saved at a financial institution	14.9	15.9	32.2
Saved at a financial institution, 2011	15.9	14.3	25.1
Saved using a savings club or person outside the family	11.9	23.9	4.9
Saved any money	53.1	59.6	62.7
Saved for old age	5.0	9.8	30.6
Saved for a farm or business	11.9	22.7	17.6
Saved for education or school fees	21.8	22.9	25.4
Credit in the Past Year (% age 15+)			
Borrowed from a financial institution	2.8	6.3	10.4
Borrowed from a financial institution, 2011	7.9	4.8	7.9
Borrowed from family or friends	20.0	41.9	24.0
Borrowed from a private informal lender	2.0	4.7	2.6
Borrowed any money	29.8	54.5	37.7
Borrowed for a farm or business	3.6	12.8	6.6
Borrowed for education or school fees	9.2	12.3	6.1
Outstanding mortgage at a financial institution	2.2	5.2	9.1

Argentina

Latin America & Caribbean			Upper middle income

Population, age 15+ (millions)	**31.4**	GNI per capita ($)		..

	Country data	Latin America & the Carib.	Upper middle income
Account (% age 15+)			
All adults	50.2	51.4	70.5
Women	50.9	48.6	67.3
Adults belonging to the poorest 40%	44.4	41.2	62.7
Young adults (% ages 15–24)	24.5	37.4	58.1
Adults living in rural areas	50.6	46.0	68.8
Financial Institution Account (% age 15+)			
All adults	50.2	51.1	70.4
All adults, 2011	33.1	39.3	57.4
Mobile Account (% age 15+)			
All adults	0.4	1.7	0.7
Access to Financial Institution Account (% age 15+)			
Has debit card	44.2	40.4	45.9
Has debit card, 2011	29.8	28.9	38.5
ATM is the main mode of withdrawal (% with an account)	78.0	71.1	55.7
ATM is the main mode of withdrawal (% with an account), 2011	80.3	57.0	42.8
Use of Account in the Past Year (% age 15+)			
Used an account to receive wages	18.1	18.0	18.1
Used an account to receive government transfers	10.3	9.0	9.6
Used a financial institution account to pay utility bills	5.9	6.3	12.3
Other Digital Payments in the Past Year (% age 15+)			
Used a debit card to make payments	25.4	27.7	19.9
Used a credit card to make payments	23.9	18.0	14.4
Used the Internet to pay bills or make purchases	8.4	6.9	15.3
Domestic Remittances in the Past Year (% age 15+)			
Sent remittances	6.2	9.5	15.4
Sent remittances via a financial institution (% senders)	..	..	37.2
Sent remittances via a mobile phone (% senders)	..	..	8.8
Sent remittances via a money transfer operator (% senders)	..	..	19.7
Received remittances	10.5	11.3	17.8
Received remittances via a financial institution (% recipients)	10.1	34.2	29.8
Received remittances via a mobile phone (% recipients)	0.0	4.3	5.6
Received remittances via a money transfer operator (% recipients)	7.5	28.4	17.9
Savings in the Past Year (% age 15+)			
Saved at a financial institution	4.1	13.5	32.2
Saved at a financial institution, 2011	3.8	9.6	25.1
Saved using a savings club or person outside the family	1.7	7.9	4.9
Saved any money	23.1	40.6	62.7
Saved for old age	4.5	10.6	30.6
Saved for a farm or business	4.8	10.6	17.6
Saved for education or school fees	8.3	17.2	25.4
Credit in the Past Year (% age 15+)			
Borrowed from a financial institution	8.3	11.3	10.4
Borrowed from a financial institution, 2011	6.6	7.9	7.9
Borrowed from family or friends	6.0	13.5	24.0
Borrowed from a private informal lender	1.2	4.7	2.6
Borrowed any money	19.1	32.7	37.7
Borrowed for a farm or business	2.0	6.1	6.6
Borrowed for education or school fees	1.3	8.3	6.1
Outstanding mortgage at a financial institution	7.9	9.6	9.1

Armenia

Population, age 15+ (millions)	2.4	GNI per capita ($)		3,800

	Country data	Europe & Central Asia	Lower middle income
Account (% age 15+)			
All adults	17.7	51.4	42.7
Women	14.7	47.4	36.3
Adults belonging to the poorest 40%	10.9	44.2	33.2
Young adults (% ages 15–24)	10.4	35.6	34.7
Adults living in rural areas	15.5	45.7	40.0
Financial Institution Account (% age 15+)			
All adults	17.2	51.4	41.8
All adults, 2011	17.5	43.3	28.7
Mobile Account (% age 15+)			
All adults	0.7	0.3	2.5
Access to Financial Institution Account (% age 15+)			
Has debit card	8.4	36.9	21.2
Has debit card, 2011	5.2	36.4	10.1
ATM is the main mode of withdrawal (% with an account)	51.6	66.7	42.4
ATM is the main mode of withdrawal (% with an account), 2011	55.4	72.5	28.1
Use of Account in the Past Year (% age 15+)			
Used an account to receive wages	7.2	22.5	5.6
Used an account to receive government transfers	0.7	7.3	3.3
Used a financial institution account to pay utility bills	1.5	12.5	3.1
Other Digital Payments in the Past Year (% age 15+)			
Used a debit card to make payments	3.9	22.9	9.6
Used a credit card to make payments	4.2	14.9	2.8
Used the Internet to pay bills or make purchases	5.0	11.9	2.6
Domestic Remittances in the Past Year (% age 15+)			
Sent remittances	3.2	12.9	14.2
Sent remittances via a financial institution (% senders)	..	31.5	30.9
Sent remittances via a mobile phone (% senders)	..	2.5	7.7
Sent remittances via a money transfer operator (% senders)	..	11.8	18.3
Received remittances	9.1	15.5	17.8
Received remittances via a financial institution (% recipients)	..	22.1	26.0
Received remittances via a mobile phone (% recipients)	..	1.0	5.7
Received remittances via a money transfer operator (% recipients)	..	15.6	16.6
Savings in the Past Year (% age 15+)			
Saved at a financial institution	1.6	8.4	14.8
Saved at a financial institution, 2011	0.8	4.9	11.1
Saved using a savings club or person outside the family	4.8	6.6	12.4
Saved any money	21.0	38.5	45.6
Saved for old age	2.1	11.8	12.6
Saved for a farm or business	3.2	5.1	11.8
Saved for education or school fees	4.7	12.1	20.0
Credit in the Past Year (% age 15+)			
Borrowed from a financial institution	19.9	12.4	7.5
Borrowed from a financial institution, 2011	18.9	7.8	7.3
Borrowed from family or friends	26.9	23.6	33.1
Borrowed from a private informal lender	2.8	2.1	8.5
Borrowed any money	47.3	39.5	47.4
Borrowed for a farm or business	8.6	2.8	9.2
Borrowed for education or school fees	5.2	6.2	10.1
Outstanding mortgage at a financial institution	15.2	10.2	4.7

Australia

High income: OECD			High income
Population, age 15+ (millions)	**18.7**	GNI per capita ($)	**65,400**

	Country data	High income: OECD
Account (% age 15+)		
All adults	98.9	94.0
Women	99.0	93.8
Adults belonging to the poorest 40%	98.4	90.6
Young adults (% ages 15-24)	94.8	84.1
Adults living in rural areas	98.7	93.8
Financial Institution Account (% age 15+)		
All adults	98.9	94.0
All adults, 2011	99.1	90.0
Mobile Account (% age 15+)		
All adults	..	..
Access to Financial Institution Account (% age 15+)		
Has debit card	88.9	79.7
Has debit card, 2011	79.1	61.9
ATM is the main mode of withdrawal (% with an account)	..	..
ATM is the main mode of withdrawal (% with an account), 2011	68.5	68.5
Use of Account In the Past Year (% age 15+)		
Used an account to receive wages	55.6	44.3
Used an account to receive government transfers	40.5	17.2
Used a financial institution account to pay utility bills	64.1	61.1
Other Digital Payments In the Past Year (% age 15+)		
Used a debit card to make payments	82.5	65.3
Used a credit card to make payments	56.3	46.7
Used the Internet to pay bills or make purchases	68.2	54.1
Domestic Remittances In the Past Year (% age 15+)		
Sent remittances	..	..
Sent remittances via a financial institution (% senders)	..	..
Sent remittances via a mobile phone (% senders)	..	..
Sent remittances via a money transfer operator (% senders)	..	..
Received remittances	..	..
Received remittances via a financial institution (% recipients)	..	..
Received remittances via a mobile phone (% recipients)	..	..
Received remittances via a money transfer operator (% recipients)	..	..
Savings In the Past Year (% age 15+)		
Saved at a financial institution	61.4	51.6
Saved at a financial institution, 2011	61.9	45.3
Saved using a savings club or person outside the family	..	..
Saved any money	81.5	70.8
Saved for old age	39.9	39.7
Saved for a farm or business	9.7	9.0
Saved for education or school fees	27.1	25.0
Credit In the Past Year (% age 15+)		
Borrowed from a financial institution	23.4	18.4
Borrowed from a financial institution, 2011	17.0	14.2
Borrowed from family or friends	16.9	14.9
Borrowed from a private informal lender	0.8	0.9
Borrowed any money	43.2	39.8
Borrowed for a farm or business	3.1	2.6
Borrowed for education or school fees	5.6	5.6
Outstanding mortgage at a financial institution	34.7	26.1

Austria

High income: OECD		**High income**
Population, age 15+ (millions)	**7.3**	GNI per capita ($)	**50,390**

	Country data	High income: OECD
Account (% age 15+)		
All adults	96.7	94.0
Women	97.4	93.8
Adults belonging to the poorest 40%	95.7	90.6
Young adults (% ages 15-24)	88.5	84.1
Adults living in rural areas	98.4	93.8
Financial Institution Account (% age 15+)		
All adults	96.7	94.0
All adults, 2011	97.1	90.0
Mobile Account (% age 15+)		
All adults	..	..
Access to Financial Institution Account (% age 15+)		
Has debit card	81.6	79.7
Has debit card, 2011	86.8	61.9
ATM is the main mode of withdrawal (% with an account)	..	..
ATM is the main mode of withdrawal (% with an account), 2011	76.7	68.5
Use of Account in the Past Year (% age 15+)		
Used an account to receive wages	48.2	44.3
Used an account to receive government transfers	22.8	17.2
Used a financial institution account to pay utility bills	74.8	61.1
Other Digital Payments in the Past Year (% age 15+)		
Used a debit card to make payments	68.5	65.3
Used a credit card to make payments	34.6	46.7
Used the Internet to pay bills or make purchases	51.0	54.1
Domestic Remittances in the Past Year (% age 15+)		
Sent remittances	..	..
Sent remittances via a financial institution (% senders)	..	..
Sent remittances via a mobile phone (% senders)	..	..
Sent remittances via a money transfer operator (% senders)	..	..
Received remittances	..	..
Received remittances via a financial institution (% recipients)	..	..
Received remittances via a mobile phone (% recipients)	..	..
Received remittances via a money transfer operator (% recipients)	..	..
Savings in the Past Year (% age 15+)		
Saved at a financial institution	60.4	51.6
Saved at a financial institution, 2011	51.6	45.3
Saved using a savings club or person outside the family	..	
Saved any money	79.6	70.8
Saved for old age	48.4	39.7
Saved for a farm or business	13.9	9.0
Saved for education or school fees	18.0	25.0
Credit in the Past Year (% age 15+)		
Borrowed from a financial institution	13.3	18.4
Borrowed from a financial institution, 2011	8.3	14.2
Borrowed from family or friends	15.0	14.9
Borrowed from a private informal lender	0.7	0.9
Borrowed any money	33.3	39.8
Borrowed for a farm or business	3.6	2.6
Borrowed for education or school fees	1.7	5.6
Outstanding mortgage at a financial institution	18.3	26.1

Azerbaijan

Europe & Central Asia			Upper middle income

Population, age 15+ (millions)	**7.3**	GNI per capita ($)	**7,350**

	Country data	Europe & Central Asia	Upper middle income
Account (% age 15+)			
All adults	29.2	51.4	70.5
Women	25.9	47.4	67.3
Adults belonging to the poorest 40%	26.9	44.2	62.7
Young adults (% ages 15–24)	10.0	35.6	58.1
Adults living in rural areas	30.1	45.7	68.8
Financial Institution Account (% age 15+)			
All adults	29.2	51.4	70.4
All adults, 2011	14.9	43.3	57.4
Mobile Account (% age 15+)			
All adults	..	0.3	0.7
Access to Financial Institution Account (% age 15+)			
Has debit card	15.7	36.9	45.9
Has debit card, 2011	10.0	36.4	38.5
ATM is the main mode of withdrawal (% with an account)	57.1	66.7	55.7
ATM is the main mode of withdrawal (% with an account), 2011	88.2	72.5	42.8
Use of Account in the Past Year (% age 15+)			
Used an account to receive wages	13.9	22.5	18.1
Used an account to receive government transfers	4.3	7.3	9.6
Used a financial institution account to pay utility bills	1.6	12.5	12.3
Other Digital Payments in the Past Year (% age 15+)			
Used a debit card to make payments	6.3	22.9	19.9
Used a credit card to make payments	8.1	14.9	14.4
Used the Internet to pay bills or make purchases	4.2	11.9	15.3
Domestic Remittances in the Past Year (% age 15+)			
Sent remittances	19.4	12.9	15.4
Sent remittances via a financial institution (% senders)	4.7	31.5	37.2
Sent remittances via a mobile phone (% senders)	0.0	2.5	8.8
Sent remittances via a money transfer operator (% senders)	15.2	11.8	19.7
Received remittances	19.9	15.5	17.8
Received remittances via a financial institution (% recipients)	3.1	22.1	29.8
Received remittances via a mobile phone (% recipients)	0.0	1.0	5.6
Received remittances via a money transfer operator (% recipients)	8.5	15.6	17.9
Savings in the Past Year (% age 15+)			
Saved at a financial institution	5.3	8.4	32.2
Saved at a financial institution, 2011	1.6	4.9	25.1
Saved using a savings club or person outside the family	1.6	6.6	4.9
Saved any money	39.5	38.5	62.7
Saved for old age	11.1	11.8	30.6
Saved for a farm or business	8.9	5.1	17.6
Saved for education or school fees	7.7	12.1	25.4
Credit in the Past Year (% age 15+)			
Borrowed from a financial institution	18.9	12.4	10.4
Borrowed from a financial institution, 2011	17.7	7.8	7.9
Borrowed from family or friends	33.3	23.6	24.0
Borrowed from a private informal lender	6.1	2.1	2.6
Borrowed any money	46.4	39.5	37.7
Borrowed for a farm or business	7.1	2.8	6.6
Borrowed for education or school fees	4.4	6.2	6.1
Outstanding mortgage at a financial institution	7.0	10.2	9.1

Bahrain

High income

	Country data	High income: OECD
Population, age 15+ (millions)	1.1	GNI per capita ($) 19,700

Account (% age 15+)

	Country data	High income: OECD
All adults	81.9	94.0
Women	66.7	93.8
Adults belonging to the poorest 40%	80.1	90.6
Young adults (% ages 15–24)	66.5	84.1
Adults living in rural areas	81.4	93.8

Financial Institution Account (% age 15+)

All adults	81.9	94.0
All adults, 2011	64.5	90.0

Mobile Account (% age 15+)

All adults	..	..

Access to Financial Institution Account (% age 15+)

Has debit card	74.9	79.7
Has debit card, 2011	62.2	61.9
ATM is the main mode of withdrawal (% with an account)	..	..
ATM is the main mode of withdrawal (% with an account), 2011	90.7	68.5

Use of Account in the Past Year (% age 15+)

Used an account to receive wages	29.1	44.3
Used an account to receive government transfers	9.1	17.2
Used a financial institution account to pay utility bills	15.6	61.1

Other Digital Payments in the Past Year (% age 15+)

Used a debit card to make payments	57.2	65.3
Used a credit card to make payments	24.4	46.7
Used the Internet to pay bills or make purchases	28.8	54.1

Domestic Remittances in the Past Year (% age 15+)

Sent remittances	..	..
Sent remittances via a financial institution (% senders)	..	..
Sent remittances via a mobile phone (% senders)	..	..
Sent remittances via a money transfer operator (% senders)	..	..
Received remittances	..	..
Received remittances via a financial institution (% recipients)	..	..
Received remittances via a mobile phone (% recipients)	..	..
Received remittances via a money transfer operator (% recipients)	..	..

Savings in the Past Year (% age 15+)

Saved at a financial institution	34.7	51.6
Saved at a financial institution, 2011	16.3	45.3
Saved using a savings club or person outside the family	..	..
Saved any money	65.3	70.8
Saved for old age	25.1	39.7
Saved for a farm or business	22.1	9.0
Saved for education or school fees	30.3	25.0

Credit in the Past Year (% age 15+)

Borrowed from a financial institution	21.3	18.4
Borrowed from a financial institution, 2011	21.9	14.2
Borrowed from family or friends	36.4	14.9
Borrowed from a private informal lender	13.3	0.9
Borrowed any money	60.1	39.8
Borrowed for a farm or business	9.8	2.6
Borrowed for education or school fees	14.1	5.6
Outstanding mortgage at a financial institution	23.5	26.1

Bangladesh

South Asia   Low income

Population, age 15+ (millions)	**109.6**	GNI per capita ($)	**1,010**

	Country data	South Asia	Low income
Account (% age 15+)			
All adults	31.0	46.4	27.5
Women	26.5	37.4	23.9
Adults belonging to the poorest 40%	23.1	38.1	19.4
Young adults (% ages 15–24)	20.8	36.7	20.2
Adults living in rural areas	25.6	43.5	24.8
Financial Institution Account (% age 15+)			
All adults	29.1	45.5	22.3
All adults, 2011	31.7	32.3	21.1
Mobile Account (% age 15+)			
All adults	2.7	2.6	10.0
Access to Financial Institution Account (% age 15+)			
Has debit card	5.2	18.0	6.6
Has debit card, 2011	2.3	7.2	6.3
ATM is the main mode of withdrawal (% with an account)	7.5	31.1	20.2
ATM is the main mode of withdrawal (% with an account), 2011	2.8	16.9	19.7
Use of Account in the Past Year (% age 15+)			
Used an account to receive wages	1.6	3.5	3.2
Used an account to receive government transfers	0.4	3.1	1.0
Used a financial institution account to pay utility bills	0.7	2.7	0.9
Other Digital Payments in the Past Year (% age 15+)			
Used a debit card to make payments	1.0	8.5	2.1
Used a credit card to make payments	0.2	2.6	0.6
Used the Internet to pay bills or make purchases	0.4	1.2	1.2
Domestic Remittances in the Past Year (% age 15+)			
Sent remittances	10.4	10.7	18.3
Sent remittances via a financial institution (% senders)	9.0	20.1	15.4
Sent remittances via a mobile phone (% senders)	33.0	7.7	42.8
Sent remittances via a money transfer operator (% senders)	5.7	13.7	14.1
Received remittances	14.1	12.2	25.6
Received remittances via a financial institution (% recipients)	8.6	15.8	13.0
Received remittances via a mobile phone (% recipients)	17.3	4.7	33.8
Received remittances via a money transfer operator (% recipients)	2.4	9.8	14.8
Savings in the Past Year (% age 15+)			
Saved at a financial institution	7.4	12.7	9.9
Saved at a financial institution, 2011	16.6	11.1	11.5
Saved using a savings club or person outside the family	5.2	8.8	16.3
Saved any money	23.9	36.2	46.5
Saved for old age	5.6	9.1	8.3
Saved for a farm or business	4.0	7.3	16.7
Saved for education or school fees	7.2	14.6	16.6
Credit in the Past Year (% age 15+)			
Borrowed from a financial institution	9.9	6.4	8.6
Borrowed from a financial institution, 2011	23.3	8.7	11.7
Borrowed from family or friends	25.2	31.4	34.9
Borrowed from a private informal lender	4.5	10.9	6.5
Borrowed any money	48.3	46.7	52.5
Borrowed for a farm or business	3.8	8.6	12.2
Borrowed for education or school fees	5.1	8.9	10.9
Outstanding mortgage at a financial institution	2.3	3.8	4.1

Belarus

Europe & Central Asia		Upper middle income		
Population, age 15+ (millions)	**8.0**	GNI per capita ($)		**6,730**

	Country data	Europe & Central Asia	Upper middle income
Account (% age 15+)			
All adults	72.0	51.4	70.5
Women	72.0	47.4	67.3
Adults belonging to the poorest 40%	66.2	44.2	62.7
Young adults (% ages 15–24)	48.2	35.6	58.1
Adults living in rural areas	62.5	45.7	68.8
Financial Institution Account (% age 15+)			
All adults	72.0	51.4	70.4
All adults, 2011	58.6	43.3	57.4
Mobile Account (% age 15+)			
All adults	..	0.3	0.7
Access to Financial Institution Account (% age 15+)			
Has debit card	39.9	36.9	45.9
Has debit card, 2011	50.3	36.4	38.5
ATM is the main mode of withdrawal (% with an account)	67.7	66.7	55.7
ATM is the main mode of withdrawal (% with an account), 2011	80.5	72.5	42.8
Use of Account in the Past Year (% age 15+)			
Used an account to receive wages	51.3	22.5	18.1
Used an account to receive government transfers	14.3	7.3	9.6
Used a financial institution account to pay utility bills	23.6	12.5	12.3
Other Digital Payments in the Past Year (% age 15+)			
Used a debit card to make payments	35.9	22.9	19.9
Used a credit card to make payments	12.7	14.9	14.4
Used the Internet to pay bills or make purchases	21.7	11.9	15.3
Domestic Remittances in the Past Year (% age 15+)			
Sent remittances	17.6	12.9	15.4
Sent remittances via a financial institution (% senders)	27.1	31.5	37.2
Sent remittances via a mobile phone (% senders)	2.4	2.5	8.8
Sent remittances via a money transfer operator (% senders)	16.4	11.8	19.7
Received remittances	15.8	15.5	17.8
Received remittances via a financial institution (% recipients)	26.7	22.1	29.8
Received remittances via a mobile phone (% recipients)	0.0	1.0	5.6
Received remittances via a money transfer operator (% recipients)	26.4	15.6	17.9
Savings in the Past Year (% age 15+)			
Saved at a financial institution	14.9	8.4	32.2
Saved at a financial institution, 2011	6.8	4.9	25.1
Saved using a savings club or person outside the family	1.2	6.6	4.9
Saved any money	50.4	38.5	62.7
Saved for old age	21.9	11.8	30.6
Saved for a farm or business	5.1	5.1	17.6
Saved for education or school fees	8.2	12.1	25.4
Credit in the Past Year (% age 15+)			
Borrowed from a financial institution	14.2	12.4	10.4
Borrowed from a financial institution, 2011	16.1	7.8	7.9
Borrowed from family or friends	21.1	23.6	24.0
Borrowed from a private informal lender	0.9	2.1	2.6
Borrowed any money	39.0	39.5	37.7
Borrowed for a farm or business	1.8	2.8	6.6
Borrowed for education or school fees	2.3	6.2	6.1
Outstanding mortgage at a financial institution	18.1	10.2	9.1

Belgium

	Country data	High income: OECD
Population, age 15+ (millions) **9.3** GNI per capita ($) **46,340**		
Account (% age 15+)		
All adults	98.1	94.0
Women	99.5	93.8
Adults belonging to the poorest 40%	98.3	90.6
Young adults (% ages 15–24)	90.9	84.1
Adults living in rural areas	98.9	93.8
Financial Institution Account (% age 15+)		
All adults	98.1	94.0
All adults, 2011	96.3	90.0
Mobile Account (% age 15+)		
All adults	..	..
Access to Financial Institution Account (% age 15+)		
Has debit card	93.6	79.7
Has debit card, 2011	85.8	61.9
ATM is the main mode of withdrawal (% with an account)	..	..
ATM is the main mode of withdrawal (% with an account), 2011	76.7	68.5
Use of Account in the Past Year (% age 15+)		
Used an account to receive wages	52.1	44.3
Used an account to receive government transfers	24.6	17.2
Used a financial institution account to pay utility bills	70.5	61.1
Other Digital Payments in the Past Year (% age 15+)		
Used a debit card to make payments	84.9	65.3
Used a credit card to make payments	37.0	46.7
Used the Internet to pay bills or make purchases	52.4	54.1
Domestic Remittances in the Past Year (% age 15+)		
Sent remittances	..	..
Sent remittances via a financial institution (% senders)	..	..
Sent remittances via a mobile phone (% senders)	..	..
Sent remittances via a money transfer operator (% senders)	..	..
Received remittances	..	..
Received remittances via a financial institution (% recipients)	..	..
Received remittances via a mobile phone (% recipients)	..	..
Received remittances via a money transfer operator (% recipients)	..	..
Savings in the Past Year (% age 15+)		
Saved at a financial institution	55.5	51.6
Saved at a financial institution, 2011	42.6	45.3
Saved using a savings club or person outside the family	..	..
Saved any money	74.7	70.8
Saved for old age	46.6	39.7
Saved for a farm or business	6.0	9.0
Saved for education or school fees	20.3	25.0
Credit in the Past Year (% age 15+)		
Borrowed from a financial institution	15.8	18.4
Borrowed from a financial institution, 2011	10.5	14.2
Borrowed from family or friends	12.2	14.9
Borrowed from a private informal lender	0.0	0.9
Borrowed any money	31.4	39.8
Borrowed for a farm or business	3.0	2.6
Borrowed for education or school fees	2.0	5.6
Outstanding mortgage at a financial institution	30.3	26.1

Belize

Latin America & Caribbean		**Upper middle income**	
Population, age 15+ (thousands)	220	GNI per capita ($)	4,510

	Country data	Latin America & the Carib.	Upper middle income
Account (% age 15+)			
All adults	48.2	51.4	70.5
Women	52.3	48.6	67.3
Adults belonging to the poorest 40%	38.4	41.2	62.7
Young adults (% ages 15–24)	39.3	37.4	58.1
Adults living in rural areas	45.3	46.0	68.8
Financial Institution Account (% age 15+)			
All adults	48.2	51.1	70.4
All adults, 2011	..	39.3	57.4
Mobile Account (% age 15+)			
All adults	..	1.7	0.7
Access to Financial Institution Account (% age 15+)			
Has debit card	24.0	40.4	45.9
Has debit card, 2011	..	28.9	38.5
ATM is the main mode of withdrawal (% with an account)	40.9	71.1	55.7
ATM is the main mode of withdrawal (% with an account), 2011	..	57.0	42.8
Use of Account in the Past Year (% age 15+)			
Used an account to receive wages	8.2	18.0	18.1
Used an account to receive government transfers	7.2	9.0	9.6
Used a financial institution account to pay utility bills	5.2	6.3	12.3
Other Digital Payments in the Past Year (% age 15+)			
Used a debit card to make payments	6.4	27.7	19.9
Used a credit card to make payments	6.6	18.0	14.4
Used the Internet to pay bills or make purchases	4.8	6.9	15.3
Domestic Remittances in the Past Year (% age 15+)			
Sent remittances	12.2	9.5	15.4
Sent remittances via a financial institution (% senders)	32.5	..	37.2
Sent remittances via a mobile phone (% senders)	3.0	..	8.8
Sent remittances via a money transfer operator (% senders)	21.6	..	19.7
Received remittances	17.9	11.3	17.8
Received remittances via a financial institution (% recipients)	32.8	34.2	29.8
Received remittances via a mobile phone (% recipients)	3.6	4.3	5.6
Received remittances via a money transfer operator (% recipients)	16.8	28.4	17.9
Savings in the Past Year (% age 15+)			
Saved at a financial institution	22.1	13.5	32.2
Saved at a financial institution, 2011	..	9.6	25.1
Saved using a savings club or person outside the family	9.8	7.9	4.9
Saved any money	59.5	40.6	62.7
Saved for old age	18.6	10.6	30.6
Saved for a farm or business	14.4	10.6	17.6
Saved for education or school fees	30.9	17.2	25.4
Credit in the Past Year (% age 15+)			
Borrowed from a financial institution	13.7	11.3	10.4
Borrowed from a financial institution, 2011	..	7.9	7.9
Borrowed from family or friends	31.6	13.5	24.0
Borrowed from a private informal lender	5.2	4.7	2.6
Borrowed any money	52.2	32.7	37.7
Borrowed for a farm or business	5.8	6.1	6.6
Borrowed for education or school fees	16.3	8.3	6.1
Outstanding mortgage at a financial institution	12.6	9.6	9.1

Benin

Low income

Population, age 15+ (millions)	5.9	GNI per capita ($)		790

	Country data	Sub-Saharan Africa	Low income
Account (% age 15+)			
All adults	16.6	34.2	27.5
Women	13.6	29.9	23.9
Adults belonging to the poorest 40%	11.0	24.6	19.4
Young adults (% ages 15–24)	8.4	25.9	20.2
Adults living in rural areas	12.6	29.2	24.8
Financial Institution Account (% age 15+)			
All adults	16.0	28.9	22.3
All adults, 2011	10.5	23.9	21.1
Mobile Account (% age 15+)			
All adults	2.0	11.5	10.0
Access to Financial Institution Account (% age 15+)			
Has debit card	5.0	17.9	6.6
Has debit card, 2011	0.7	15.0	6.3
ATM is the main mode of withdrawal (% with an account)	39.1	53.8	20.2
ATM is the main mode of withdrawal (% with an account), 2011	0.4	51.7	19.7
Use of Account in the Past Year (% age 15+)			
Used an account to receive wages	3.2	7.3	3.2
Used an account to receive government transfers	0.9	3.8	1.0
Used a financial institution account to pay utility bills	0.5	2.8	0.9
Other Digital Payments in the Past Year (% age 15+)			
Used a debit card to make payments	1.2	8.7	2.1
Used a credit card to make payments	0.3	1.9	0.6
Used the Internet to pay bills or make purchases	2.5	2.4	1.2
Domestic Remittances in the Past Year (% age 15+)			
Sent remittances	18.7	28.7	18.3
Sent remittances via a financial institution (% senders)	13.0	31.0	15.4
Sent remittances via a mobile phone (% senders)	4.8	30.8	42.8
Sent remittances via a money transfer operator (% senders)	15.8	21.0	14.1
Received remittances	24.2	37.2	25.6
Received remittances via a financial institution (% recipients)	10.8	26.6	13.0
Received remittances via a mobile phone (% recipients)	4.5	27.6	33.8
Received remittances via a money transfer operator (% recipients)	10.4	22.1	14.8
Savings in the Past Year (% age 15+)			
Saved at a financial institution	7.1	15.9	9.9
Saved at a financial institution, 2011	7.0	14.3	11.5
Saved using a savings club or person outside the family	36.8	23.9	16.3
Saved any money	61.1	59.6	46.5
Saved for old age	5.5	9.8	8.3
Saved for a farm or business	16.5	22.7	16.7
Saved for education or school fees	17.8	22.9	16.6
Credit in the Past Year (% age 15+)			
Borrowed from a financial institution	7.6	6.3	8.6
Borrowed from a financial institution, 2011	4.2	4.8	11.7
Borrowed from family or friends	24.2	41.9	34.9
Borrowed from a private informal lender	2.7	4.7	6.5
Borrowed any money	39.6	54.5	52.5
Borrowed for a farm or business	12.7	12.8	12.2
Borrowed for education or school fees	7.3	12.3	10.9
Outstanding mortgage at a financial institution	5.5	5.2	4.1

Bhutan

Lower middle income

Population, age 15+ (thousands)	**542**	GNI per capita ($)		**2,330**

	Country data	South Asia	Lower middle income
Account (% age 15+)			
All adults	33.7	46.4	42.7
Women	27.7	37.4	36.3
Adults belonging to the poorest 40%	25.4	38.1	33.2
Young adults (% ages 15-24)	22.2	36.7	34.7
Adults living in rural areas	24.9	43.5	40.0
Financial Institution Account (% age 15+)			
All adults	33.7	45.5	41.8
All adults, 2011	..	32.3	28.7
Mobile Account (% age 15+)			
All adults	..	2.6	2.5
Access to Financial Institution Account (% age 15+)			
Has debit card	17.2	18.0	21.2
Has debit card, 2011	..	7.2	10.1
ATM is the main mode of withdrawal (% with an account)	51.3	31.1	42.4
ATM is the main mode of withdrawal (% with an account), 2011	..	16.9	28.1
Use of Account in the Past Year (% age 15+)			
Used an account to receive wages	6.4	3.5	5.6
Used an account to receive government transfers	0.5	3.1	3.3
Used a financial institution account to pay utility bills	1.1	2.7	3.1
Other Digital Payments in the Past Year (% age 15+)			
Used a debit card to make payments	10.1	8.5	9.6
Used a credit card to make payments	0.0	2.6	2.8
Used the Internet to pay bills or make purchases	0.8	1.2	2.6
Domestic Remittances in the Past Year (% age 15+)			
Sent remittances	7.8	10.7	14.2
Sent remittances via a financial institution (% senders)	..	20.1	30.9
Sent remittances via a mobile phone (% senders)	..	7.7	7.7
Sent remittances via a money transfer operator (% senders)	..	13.7	18.3
Received remittances	12.5	12.2	17.8
Received remittances via a financial institution (% recipients)	23.0	15.8	26.0
Received remittances via a mobile phone (% recipients)	0.2	4.7	5.7
Received remittances via a money transfer operator (% recipients)	10.9	9.8	16.6
Savings in the Past Year (% age 15+)			
Saved at a financial institution	22.6	12.7	14.8
Saved at a financial institution, 2011	..	11.1	11.1
Saved using a savings club or person outside the family	1.1	8.8	12.4
Saved any money	32.7	36.2	45.6
Saved for old age	7.3	9.1	12.6
Saved for a farm or business	9.4	7.3	11.8
Saved for education or school fees	24.4	14.6	20.0
Credit in the Past Year (% age 15+)			
Borrowed from a financial institution	4.2	6.4	7.5
Borrowed from a financial institution, 2011	..	8.7	7.3
Borrowed from family or friends	10.2	31.4	33.1
Borrowed from a private informal lender	1.3	10.9	8.5
Borrowed any money	18.4	46.7	47.4
Borrowed for a farm or business	3.2	8.6	9.2
Borrowed for education or school fees	6.0	8.9	10.1
Outstanding mortgage at a financial institution	5.7	3.8	4.7

Bolivia

Latin America & Caribbean			Lower middle income

Population, age 15+ (millions)	7.0	GNI per capita ($)	2,550

	Country data	Latin America & the Carib.	Lower middle income
Account (% age 15+)			
All adults	41.8	51.4	42.7
Women	38.0	48.6	36.3
Adults belonging to the poorest 40%	26.3	41.2	33.2
Young adults (% ages 15–24)	31.4	37.4	34.7
Adults living in rural areas	35.4	46.0	40.0
Financial Institution Account (% age 15+)			
All adults	40.7	51.1	41.8
All adults, 2011	28.0	39.3	28.7
Mobile Account (% age 15+)			
All adults	2.8	1.7	2.5
Access to Financial Institution Account (% age 15+)			
Has debit card	23.1	40.4	21.2
Has debit card, 2011	12.8	28.9	10.1
ATM is the main mode of withdrawal (% with an account)	40.3	71.1	42.4
ATM is the main mode of withdrawal (% with an account), 2011	38.0	57.0	28.1
Use of Account in the Past Year (% age 15+)			
Used an account to receive wages	10.4	18.0	5.6
Used an account to receive government transfers	2.6	9.0	3.3
Used a financial institution account to pay utility bills	2.3	6.3	3.1
Other Digital Payments in the Past Year (% age 15+)			
Used a debit card to make payments	11.1	27.7	9.6
Used a credit card to make payments	4.6	18.0	2.8
Used the Internet to pay bills or make purchases	0.9	6.9	2.6
Domestic Remittances in the Past Year (% age 15+)			
Sent remittances	17.7	9.5	14.2
Sent remittances via a financial institution (% senders)	42.0	..	30.9
Sent remittances via a mobile phone (% senders)	7.9	..	7.7
Sent remittances via a money transfer operator (% senders)	23.9	..	18.3
Received remittances	18.8	11.3	17.8
Received remittances via a financial institution (% recipients)	33.7	34.2	26.0
Received remittances via a mobile phone (% recipients)	4.4	4.3	5.7
Received remittances via a money transfer operator (% recipients)	23.4	28.4	16.6
Savings in the Past Year (% age 15+)			
Saved at a financial institution	23.5	13.5	14.8
Saved at a financial institution, 2011	17.1	9.6	11.1
Saved using a savings club or person outside the family	14.2	7.9	12.4
Saved any money	64.4	40.6	45.6
Saved for old age	17.5	10.6	12.6
Saved for a farm or business	25.4	10.6	11.8
Saved for education or school fees	35.8	17.2	20.0
Credit in the Past Year (% age 15+)			
Borrowed from a financial institution	19.7	11.3	7.5
Borrowed from a financial institution, 2011	16.6	7.9	7.3
Borrowed from family or friends	13.2	13.5	33.1
Borrowed from a private informal lender	2.8	4.7	8.5
Borrowed any money	35.7	32.7	47.4
Borrowed for a farm or business	11.8	6.1	9.2
Borrowed for education or school fees	7.0	8.3	10.1
Outstanding mortgage at a financial institution	20.6	9.6	4.7

Bosnia and Herzegovina

Europe & Central Asia			Upper middle income

Population, age 15+ (millions)	**3.2**	GNI per capita ($)		**4,780**

	Country data	Europe & Central Asia	Upper middle income
Account (% age 15+)			
All adults	52.7	51.4	70.5
Women	47.1	47.4	67.3
Adults belonging to the poorest 40%	42.3	44.2	62.7
Young adults (% ages 15-24)	34.4	35.6	58.1
Adults living in rural areas	52.3	45.7	68.8
Financial Institution Account (% age 15+)			
All adults	52.7	51.4	70.4
All adults, 2011	56.2	43.3	57.4
Mobile Account (% age 15+)			
All adults	..	0.3	0.7
Access to Financial Institution Account (% age 15+)			
Has debit card	34.4	36.9	45.9
Has debit card, 2011	34.4	36.4	38.5
ATM is the main mode of withdrawal (% with an account)	44.8	66.7	55.7
ATM is the main mode of withdrawal (% with an account), 2011	42.9	72.5	42.8
Use of Account in the Past Year (% age 15+)			
Used an account to receive wages	18.6	22.5	18.1
Used an account to receive government transfers	2.1	7.3	9.6
Used a financial institution account to pay utility bills	3.0	12.5	12.3
Other Digital Payments in the Past Year (% age 15+)			
Used a debit card to make payments	18.7	22.9	19.9
Used a credit card to make payments	6.2	14.9	14.4
Used the Internet to pay bills or make purchases	3.3	11.9	15.3
Domestic Remittances in the Past Year (% age 15+)			
Sent remittances	8.0	12.9	15.4
Sent remittances via a financial institution (% senders)	..	31.5	37.2
Sent remittances via a mobile phone (% senders)	..	2.5	8.8
Sent remittances via a money transfer operator (% senders)	..	11.8	19.7
Received remittances	8.6	15.5	17.8
Received remittances via a financial institution (% recipients)	..	22.1	29.8
Received remittances via a mobile phone (% recipients)	..	1.0	5.6
Received remittances via a money transfer operator (% recipients)	..	15.6	17.9
Savings in the Past Year (% age 15+)			
Saved at a financial institution	8.8	8.4	32.2
Saved at a financial institution, 2011	6.1	4.9	25.1
Saved using a savings club or person outside the family	2.4	6.6	4.9
Saved any money	25.6	38.5	62.7
Saved for old age	10.0	11.8	30.6
Saved for a farm or business	2.6	5.1	17.6
Saved for education or school fees	7.8	12.1	25.4
Credit in the Past Year (% age 15+)			
Borrowed from a financial institution	14.0	12.4	10.4
Borrowed from a financial institution, 2011	13.0	7.8	7.9
Borrowed from family or friends	6.6	23.6	24.0
Borrowed from a private informal lender	0.1	2.1	2.6
Borrowed any money	25.1	39.5	37.7
Borrowed for a farm or business	2.3	2.8	6.6
Borrowed for education or school fees	1.6	6.2	6.1
Outstanding mortgage at a financial institution	16.7	10.2	9.1

Botswana

| | Population, age 15+ (millions) | 1.3 | GNI per capita ($) | 7,770 |

	Country data	Sub-Saharan Africa	Upper middle income
Account (% age 15+)			
All adults	52.0	34.2	70.5
Women	48.7	29.9	67.3
Adults belonging to the poorest 40%	36.6	24.6	62.7
Young adults (% ages 15–24)	47.7	25.9	58.1
Adults living in rural areas	52.3	29.2	68.8
Financial Institution Account (% age 15+)			
All adults	49.2	28.9	70.4
All adults, 2011	30.3	23.9	57.4
Mobile Account (% age 15+)			
All adults	20.8	11.5	0.7
Access to Financial Institution Account (% age 15+)			
Has debit card	35.1	17.9	45.9
Has debit card, 2011	15.6	38.5	38.5
ATM is the main mode of withdrawal (% with an account)	78.2	53.8	55.7
ATM is the main mode of withdrawal (% with an account), 2011	78.0	51.7	42.8
Use of Account in the Past Year (% age 15+)			
Used an account to receive wages	18.9	7.3	18.1
Used an account to receive government transfers	12.6	3.8	9.6
Used a financial institution account to pay utility bills	8.1	2.8	12.3
Other Digital Payments in the Past Year (% age 15+)			
Used a debit card to make payments	26.9	8.7	19.9
Used a credit card to make payments	7.8	1.9	14.4
Used the Internet to pay bills or make purchases	6.3	2.4	15.3
Domestic Remittances in the Past Year (% age 15+)			
Sent remittances	36.1	28.7	15.4
Sent remittances via a financial institution (% senders)	57.6	31.0	37.2
Sent remittances via a mobile phone (% senders)	36.9	30.8	8.8
Sent remittances via a money transfer operator (% senders)	26.2	21.0	19.7
Received remittances	48.3	37.2	17.8
Received remittances via a financial institution (% recipients)	45.4	26.6	29.8
Received remittances via a mobile phone (% recipients)	34.9	27.6	5.6
Received remittances via a money transfer operator (% recipients)	24.0	22.1	17.9
Savings in the Past Year (% age 15+)			
Saved at a financial institution	26.6	15.9	32.2
Saved at a financial institution, 2011	16.5	14.3	25.1
Saved using a savings club or person outside the family	35.4	23.9	4.9
Saved any money	58.2	59.6	62.7
Saved for old age	16.7	9.8	30.6
Saved for a farm or business	16.5	22.7	17.6
Saved for education or school fees	22.1	22.9	25.4
Credit in the Past Year (% age 15+)			
Borrowed from a financial institution	13.0	6.3	10.4
Borrowed from a financial institution, 2011	5.6	4.8	7.9
Borrowed from family or friends	61.2	41.9	24.0
Borrowed from a private informal lender	9.1	4.7	2.6
Borrowed any money	69.0	54.5	37.7
Borrowed for a farm or business	10.3	12.8	6.6
Borrowed for education or school fees	11.3	12.3	6.1
Outstanding mortgage at a financial institution	9.6	5.2	9.1

Brazil

Latin America & Caribbean			Upper middle income

Population, age 15+ (millions)	**152.1**	GNI per capita ($)	**11,690**

	Country data	Latin America & the Carib.	Upper middle income
Account (% age 15+)			
All adults	68.1	51.4	70.5
Women	64.8	48.6	67.3
Adults belonging to the poorest 40%	58.5	41.2	62.7
Young adults (% ages 15–24)	52.6	37.4	58.1
Adults living in rural areas	63.0	46.0	68.8
Financial Institution Account (% age 15+)			
All adults	68.1	51.1	70.4
All adults, 2011	55.9	39.3	57.4
Mobile Account (% age 15+)			
All adults	0.9	1.7	0.7
Access to Financial Institution Account (% age 15+)			
Has debit card	59.2	40.4	45.9
Has debit card, 2011	41.2	28.9	38.5
ATM is the main mode of withdrawal (% with an account)	75.4	71.1	55.7
ATM is the main mode of withdrawal (% with an account), 2011	57.5	57.0	42.8
Use of Account in the Past Year (% age 15+)			
Used an account to receive wages	22.9	18.0	18.1
Used an account to receive government transfers	13.2	9.0	9.6
Used a financial institution account to pay utility bills	9.4	6.3	12.3
Other Digital Payments in the Past Year (% age 15+)			
Used a debit card to make payments	41.7	27.7	19.9
Used a credit card to make payments	28.3	18.0	14.4
Used the Internet to pay bills or make purchases	8.8	6.9	15.3
Domestic Remittances in the Past Year (% age 15+)			
Sent remittances	5.8	9.5	15.4
Sent remittances via a financial institution (% senders)	..	..	37.2
Sent remittances via a mobile phone (% senders)	..	..	8.8
Sent remittances via a money transfer operator (% senders)	..	..	19.7
Received remittances	6.4	11.3	17.8
Received remittances via a financial institution (% recipients)	..	34.2	29.8
Received remittances via a mobile phone (% recipients)	..	4.3	5.6
Received remittances via a money transfer operator (% recipients)	..	28.4	17.9
Savings in the Past Year (% age 15+)			
Saved at a financial institution	12.3	13.5	32.2
Saved at a financial institution, 2011	10.3	9.6	25.1
Saved using a savings club or person outside the family	3.5	7.9	4.9
Saved any money	28.0	40.6	62.7
Saved for old age	3.6	10.6	30.6
Saved for a farm or business	6.9	10.6	17.6
Saved for education or school fees	6.1	17.2	25.4
Credit in the Past Year (% age 15+)			
Borrowed from a financial institution	11.9	11.3	10.4
Borrowed from a financial institution, 2011	6.3	7.9	7.9
Borrowed from family or friends	5.9	13.5	24.0
Borrowed from a private informal lender	1.1	4.7	2.6
Borrowed any money	22.3	32.7	37.7
Borrowed for a farm or business	3.5	6.1	6.6
Borrowed for education or school fees	1.7	8.3	6.1
Outstanding mortgage at a financial institution	10.5	9.6	9.1

Bulgaria

Europe & Central Asia			Upper middle income

Population, age 15+ (millions)	6.3	GNI per capita ($)		7,360

	Country data	Europe & Central Asia	Upper middle income
Account (% age 15+)			
All adults	63.0	51.4	70.5
Women	63.2	47.4	67.3
Adults belonging to the poorest 40%	49.9	44.2	62.7
Young adults (% ages 15–24)	32.6	35.6	58.1
Adults living in rural areas	54.3	45.7	68.8
Financial Institution Account (% age 15+)			
All adults	63.0	51.4	70.4
All adults, 2011	52.8	43.3	57.4
Mobile Account (% age 15+)			
All adults	..	0.3	0.7
Access to Financial Institution Account (% age 15+)			
Has debit card	55.9	36.9	45.9
Has debit card, 2011	45.8	36.4	38.5
ATM is the main mode of withdrawal (% with an account)	76.2	66.7	55.7
ATM is the main mode of withdrawal (% with an account), 2011	76.5	72.5	42.8
Use of Account in the Past Year (% age 15+)			
Used an account to receive wages	32.3	22.5	18.1
Used an account to receive government transfers	10.0	7.3	9.6
Used a financial institution account to pay utility bills	5.9	12.5	12.3
Other Digital Payments in the Past Year (% age 15+)			
Used a debit card to make payments	34.5	22.9	19.9
Used a credit card to make payments	9.2	14.9	14.4
Used the Internet to pay bills or make purchases	16.1	11.9	15.3
Domestic Remittances in the Past Year (% age 15+)			
Sent remittances	17.8	12.9	15.4
Sent remittances via a financial institution (% senders)	14.7	31.5	37.2
Sent remittances via a mobile phone (% senders)	0.0	2.5	8.8
Sent remittances via a money transfer operator (% senders)	11.7	11.8	19.7
Received remittances	20.1	15.5	17.8
Received remittances via a financial institution (% recipients)	8.6	22.1	29.8
Received remittances via a mobile phone (% recipients)	0.0	1.0	5.6
Received remittances via a money transfer operator (% recipients)	8.3	15.6	17.9
Savings in the Past Year (% age 15+)			
Saved at a financial institution	14.3	8.4	32.2
Saved at a financial institution, 2011	4.8	4.9	25.1
Saved using a savings club or person outside the family	0.8	6.6	4.9
Saved any money	27.3	38.5	62.7
Saved for old age	11.5	11.8	30.6
Saved for a farm or business	5.6	5.1	17.6
Saved for education or school fees	7.5	12.1	25.4
Credit in the Past Year (% age 15+)			
Borrowed from a financial institution	13.3	12.4	10.4
Borrowed from a financial institution, 2011	7.8	7.8	7.9
Borrowed from family or friends	19.8	23.6	24.0
Borrowed from a private informal lender	1.6	1.6	2.6
Borrowed any money	33.1	39.5	37.7
Borrowed for a farm or business	1.6	2.8	6.6
Borrowed for education or school fees	2.1	6.2	6.1
Outstanding mortgage at a financial institution	14.7	10.2	9.1

Burkina Faso

Population, age 15+ (millions)	**9.2**	GNI per capita ($)	**750**

	Country data	Sub-Saharan Africa	Low income
Account (% age 15+)			
All adults	14.4	34.2	27.5
Women	12.6	29.9	23.9
Adults belonging to the poorest 40%	8.9	24.6	19.4
Young adults (% ages 15–24)	8.3	25.9	20.2
Adults living in rural areas	13.0	29.2	24.8
Financial Institution Account (% age 15+)			
All adults	13.4	28.9	22.3
All adults, 2011	13.4	23.9	21.1
Mobile Account (% age 15+)			
All adults	3.1	11.5	10.0
Access to Financial Institution Account (% age 15+)			
Has debit card	4.3	17.9	6.6
Has debit card, 2011	2.0	15.0	6.3
ATM is the main mode of withdrawal (% with an account)	20.2	53.8	20.2
ATM is the main mode of withdrawal (% with an account), 2011	3.6	51.7	19.7
Use of Account in the Past Year (% age 15+)			
Used an account to receive wages	3.9	7.3	3.2
Used an account to receive government transfers	2.0	3.8	1.0
Used a financial institution account to pay utility bills	0.9	2.8	0.9
Other Digital Payments in the Past Year (% age 15+)			
Used a debit card to make payments	1.4	8.7	2.1
Used a credit card to make payments	1.4	1.9	0.6
Used the Internet to pay bills or make purchases	1.7	2.4	1.2
Domestic Remittances in the Past Year (% age 15+)			
Sent remittances	18.5	28.7	18.3
Sent remittances via a financial institution (% senders)	13.0	31.0	15.4
Sent remittances via a mobile phone (% senders)	16.5	30.8	42.8
Sent remittances via a money transfer operator (% senders)	30.2	21.0	14.1
Received remittances	26.7	37.2	25.6
Received remittances via a financial institution (% recipients)	9.2	26.6	13.0
Received remittances via a mobile phone (% recipients)	6.9	27.6	33.8
Received remittances via a money transfer operator (% recipients)	24.0	22.1	14.8
Savings in the Past Year (% age 15+)			
Saved at a financial institution	8.7	15.9	9.9
Saved at a financial institution, 2011	7.9	14.3	11.5
Saved using a savings club or person outside the family	18.0	23.9	16.3
Saved any money	50.8	59.6	46.5
Saved for old age	7.5	9.8	8.3
Saved for a farm or business	15.3	22.7	16.7
Saved for education or school fees	20.4	22.9	16.6
Credit in the Past Year (% age 15+)			
Borrowed from a financial institution	5.0	6.3	8.6
Borrowed from a financial institution, 2011	3.1	4.8	11.7
Borrowed from family or friends	30.5	41.9	34.9
Borrowed from a private informal lender	2.4	4.7	6.5
Borrowed any money	46.4	54.5	52.5
Borrowed for a farm or business	8.5	12.8	12.2
Borrowed for education or school fees	9.9	12.3	10.9
Outstanding mortgage at a financial institution	3.4	5.2	4.1

Burundi

Population, age 15+ (millions)	5.6	GNI per capita ($)	260

	Country data	Sub-Saharan Africa	Low income
Account (% age 15+)			
All adults	7.1	34.2	27.5
Women	6.7	29.9	23.9
Adults belonging to the poorest 40%	2.3	24.6	19.4
Young adults (% ages 15–24)	4.9	25.9	20.2
Adults living in rural areas	6.5	29.2	24.8
Financial Institution Account (% age 15+)			
All adults	6.9	28.9	22.3
All adults, 2011	7.2	23.9	21.1
Mobile Account (% age 15+)			
All adults	0.7	11.5	10.0
Access to Financial Institution Account (% age 15+)			
Has debit card	1.3	17.9	6.6
Has debit card, 2011	0.8	15.0	6.3
ATM is the main mode of withdrawal (% with an account)	..	53.8	20.2
ATM is the main mode of withdrawal (% with an account), 2011	..	51.7	19.7
Use of Account in the Past Year (% age 15+)			
Used an account to receive wages	1.6	7.3	3.2
Used an account to receive government transfers	0.3	3.8	1.0
Used a financial institution account to pay utility bills	0.1	2.8	0.9
Other Digital Payments in the Past Year (% age 15+)			
Used a debit card to make payments	0.6	8.7	2.1
Used a credit card to make payments	0.2	1.9	0.6
Used the Internet to pay bills or make purchases	0.2	2.4	1.2
Domestic Remittances in the Past Year (% age 15+)			
Sent remittances	9.9	28.7	18.3
Sent remittances via a financial institution (% senders)	..	31.0	15.4
Sent remittances via a mobile phone (% senders)	..	30.8	42.8
Sent remittances via a money transfer operator (% senders)	..	21.0	14.1
Received remittances	15.4	37.2	25.6
Received remittances via a financial institution (% recipients)	7.3	26.6	13.0
Received remittances via a mobile phone (% recipients)	2.2	27.6	33.8
Received remittances via a money transfer operator (% recipients)	6.0	22.1	14.8
Savings in the Past Year (% age 15+)			
Saved at a financial institution	4.0	15.9	9.9
Saved at a financial institution, 2011	3.3	14.3	11.5
Saved using a savings club or person outside the family	8.1	23.9	16.3
Saved any money	34.9	59.6	46.5
Saved for old age	3.2	9.8	8.3
Saved for a farm or business	6.1	22.7	16.7
Saved for education or school fees	14.2	22.9	16.6
Credit in the Past Year (% age 15+)			
Borrowed from a financial institution	1.5	6.3	8.6
Borrowed from a financial institution, 2011	1.7	4.8	11.7
Borrowed from family or friends	45.9	41.9	34.9
Borrowed from a private informal lender	6.0	4.7	6.5
Borrowed any money	60.3	54.5	52.5
Borrowed for a farm or business	5.8	12.8	12.2
Borrowed for education or school fees	17.6	12.3	10.9
Outstanding mortgage at a financial institution	1.4	5.2	4.1

Cambodia

Population, age 15+ (millions)	**10.4**	GNI per capita ($)	**950**

	Country data	East Asia & Pacific	Low income
Account (% age 15+)			
All adults	22.2	69.0	27.5
Women	20.5	67.0	23.9
Adults belonging to the poorest 40%	17.9	60.9	19.4
Young adults (% ages 15–24)	26.3	60.7	20.2
Adults living in rural areas	20.4	64.5	24.8
Financial Institution Account (% age 15+)			
All adults	12.6	68.8	22.3
All adults, 2011	3.7	55.1	21.1
Mobile Account (% age 15+)			
All adults	13.3	0.4	10.0
Access to Financial Institution Account (% age 15+)			
Has debit card	5.4	42.9	6.6
Has debit card, 2011	2.9	34.7	6.3
ATM is the main mode of withdrawal (% with an account)	30.5	53.3	20.2
ATM is the main mode of withdrawal (% with an account), 2011	..	37.0	19.7
Use of Account in the Past Year (% age 15+)			
Used an account to receive wages	3.2	15.1	3.2
Used an account to receive government transfers	0.4	8.1	1.0
Used a financial institution account to pay utility bills	1.7	11.8	0.9
Other Digital Payments in the Past Year (% age 15+)			
Used a debit card to make payments	0.7	14.8	2.1
Used a credit card to make payments	2.3	10.8	0.6
Used the Internet to pay bills or make purchases	0.6	15.6	1.2
Domestic Remittances in the Past Year (% age 15+)			
Sent remittances	19.8	16.6	18.3
Sent remittances via a financial institution (% senders)	26.4	36.9	15.4
Sent remittances via a mobile phone (% senders)	28.0	8.7	42.8
Sent remittances via a money transfer operator (% senders)	55.4	18.5	14.1
Received remittances	23.7	20.6	25.6
Received remittances via a financial institution (% recipients)	20.4	29.0	13.0
Received remittances via a mobile phone (% recipients)	26.4	4.9	33.8
Received remittances via a money transfer operator (% recipients)	39.3	15.8	14.8
Savings in the Past Year (% age 15+)			
Saved at a financial institution	3.6	36.5	9.9
Saved at a financial institution, 2011	0.8	28.5	11.5
Saved using a savings club or person outside the family	14.1	6.0	16.3
Saved any money	67.0	71.0	46.5
Saved for old age	28.6	36.5	8.3
Saved for a farm or business	24.7	21.3	16.7
Saved for education or school fees	37.3	30.7	16.6
Credit in the Past Year (% age 15+)			
Borrowed from a financial institution	27.7	11.0	8.6
Borrowed from a financial institution, 2011	19.5	8.6	11.7
Borrowed from family or friends	36.2	28.3	34.9
Borrowed from a private informal lender	18.2	2.5	6.5
Borrowed any money	62.0	41.2	52.5
Borrowed for a farm or business	14.8	8.3	12.2
Borrowed for education or school fees	8.1	7.1	10.9
Outstanding mortgage at a financial institution	12.4	8.0	4.1

Cameroon

Sub-Saharan Africa   **Lower middle income**

Population, age 15+ (millions)	**12.7**	GNI per capita ($)	**1,290**

	Country data	Sub-Saharan Africa	Lower middle income
Account (% age 15+)			
All adults	12.2	34.2	42.7
Women	10.2	29.9	36.3
Adults belonging to the poorest 40%	2.7	24.6	33.2
Young adults (% ages 15–24)	5.3	25.9	34.7
Adults living in rural areas	11.1	29.2	40.0
Financial Institution Account (% age 15+)			
All adults	11.4	28.9	41.8
All adults, 2011	14.8	23.9	28.7
Mobile Account (% age 15+)			
All adults	1.8	11.5	2.5
Access to Financial Institution Account (% age 15+)			
Has debit card	6.1	17.9	21.2
Has debit card, 2011	2.1	15.0	10.1
ATM is the main mode of withdrawal (% with an account)	27.1	53.8	42.4
ATM is the main mode of withdrawal (% with an account), 2011	5.8	51.7	28.1
Use of Account in the Past Year (% age 15+)			
Used an account to receive wages	3.7	7.3	5.6
Used an account to receive government transfers	0.4	3.8	3.3
Used a financial institution account to pay utility bills	0.2	2.8	3.1
Other Digital Payments in the Past Year (% age 15+)			
Used a debit card to make payments	1.5	8.7	9.6
Used a credit card to make payments	0.3	1.9	2.8
Used the Internet to pay bills or make purchases	0.7	2.4	2.6
Domestic Remittances in the Past Year (% age 15+)			
Sent remittances	28.5	28.7	14.2
Sent remittances via a financial institution (% senders)	4.3	31.0	30.9
Sent remittances via a mobile phone (% senders)	2.3	30.8	7.7
Sent remittances via a money transfer operator (% senders)	62.1	21.0	18.3
Received remittances	38.9	37.2	17.8
Received remittances via a financial institution (% recipients)	7.0	26.6	26.0
Received remittances via a mobile phone (% recipients)	1.6	27.6	5.7
Received remittances via a money transfer operator (% recipients)	57.1	22.1	16.6
Savings in the Past Year (% age 15+)			
Saved at a financial institution	7.7	15.9	14.8
Saved at a financial institution, 2011	9.9	14.3	11.1
Saved using a savings club or person outside the family	34.6	23.9	12.4
Saved any money	64.0	59.6	45.6
Saved for old age	7.2	9.8	12.6
Saved for a farm or business	16.7	22.7	11.8
Saved for education or school fees	25.5	22.9	20.0
Credit in the Past Year (% age 15+)			
Borrowed from a financial institution	1.9	6.3	7.5
Borrowed from a financial institution, 2011	4.5	4.8	7.3
Borrowed from family or friends	42.2	41.9	33.1
Borrowed from a private informal lender	1.6	4.7	8.5
Borrowed any money	56.6	54.5	47.4
Borrowed for a farm or business	11.0	12.8	9.2
Borrowed for education or school fees	12.5	12.3	10.1
Outstanding mortgage at a financial institution	2.7	5.2	4.7

Canada

Population, age 15+ (millions)	**29.4**	GNI per capita ($)	**52,210**

	Country data	High income: OECD
Account (% age 15+)		
All adults	99.1	94.0
Women	99.2	93.8
Adults belonging to the poorest 40%	98.4	90.6
Young adults (% ages 15–24)	97.4	84.1
Adults living in rural areas	98.3	93.8
Financial Institution Account (% age 15+)		
All adults	99.1	94.0
All adults, 2011	95.8	90.0
Mobile Account (% age 15+)		
All adults	..	..
Access to Financial Institution Account (% age 15+)		
Has debit card	93.2	79.7
Has debit card, 2011	88.0	61.9
ATM is the main mode of withdrawal (% with an account)	..	..
ATM is the main mode of withdrawal (% with an account), 2011	69.9	68.5
Use of Account in the Past Year (% age 15+)		
Used an account to receive wages	52.4	44.3
Used an account to receive government transfers	28.6	17.2
Used a financial institution account to pay utility bills	69.4	61.1
Other Digital Payments in the Past Year (% age 15+)		
Used a debit card to make payments	83.0	65.3
Used a credit card to make payments	73.1	46.7
Used the Internet to pay bills or make purchases	65.7	54.1
Domestic Remittances in the Past Year (% age 15+)		
Sent remittances	..	..
Sent remittances via a financial institution (% senders)	..	..
Sent remittances via a mobile phone (% senders)	..	..
Sent remittances via a money transfer operator (% senders)	..	..
Received remittances	..	..
Received remittances via a financial institution (% recipients)	..	..
Received remittances via a mobile phone (% recipients)	..	..
Received remittances via a money transfer operator (% recipients)	..	..
Savings in the Past Year (% age 15+)		
Saved at a financial institution	62.6	51.6
Saved at a financial institution, 2011	53.2	45.3
Saved using a savings club or person outside the family	..	..
Saved any money	82.2	70.8
Saved for old age	51.7	39.7
Saved for a farm or business	7.3	9.0
Saved for education or school fees	31.9	25.0
Credit in the Past Year (% age 15+)		
Borrowed from a financial institution	27.0	18.4
Borrowed from a financial institution, 2011	20.3	14.2
Borrowed from family or friends	17.1	14.9
Borrowed from a private informal lender	1.3	0.9
Borrowed any money	50.7	39.8
Borrowed for a farm or business	3.2	2.6
Borrowed for education or school fees	7.4	5.6
Outstanding mortgage at a financial institution	32.4	26.1

Chad

Population, age 15+ (millions)	6.6	GNI per capita ($)		1,030

	Country data	Sub-Saharan Africa	Low income
Account (% age 15+)			
All adults	12.4	34.2	27.5
Women	7.8	29.9	23.9
Adults belonging to the poorest 40%	8.3	24.6	19.4
Young adults (% ages 15–24)	8.1	25.9	20.2
Adults living in rural areas	12.1	29.2	24.8
Financial Institution Account (% age 15+)			
All adults	7.7	28.9	22.3
All adults, 2011	9.0	23.9	21.1
Mobile Account (% age 15+)			
All adults	5.8	11.5	10.0
Access to Financial Institution Account (% age 15+)			
Has debit card	2.8	17.9	6.6
Has debit card, 2011	5.3	15.0	6.3
ATM is the main mode of withdrawal (% with an account)	..	53.8	20.2
ATM is the main mode of withdrawal (% with an account), 2011	..	51.7	19.7
Use of Account in the Past Year (% age 15+)			
Used an account to receive wages	0.8	7.3	3.2
Used an account to receive government transfers	1.4	3.8	1.0
Used a financial institution account to pay utility bills	0.2	2.8	0.9
Other Digital Payments in the Past Year (% age 15+)			
Used a debit card to make payments	0.5	8.7	2.1
Used a credit card to make payments	0.5	1.9	0.6
Used the Internet to pay bills or make purchases	2.3	2.4	1.2
Domestic Remittances in the Past Year (% age 15+)			
Sent remittances	18.5	28.7	18.3
Sent remittances via a financial institution (% senders)	9.1	31.0	15.4
Sent remittances via a mobile phone (% senders)	33.9	30.8	42.8
Sent remittances via a money transfer operator (% senders)	29.7	21.0	14.1
Received remittances	30.9	37.2	25.6
Received remittances via a financial institution (% recipients)	4.6	26.6	13.0
Received remittances via a mobile phone (% recipients)	24.3	27.6	33.8
Received remittances via a money transfer operator (% recipients)	11.1	22.1	14.8
Savings in the Past Year (% age 15+)			
Saved at a financial institution	4.6	15.9	9.9
Saved at a financial institution, 2011	6.8	14.3	11.5
Saved using a savings club or person outside the family	20.1	23.9	16.3
Saved any money	48.6	59.6	46.5
Saved for old age	2.5	9.8	8.3
Saved for a farm or business	22.4	22.7	16.7
Saved for education or school fees	14.1	22.9	16.6
Credit in the Past Year (% age 15+)			
Borrowed from a financial institution	2.4	6.3	8.6
Borrowed from a financial institution, 2011	6.2	4.8	11.7
Borrowed from family or friends	24.5	41.9	34.9
Borrowed from a private informal lender	3.1	4.7	6.5
Borrowed any money	41.0	54.5	52.5
Borrowed for a farm or business	11.4	12.8	12.2
Borrowed for education or school fees	4.8	12.3	10.9
Outstanding mortgage at a financial institution	4.5	5.2	4.1

Chile

Population, age 15+ (millions)	**13.9**	GNI per capita ($)	**15,230**

	Country data	High income: OECD
Account (% age 15+)		
All adults	63.3	94.0
Women	59.2	93.8
Adults belonging to the poorest 40%	56.4	90.6
Young adults (% ages 15–24)	62.5	84.1
Adults living in rural areas	61.2	93.8
Financial Institution Account (% age 15+)		
All adults	63.2	94.0
All adults, 2011	42.2	90.0
Mobile Account (% age 15+)		
All adults	3.8	..
Access to Financial Institution Account (% age 15+)		
Has debit card	54.1	79.7
Has debit card, 2011	25.8	61.9
ATM is the main mode of withdrawal (% with an account)	80.8	..
ATM is the main mode of withdrawal (% with an account), 2011	61.8	68.5
Use of Account in the Past Year (% age 15+)		
Used an account to receive wages	27.7	44.3
Used an account to receive government transfers	5.5	17.2
Used a financial institution account to pay utility bills	8.6	61.1
Other Digital Payments in the Past Year (% age 15+)		
Used a debit card to make payments	39.8	65.3
Used a credit card to make payments	22.6	46.7
Used the Internet to pay bills or make purchases	14.6	54.1
Domestic Remittances in the Past Year (% age 15+)		
Sent remittances	14.9	..
Sent remittances via a financial institution (% senders)	55.8	..
Sent remittances via a mobile phone (% senders)	2.7	..
Sent remittances via a money transfer operator (% senders)	23.0	..
Received remittances	15.4	..
Received remittances via a financial institution (% recipients)	40.5	..
Received remittances via a mobile phone (% recipients)	2.5	..
Received remittances via a money transfer operator (% recipients)	23.4	..
Savings in the Past Year (% age 15+)		
Saved at a financial institution	15.0	51.6
Saved at a financial institution, 2011	12.4	45.3
Saved using a savings club or person outside the family	1.8	..
Saved any money	35.9	70.8
Saved for old age	12.9	39.7
Saved for a farm or business	5.9	9.0
Saved for education or school fees	13.8	25.0
Credit in the Past Year (% age 15+)		
Borrowed from a financial institution	15.6	18.4
Borrowed from a financial institution, 2011	7.8	14.2
Borrowed from family or friends	6.3	14.9
Borrowed from a private informal lender	0.6	0.9
Borrowed any money	28.6	39.8
Borrowed for a farm or business	3.0	2.6
Borrowed for education or school fees	4.7	5.6
Outstanding mortgage at a financial institution	13.3	26.1

China

	Country data	East Asia & Pacific	Upper middle income
East Asia & Pacific		**Upper middle income**	
Population, age 15+ (millions)	**1,112.6**	GNI per capita ($)	**6,560**

	Country data	East Asia & Pacific	Upper middle income
Account (% age 15+)			
All adults	78.9	69.0	70.5
Women	76.4	67.0	67.3
Adults belonging to the poorest 40%	72.0	60.9	62.7
Young adults (% ages 15–24)	74.2	60.7	58.1
Adults living in rural areas	74.3	64.5	68.8
Financial Institution Account (% age 15+)			
All adults	78.9	68.8	70.4
All adults, 2011	63.8	55.1	57.4
Mobile Account (% age 15+)			
All adults	..	0.4	0.7
Access to Financial Institution Account (% age 15+)			
Has debit card	48.6	42.9	45.9
Has debit card, 2011	41.0	34.7	38.5
ATM is the main mode of withdrawal (% with an account)	51.2	53.3	55.7
ATM is the main mode of withdrawal (% with an account), 2011	33.4	37.0	42.8
Use of Account in the Past Year (% age 15+)			
Used an account to receive wages	17.7	15.1	18.1
Used an account to receive government transfers	9.5	8.1	9.6
Used a financial institution account to pay utility bills	15.1	11.8	12.3
Other Digital Payments in the Past Year (% age 15+)			
Used a debit card to make payments	17.3	14.8	19.9
Used a credit card to make payments	13.8	10.8	14.4
Used the Internet to pay bills or make purchases	19.2	15.6	15.3
Domestic Remittances in the Past Year (% age 15+)			
Sent remittances	15.5	16.6	15.4
Sent remittances via a financial institution (% senders)	34.3	36.9	37.2
Sent remittances via a mobile phone (% senders)	10.1	8.7	8.8
Sent remittances via a money transfer operator (% senders)	15.0	18.5	19.7
Received remittances	17.6	20.6	17.8
Received remittances via a financial institution (% recipients)	27.3	29.0	29.8
Received remittances via a mobile phone (% recipients)	6.0	4.9	5.6
Received remittances via a money transfer operator (% recipients)	12.3	15.8	17.9
Savings in the Past Year (% age 15+)			
Saved at a financial institution	41.2	36.5	32.2
Saved at a financial institution, 2011	32.1	28.5	25.1
Saved using a savings club or person outside the family	2.5	6.0	4.9
Saved any money	72.1	71.0	62.7
Saved for old age	38.7	36.5	30.6
Saved for a farm or business	21.9	21.3	17.6
Saved for education or school fees	29.9	30.7	25.4
Credit in the Past Year (% age 15+)			
Borrowed from a financial institution	9.6	11.0	10.4
Borrowed from a financial institution, 2011	7.3	8.6	7.9
Borrowed from family or friends	25.1	28.3	24.0
Borrowed from a private informal lender	1.1	2.5	2.6
Borrowed any money	36.3	41.2	37.7
Borrowed for a farm or business	7.0	8.3	6.6
Borrowed for education or school fees	4.9	7.1	6.1
Outstanding mortgage at a financial institution	8.5	8.0	9.1

Colombia

Latin America & Caribbean		Upper middle income	

Population, age 15+ (millions)	**34.9**	GNI per capita ($)	**7,590**

	Country data	Latin America & the Carib.	Upper middle income
Account (% age 15+)			
All adults	39.0	51.4	70.5
Women	34.0	48.6	67.3
Adults belonging to the poorest 40%	24.4	41.2	62.7
Young adults (% ages 15–24)	28.4	37.4	58.1
Adults living in rural areas	35.9	46.0	68.8
Financial Institution Account (% age 15+)			
All adults	38.4	51.1	70.4
All adults, 2011	30.4	39.3	57.4
Mobile Account (% age 15+)			
All adults	2.2	1.7	0.7
Access to Financial Institution Account (% age 15+)			
Has debit card	30.0	40.4	45.9
Has debit card, 2011	22.7	28.9	38.5
ATM is the main mode of withdrawal (% with an account)	80.8	71.1	55.7
ATM is the main mode of withdrawal (% with an account), 2011	61.2	57.0	42.8
Use of Account in the Past Year (% age 15+)			
Used an account to receive wages	15.4	18.0	18.1
Used an account to receive government transfers	4.8	9.0	9.6
Used a financial institution account to pay utility bills	1.9	6.3	12.3
Other Digital Payments in the Past Year (% age 15+)			
Used a debit card to make payments	17.5	27.7	19.9
Used a credit card to make payments	12.2	18.0	14.4
Used the Internet to pay bills or make purchases	6.4	6.9	15.3
Domestic Remittances in the Past Year (% age 15+)			
Sent remittances	19.8	9.5	15.4
Sent remittances via a financial institution (% senders)	18.8	..	37.2
Sent remittances via a mobile phone (% senders)	0.9	..	8.8
Sent remittances via a money transfer operator (% senders)	63.4	..	19.7
Received remittances	19.1	11.3	17.8
Received remittances via a financial institution (% recipients)	17.9	34.2	29.8
Received remittances via a mobile phone (% recipients)	0.7	4.3	5.6
Received remittances via a money transfer operator (% recipients)	63.3	28.4	17.9
Savings in the Past Year (% age 15+)			
Saved at a financial institution	12.3	13.5	32.2
Saved at a financial institution, 2011	9.2	9.6	25.1
Saved using a savings club or person outside the family	5.4	7.9	4.9
Saved any money	43.9	40.6	62.7
Saved for old age	13.0	10.6	30.6
Saved for a farm or business	13.1	10.6	17.6
Saved for education or school fees	20.4	17.2	25.4
Credit in the Past Year (% age 15+)			
Borrowed from a financial institution	15.6	11.3	10.4
Borrowed from a financial institution, 2011	11.9	7.9	7.9
Borrowed from family or friends	15.9	13.5	24.0
Borrowed from a private informal lender	8.1	4.7	2.6
Borrowed any money	38.9	32.7	37.7
Borrowed for a farm or business	10.2	6.1	6.6
Borrowed for education or school fees	10.1	8.3	6.1
Outstanding mortgage at a financial institution	9.7	9.6	9.1

Congo, Dem. Rep.

Sub-Saharan Africa			Low income
Population, age 15+ (millions)	**37.1**	GNI per capita ($)	**430**

	Country data	Sub-Saharan Africa	Low income
Account (% age 15+)			
All adults	17.5	34.2	27.5
Women	14.3	29.9	23.9
Adults belonging to the poorest 40%	12.2	24.6	19.4
Young adults (% ages 15–24)	12.3	25.9	20.2
Adults living in rural areas	14.1	29.2	24.8
Financial Institution Account (% age 15+)			
All adults	10.9	28.9	22.3
All adults, 2011	3.7	23.9	21.1
Mobile Account (% age 15+)			
All adults	9.2	11.5	10.0
Access to Financial Institution Account (% age 15+)			
Has debit card	3.8	17.9	6.6
Has debit card, 2011	1.7	15.0	6.3
ATM is the main mode of withdrawal (% with an account)	..	53.8	20.2
ATM is the main mode of withdrawal (% with an account), 2011	..	51.7	19.7
Use of Account in the Past Year (% age 15+)			
Used an account to receive wages	3.7	7.3	3.2
Used an account to receive government transfers	1.5	3.8	1.0
Used a financial institution account to pay utility bills	0.2	2.8	0.9
Other Digital Payments in the Past Year (% age 15+)			
Used a debit card to make payments	1.6	8.7	2.1
Used a credit card to make payments	1.0	1.9	0.6
Used the Internet to pay bills or make purchases	2.7	2.4	1.2
Domestic Remittances in the Past Year (% age 15+)			
Sent remittances	15.3	28.7	18.3
Sent remittances via a financial institution (% senders)	9.4	31.0	15.4
Sent remittances via a mobile phone (% senders)	13.6	30.8	42.8
Sent remittances via a money transfer operator (% senders)	53.4	21.0	14.1
Received remittances	37.2	37.2	25.6
Received remittances via a financial institution (% recipients)	10.3	26.6	13.0
Received remittances via a mobile phone (% recipients)	9.2	27.6	33.8
Received remittances via a money transfer operator (% recipients)	46.1	22.1	14.8
Savings in the Past Year (% age 15+)			
Saved at a financial institution	4.7	15.9	9.9
Saved at a financial institution, 2011	1.5	14.3	11.5
Saved using a savings club or person outside the family	15.4	23.9	16.3
Saved any money	65.2	59.6	46.5
Saved for old age	4.4	9.8	8.3
Saved for a farm or business	25.7	22.7	16.7
Saved for education or school fees	21.4	22.9	16.6
Credit in the Past Year (% age 15+)			
Borrowed from a financial institution	2.4	6.3	8.6
Borrowed from a financial institution, 2011	1.5	4.8	11.7
Borrowed from family or friends	40.9	41.9	34.9
Borrowed from a private informal lender	6.0	4.7	6.5
Borrowed any money	56.9	54.5	52.5
Borrowed for a farm or business	11.2	12.8	12.2
Borrowed for education or school fees	10.8	12.3	10.9
Outstanding mortgage at a financial institution	2.7	5.2	4.1

Congo, Rep.

Sub-Saharan Africa		Lower middle income	

Population, age 15+ (millions)	2.6	GNI per capita ($)	2,590

	Country data	Sub-Saharan Africa	Lower middle income
Account (% age 15+)			
All adults	17.1	34.2	42.7
Women	15.0	29.9	36.3
Adults belonging to the poorest 40%	6.6	24.6	33.2
Young adults (% ages 15–24)	7.4	25.9	34.7
Adults living in rural areas	11.8	29.2	40.0
Financial Institution Account (% age 15+)			
All adults	16.7	28.9	41.8
All adults, 2011	10.0	23.9	28.7
Mobile Account (% age 15+)			
All adults	2.0	11.5	2.5
Access to Financial Institution Account (% age 15+)			
Has debit card	10.2	17.9	21.2
Has debit card, 2011	4.1	15.0	10.1
ATM is the main mode of withdrawal (% with an account)	16.3	53.8	42.4
ATM is the main mode of withdrawal (% with an account), 2011	6.8	51.7	28.1
Use of Account in the Past Year (% age 15+)			
Used an account to receive wages	5.0	7.3	5.6
Used an account to receive government transfers	1.8	3.8	3.3
Used a financial institution account to pay utility bills	0.6	2.8	3.1
Other Digital Payments in the Past Year (% age 15+)			
Used a debit card to make payments	2.5	8.7	9.6
Used a credit card to make payments	1.0	1.9	2.8
Used the Internet to pay bills or make purchases	0.8	2.4	2.6
Domestic Remittances in the Past Year (% age 15+)			
Sent remittances	25.1	28.7	14.2
Sent remittances via a financial institution (% senders)	24.5	31.0	30.9
Sent remittances via a mobile phone (% senders)	1.7	30.8	7.7
Sent remittances via a money transfer operator (% senders)	69.5	21.0	18.3
Received remittances	27.0	37.2	17.8
Received remittances via a financial institution (% recipients)	16.3	26.6	26.0
Received remittances via a mobile phone (% recipients)	2.6	27.6	5.7
Received remittances via a money transfer operator (% recipients)	61.2	22.1	16.6
Savings in the Past Year (% age 15+)			
Saved at a financial institution	9.8	15.9	14.8
Saved at a financial institution, 2011	5.9	14.3	11.1
Saved using a savings club or person outside the family	24.1	23.9	12.4
Saved any money	55.9	59.6	45.6
Saved for old age	11.9	9.8	12.6
Saved for a farm or business	19.3	22.7	11.8
Saved for education or school fees	20.4	22.9	20.0
Credit in the Past Year (% age 15+)			
Borrowed from a financial institution	4.4	6.3	7.5
Borrowed from a financial institution, 2011	3.2	4.8	7.3
Borrowed from family or friends	23.6	41.9	33.1
Borrowed from a private informal lender	6.4	4.7	8.5
Borrowed any money	41.6	54.5	47.4
Borrowed for a farm or business	10.3	12.8	9.2
Borrowed for education or school fees	7.2	12.3	10.1
Outstanding mortgage at a financial institution	3.2	5.2	4.7

Costa Rica

Population, age 15+ (millions)	3.7	GNI per capita ($)	9,550

	Country data	Latin America & the Carib.	Upper middle income
Account (% age 15+)			
All adults	64.6	51.4	70.5
Women	60.2	48.6	67.3
Adults belonging to the poorest 40%	61.3	41.2	62.7
Young adults (% ages 15–24)	61.6	37.4	58.1
Adults living in rural areas	67.3	46.0	68.8
Financial Institution Account (% age 15+)			
All adults	64.6	51.1	70.4
All adults, 2011	50.4	39.3	57.4
Mobile Account (% age 15+)			
All adults	..	1.7	0.7
Access to Financial Institution Account (% age 15+)			
Has debit card	53.6	40.4	45.9
Has debit card, 2011	43.8	28.9	38.5
ATM is the main mode of withdrawal (% with an account)	83.2	71.1	55.7
ATM is the main mode of withdrawal (% with an account), 2011	72.2	57.0	42.8
Use of Account in the Past Year (% age 15+)			
Used an account to receive wages	18.7	18.0	18.1
Used an account to receive government transfers	7.9	9.0	9.6
Used a financial institution account to pay utility bills	9.4	6.3	12.3
Other Digital Payments in the Past Year (% age 15+)			
Used a debit card to make payments	35.3	27.7	19.9
Used a credit card to make payments	10.8	18.0	14.4
Used the Internet to pay bills or make purchases	10.4	6.9	15.3
Domestic Remittances in the Past Year (% age 15+)			
Sent remittances	16.4	9.5	15.4
Sent remittances via a financial institution (% senders)	48.2	..	37.2
Sent remittances via a mobile phone (% senders)	2.4	..	8.8
Sent remittances via a money transfer operator (% senders)	36.2	..	19.7
Received remittances	19.2	11.3	17.8
Received remittances via a financial institution (% recipients)	43.1	34.2	29.8
Received remittances via a mobile phone (% recipients)	0.6	4.3	5.6
Received remittances via a money transfer operator (% recipients)	19.1	28.4	17.9
Savings in the Past Year (% age 15+)			
Saved at a financial institution	24.2	13.5	32.2
Saved at a financial institution, 2011	19.9	9.6	25.1
Saved using a savings club or person outside the family	6.5	7.9	4.9
Saved any money	59.4	40.6	62.7
Saved for old age	19.2	10.6	30.6
Saved for a farm or business	14.7	10.6	17.6
Saved for education or school fees	26.8	17.2	25.4
Credit in the Past Year (% age 15+)			
Borrowed from a financial institution	12.7	11.3	10.4
Borrowed from a financial institution, 2011	10.0	7.9	7.9
Borrowed from family or friends	14.3	13.5	24.0
Borrowed from a private informal lender	4.8	4.7	2.6
Borrowed any money	40.0	32.7	37.7
Borrowed for a farm or business	5.6	6.1	6.6
Borrowed for education or school fees	8.7	8.3	6.1
Outstanding mortgage at a financial institution	11.0	9.6	9.1

Côte d'Ivoire

Sub-Saharan Africa			Lower middle income
Population, age 15+ (millions)	**11.9**	GNI per capita ($)	**1,450**

	Country data	Sub-Saharan Africa	Lower middle income
Account (% age 15+)			
All adults	34.3	34.2	42.7
Women	29.2	29.9	36.3
Adults belonging to the poorest 40%	25.1	24.6	33.2
Young adults (% ages 15–24)	24.1	25.9	34.7
Adults living in rural areas	34.0	29.2	40.0
Financial Institution Account (% age 15+)			
All adults	15.1	28.9	41.8
All adults, 2011	..	23.9	28.7
Mobile Account (% age 15+)			
All adults	24.3	11.5	2.5
Access to Financial Institution Account (% age 15+)			
Has debit card	5.5	17.9	21.2
Has debit card, 2011	..	15.0	10.1
ATM is the main mode of withdrawal (% with an account)	8.0	53.8	42.4
ATM is the main mode of withdrawal (% with an account), 2011	..	51.7	28.1
Use of Account in the Past Year (% age 15+)			
Used an account to receive wages	2.9	7.3	5.6
Used an account to receive government transfers	1.2	3.8	3.3
Used a financial institution account to pay utility bills	1.3	2.8	3.1
Other Digital Payments in the Past Year (% age 15+)			
Used a debit card to make payments	0.7	8.7	9.6
Used a credit card to make payments	0.6	1.9	2.8
Used the Internet to pay bills or make purchases	1.7	2.4	2.6
Domestic Remittances in the Past Year (% age 15+)			
Sent remittances	39.1	28.7	14.2
Sent remittances via a financial institution (% senders)	6.6	31.0	30.9
Sent remittances via a mobile phone (% senders)	41.7	30.8	7.7
Sent remittances via a money transfer operator (% senders)	31.5	21.0	18.3
Received remittances	36.4	37.2	17.8
Received remittances via a financial institution (% recipients)	4.7	26.6	26.0
Received remittances via a mobile phone (% recipients)	50.0	27.6	5.7
Received remittances via a money transfer operator (% recipients)	24.6	22.1	16.6
Savings in the Past Year (% age 15+)			
Saved at a financial institution	8.9	15.9	14.8
Saved at a financial institution, 2011	..	14.3	11.1
Saved using a savings club or person outside the family	22.9	23.9	12.4
Saved any money	63.2	59.6	45.6
Saved for old age	11.8	9.8	12.6
Saved for a farm or business	22.6	22.7	11.8
Saved for education or school fees	19.0	22.9	20.0
Credit in the Past Year (% age 15+)			
Borrowed from a financial institution	2.3	6.3	7.5
Borrowed from a financial institution, 2011	..	4.8	7.3
Borrowed from family or friends	35.5	41.9	33.1
Borrowed from a private informal lender	0.8	4.7	8.5
Borrowed any money	48.4	54.5	47.4
Borrowed for a farm or business	9.6	12.8	9.2
Borrowed for education or school fees	7.4	12.3	10.1
Outstanding mortgage at a financial institution	2.9	5.2	4.7

Croatia

		High income
Population, age 15+ (millions)	3.6	GNI per capita ($) 13,420

	Country data	High income: OECD
Account (% age 15+)		
All adults	86.0	94.0
Women	87.7	93.8
Adults belonging to the poorest 40%	81.5	90.6
Young adults (% ages 15–24)	57.8	84.1
Adults living in rural areas	84.2	93.8
Financial Institution Account (% age 15+)		
All adults	86.0	94.0
All adults, 2011	88.4	90.0
Mobile Account (% age 15+)		
All adults	..	..
Access to Financial Institution Account (% age 15+)		
Has debit card	71.1	79.7
Has debit card, 2011	74.8	61.9
ATM is the main mode of withdrawal (% with an account)	70.4	..
ATM is the main mode of withdrawal (% with an account), 2011	70.6	68.5
Use of Account in the Past Year (% age 15+)		
Used an account to receive wages	43.2	44.3
Used an account to receive government transfers	11.4	17.2
Used a financial institution account to pay utility bills	9.8	61.1
Other Digital Payments in the Past Year (% age 15+)		
Used a debit card to make payments	50.4	65.3
Used a credit card to make payments	32.8	46.7
Used the Internet to pay bills or make purchases	19.9	54.1
Domestic Remittances in the Past Year (% age 15+)		
Sent remittances	13.0	..
Sent remittances via a financial institution (% senders)	63.8	..
Sent remittances via a mobile phone (% senders)	2.6	..
Sent remittances via a money transfer operator (% senders)	4.7	..
Received remittances	15.8	..
Received remittances via a financial institution (% recipients)	54.6	..
Received remittances via a mobile phone (% recipients)	4.7	..
Received remittances via a money transfer operator (% recipients)	2.8	..
Savings in the Past Year (% age 15+)		
Saved at a financial institution	27.3	51.6
Saved at a financial institution, 2011	12.2	45.3
Saved using a savings club or person outside the family	9.8	..
Saved any money	51.8	70.8
Saved for old age	34.8	39.7
Saved for a farm or business	6.8	9.0
Saved for education or school fees	16.3	25.0
Credit in the Past Year (% age 15+)		
Borrowed from a financial institution	23.1	18.4
Borrowed from a financial institution, 2011	14.4	14.2
Borrowed from family or friends	26.7	14.9
Borrowed from a private informal lender	1.5	0.9
Borrowed any money	56.1	39.8
Borrowed for a farm or business	4.2	2.6
Borrowed for education or school fees	8.7	5.6
Outstanding mortgage at a financial institution	23.4	26.1

Cyprus

High income

Population, age 15+ (thousands)	**948**	GNI per capita ($)	**25,210**

	Country data	High income: OECD
Account (% age 15+)		
All adults	90.2	94.0
Women	90.3	93.8
Adults belonging to the poorest 40%	92.7	90.6
Young adults (% ages 15–24)	74.4	84.1
Adults living in rural areas	91.1	93.8
Financial Institution Account (% age 15+)		
All adults	90.2	94.0
All adults, 2011	85.2	90.0
Mobile Account (% age 15+)		
All adults	..	..
Access to Financial Institution Account (% age 15+)		
Has debit card	48.9	79.7
Has debit card, 2011	46.4	61.9
ATM is the main mode of withdrawal (% with an account)	..	..
ATM is the main mode of withdrawal (% with an account), 2011	43.2	68.5
Use of Account in the Past Year (% age 15+)		
Used an account to receive wages	26.3	44.3
Used an account to receive government transfers	24.0	17.2
Used a financial institution account to pay utility bills	32.8	61.1
Other Digital Payments in the Past Year (% age 15+)		
Used a debit card to make payments	37.5	65.3
Used a credit card to make payments	21.9	46.7
Used the Internet to pay bills or make purchases	31.1	54.1
Domestic Remittances in the Past Year (% age 15+)		
Sent remittances	..	..
Sent remittances via a financial institution (% senders)	..	..
Sent remittances via a mobile phone (% senders)	..	..
Sent remittances via a money transfer operator (% senders)	..	..
Received remittances	..	..
Received remittances via a financial institution (% recipients)	..	..
Received remittances via a mobile phone (% recipients)	..	..
Received remittances via a money transfer operator (% recipients)	..	..
Savings in the Past Year (% age 15+)		
Saved at a financial institution	22.0	51.6
Saved at a financial institution, 2011	30.4	45.3
Saved using a savings club or person outside the family	..	..
Saved any money	41.2	70.8
Saved for old age	12.9	39.7
Saved for a farm or business	4.5	9.0
Saved for education or school fees	16.3	25.0
Credit in the Past Year (% age 15+)		
Borrowed from a financial institution	9.6	18.4
Borrowed from a financial institution, 2011	27.0	14.2
Borrowed from family or friends	20.7	14.9
Borrowed from a private informal lender	0.4	0.9
Borrowed any money	32.8	39.8
Borrowed for a farm or business	1.7	2.6
Borrowed for education or school fees	9.7	5.6
Outstanding mortgage at a financial institution	28.4	26.1

Czech Republic

Population, age 15+ (millions)	9.0	GNI per capita ($)	18,970

	Country data	High income: OECD
Account (% age 15+)		
All adults	82.2	94.0
Women	79.4	93.8
Adults belonging to the poorest 40%	79.1	90.6
Young adults (% ages 15–24)	64.9	84.1
Adults living in rural areas	79.9	93.8
Financial Institution Account (% age 15+)		
All adults	82.2	94.0
All adults, 2011	80.7	90.0
Mobile Account (% age 15+)		
All adults	..	..
Access to Financial Institution Account (% age 15+)		
Has debit card	64.0	79.7
Has debit card, 2011	61.0	61.9
ATM is the main mode of withdrawal (% with an account)	80.2	..
ATM is the main mode of withdrawal (% with an account), 2011	81.0	68.5
Use of Account in the Past Year (% age 15+)		
Used an account to receive wages	45.4	44.3
Used an account to receive government transfers	19.4	17.2
Used a financial institution account to pay utility bills	53.8	61.1
Other Digital Payments in the Past Year (% age 15+)		
Used a debit card to make payments	52.2	65.3
Used a credit card to make payments	20.0	46.7
Used the Internet to pay bills or make purchases	45.7	54.1
Domestic Remittances in the Past Year (% age 15+)		
Sent remittances	14.3	..
Sent remittances via a financial institution (% senders)	40.2	..
Sent remittances via a mobile phone (% senders)	4.2	..
Sent remittances via a money transfer operator (% senders)	3.0	..
Received remittances	15.9	..
Received remittances via a financial institution (% recipients)	25.6	..
Received remittances via a mobile phone (% recipients)	1.2	..
Received remittances via a money transfer operator (% recipients)	1.9	..
Savings in the Past Year (% age 15+)		
Saved at a financial institution	37.6	51.6
Saved at a financial institution, 2011	35.5	45.3
Saved using a savings club or person outside the family	3.8	..
Saved any money	62.6	70.8
Saved for old age	38.8	39.7
Saved for a farm or business	6.4	9.0
Saved for education or school fees	15.6	25.0
Credit in the Past Year (% age 15+)		
Borrowed from a financial institution	13.0	18.4
Borrowed from a financial institution, 2011	9.5	14.2
Borrowed from family or friends	14.1	14.9
Borrowed from a private informal lender	1.8	0.9
Borrowed any money	31.4	39.8
Borrowed for a farm or business	1.5	2.6
Borrowed for education or school fees	2.7	5.6
Outstanding mortgage at a financial institution	21.5	26.1

Denmark

High income: OECD			High income
Population, age 15+ (millions)	**4.6**	GNI per capita ($)	**61,670**

	Country data	High income: OECD
Account (% age 15+)		
All adults	100.0	94.0
Women	100.0	93.8
Adults belonging to the poorest 40%	100.0	90.6
Young adults (% ages 15–24)	100.0	84.1
Adults living in rural areas	100.0	93.8
Financial Institution Account (% age 15+)		
All adults	100.0	94.0
All adults, 2011	99.7	90.0
Mobile Account (% age 15+)		
All adults	..	..
Access to Financial Institution Account (% age 15+)		
Has debit card	95.5	79.7
Has debit card, 2011	90.1	61.9
ATM is the main mode of withdrawal (% with an account)	..	..
ATM is the main mode of withdrawal (% with an account), 2011	46.8	68.5
Use of Account in the Past Year (% age 15+)		
Used an account to receive wages	64.4	44.3
Used an account to receive government transfers	42.7	17.2
Used a financial institution account to pay utility bills	82.4	61.1
Other Digital Payments in the Past Year (% age 15+)		
Used a debit card to make payments	91.2	65.3
Used a credit card to make payments	28.5	46.7
Used the Internet to pay bills or make purchases	73.8	54.1
Domestic Remittances in the Past Year (% age 15+)		
Sent remittances	..	..
Sent remittances via a financial institution (% senders)	..	..
Sent remittances via a mobile phone (% senders)	..	..
Sent remittances via a money transfer operator (% senders)	..	..
Received remittances	..	..
Received remittances via a financial institution (% recipients)	..	..
Received remittances via a mobile phone (% recipients)	..	..
Received remittances via a money transfer operator (% recipients)	..	..
Savings in the Past Year (% age 15+)		
Saved at a financial institution	64.7	51.6
Saved at a financial institution, 2011	56.5	45.3
Saved using a savings club or person outside the family	..	..
Saved any money	81.2	70.8
Saved for old age	45.0	39.7
Saved for a farm or business	3.3	9.0
Saved for education or school fees	13.9	25.0
Credit in the Past Year (% age 15+)		
Borrowed from a financial institution	21.6	18.4
Borrowed from a financial institution, 2011	18.8	14.2
Borrowed from family or friends	14.9	14.9
Borrowed from a private informal lender	0.3	0.9
Borrowed any money	38.9	39.8
Borrowed for a farm or business	1.4	2.6
Borrowed for education or school fees	4.4	5.6
Outstanding mortgage at a financial institution	38.2	26.1

Dominican Republic

Latin America & Caribbean			Upper middle income	
Population, age 15+ (millions)	7.3	GNI per capita ($)		5,770

	Country data	Latin America & the Carib.	Upper middle income
Account (% age 15+)			
All adults	54.1	51.4	70.5
Women	56.0	48.6	67.3
Adults belonging to the poorest 40%	41.8	41.2	62.7
Young adults (% ages 15–24)	38.0	37.4	58.1
Adults living in rural areas	46.5	46.0	68.8
Financial Institution Account (% age 15+)			
All adults	54.0	51.1	70.4
All adults, 2011	38.2	39.3	57.4
Mobile Account (% age 15+)			
All adults	2.3	1.7	0.7
Access to Financial Institution Account (% age 15+)			
Has debit card	22.6	40.4	45.9
Has debit card, 2011	21.3	28.9	38.5
ATM is the main mode of withdrawal (% with an account)	39.5	71.1	55.7
ATM is the main mode of withdrawal (% with an account), 2011	41.3	57.0	42.8
Use of Account in the Past Year (% age 15+)			
Used an account to receive wages	17.8	18.0	18.1
Used an account to receive government transfers	9.8	9.0	9.6
Used a financial institution account to pay utility bills	3.9	6.3	12.3
Other Digital Payments in the Past Year (% age 15+)			
Used a debit card to make payments	11.4	27.7	19.9
Used a credit card to make payments	9.3	18.0	14.4
Used the Internet to pay bills or make purchases	4.2	6.9	15.3
Domestic Remittances in the Past Year (% age 15+)			
Sent remittances	20.5	9.5	15.4
Sent remittances via a financial institution (% senders)	32.0	..	37.2
Sent remittances via a mobile phone (% senders)	4.6	..	8.8
Sent remittances via a money transfer operator (% senders)	26.3	..	19.7
Received remittances	29.6	11.3	17.8
Received remittances via a financial institution (% recipients)	28.9	34.2	29.8
Received remittances via a mobile phone (% recipients)	2.3	4.3	5.6
Received remittances via a money transfer operator (% recipients)	31.5	28.4	17.9
Savings in the Past Year (% age 15+)			
Saved at a financial institution	26.5	13.5	32.2
Saved at a financial institution, 2011	16.0	9.6	25.1
Saved using a savings club or person outside the family	14.2	7.9	4.9
Saved any money	57.3	40.6	62.7
Saved for old age	11.3	10.6	30.6
Saved for a farm or business	16.2	10.6	17.6
Saved for education or school fees	25.3	17.2	25.4
Credit in the Past Year (% age 15+)			
Borrowed from a financial institution	18.2	11.3	10.4
Borrowed from a financial institution, 2011	13.9	7.9	7.9
Borrowed from family or friends	22.2	13.5	24.0
Borrowed from a private informal lender	20.9	4.7	2.6
Borrowed any money	53.6	32.7	37.7
Borrowed for a farm or business	11.3	6.1	6.6
Borrowed for education or school fees	15.5	8.3	6.1
Outstanding mortgage at a financial institution	13.9	9.6	9.1

Ecuador

Latin America & Caribbean			Upper middle income

Population, age 15+ (millions)	**11.0**	GNI per capita ($)	**5,760**

	Country data	Latin America & the Carib.	Upper middle income
Account (% age 15+)			
All adults	46.2	51.4	70.5
Women	40.8	48.6	67.3
Adults belonging to the poorest 40%	32.4	41.2	62.7
Young adults (% ages 15–24)	33.5	37.4	58.1
Adults living in rural areas	48.2	46.0	68.8
Financial Institution Account (% age 15+)			
All adults	46.2	51.1	70.4
All adults, 2011	36.7	39.3	57.4
Mobile Account (% age 15+)			
All adults	..	1.7	0.7
Access to Financial Institution Account (% age 15+)			
Has debit card	25.6	40.4	45.9
Has debit card, 2011	17.1	28.9	38.5
ATM is the main mode of withdrawal (% with an account)	46.5	71.1	55.7
ATM is the main mode of withdrawal (% with an account), 2011	36.1	57.0	42.8
Use of Account in the Past Year (% age 15+)			
Used an account to receive wages	11.9	18.0	18.1
Used an account to receive government transfers	0.9	9.0	9.6
Used a financial institution account to pay utility bills	0.6	6.3	12.3
Other Digital Payments in the Past Year (% age 15+)			
Used a debit card to make payments	11.8	27.7	19.9
Used a credit card to make payments	4.9	18.0	14.4
Used the Internet to pay bills or make purchases	2.0	6.9	15.3
Domestic Remittances in the Past Year (% age 15+)			
Sent remittances	7.2	9.5	15.4
Sent remittances via a financial institution (% senders)	..	..	37.2
Sent remittances via a mobile phone (% senders)	..	..	8.8
Sent remittances via a money transfer operator (% senders)	..	..	19.7
Received remittances	7.9	11.3	17.8
Received remittances via a financial institution (% recipients)	..	34.2	29.8
Received remittances via a mobile phone (% recipients)	..	4.3	5.6
Received remittances via a money transfer operator (% recipients)	..	28.4	17.9
Savings in the Past Year (% age 15+)			
Saved at a financial institution	14.3	13.5	32.2
Saved at a financial institution, 2011	14.5	9.6	25.1
Saved using a savings club or person outside the family	1.4	7.9	4.9
Saved any money	32.1	40.6	62.7
Saved for old age	6.8	10.6	30.6
Saved for a farm or business	9.5	10.6	17.6
Saved for education or school fees	17.3	17.2	25.4
Credit in the Past Year (% age 15+)			
Borrowed from a financial institution	13.4	11.3	10.4
Borrowed from a financial institution, 2011	10.6	7.9	7.9
Borrowed from family or friends	6.1	13.5	24.0
Borrowed from a private informal lender	1.9	4.7	2.6
Borrowed any money	22.8	32.7	37.7
Borrowed for a farm or business	5.6	6.1	6.6
Borrowed for education or school fees	4.0	8.3	6.1
Outstanding mortgage at a financial institution	13.4	9.6	9.1

Egypt, Arab Rep.

Middle East			**Lower middle income**
Population, age 15+ (millions)	**56.5**	GNI per capita ($)	**3,140**

	Country data	Middle East	Lower middle income
Account (% age 15+)			
All adults	14.1	14.2	42.7
Women	9.3	9.2	36.3
Adults belonging to the poorest 40%	5.6	7.3	33.2
Young adults (% ages 15–24)	7.3	7.6	34.7
Adults living in rural areas	10.5	10.7	40.0
Financial Institution Account (% age 15+)			
All adults	13.7	14.0	41.8
All adults, 2011	9.7	10.9	28.7
Mobile Account (% age 15+)			
All adults	1.1	0.7	2.5
Access to Financial Institution Account (% age 15+)			
Has debit card	9.6	8.5	21.2
Has debit card, 2011	5.1	5.5	10.1
ATM is the main mode of withdrawal (% with an account)	51.3	44.9	42.4
ATM is the main mode of withdrawal (% with an account), 2011	..	42.4	28.1
Use of Account in the Past Year (% age 15+)			
Used an account to receive wages	2.9	3.3	5.6
Used an account to receive government transfers	0.3	0.9	3.3
Used a financial institution account to pay utility bills	0.1	0.2	3.1
Other Digital Payments in the Past Year (% age 15+)			
Used a debit card to make payments	3.5	3.3	9.6
Used a credit card to make payments	1.4	1.5	2.8
Used the Internet to pay bills or make purchases	1.4	2.1	2.6
Domestic Remittances in the Past Year (% age 15+)			
Sent remittances	5.4	9.3	14.2
Sent remittances via a financial institution (% senders)	..	..	30.9
Sent remittances via a mobile phone (% senders)	..	..	7.7
Sent remittances via a money transfer operator (% senders)	..	..	18.3
Received remittances	8.1	11.3	17.8
Received remittances via a financial institution (% recipients)	..	9.8	26.0
Received remittances via a mobile phone (% recipients)	..	0.2	5.7
Received remittances via a money transfer operator (% recipients)	..	15.6	16.6
Savings in the Past Year (% age 15+)			
Saved at a financial institution	4.1	4.0	14.8
Saved at a financial institution, 2011	0.7	2.7	11.1
Saved using a savings club or person outside the family	11.8	11.5	12.4
Saved any money	25.9	30.5	45.6
Saved for old age	2.1	5.0	12.6
Saved for a farm or business	2.7	5.1	11.8
Saved for education or school fees	8.0	9.1	20.0
Credit in the Past Year (% age 15+)			
Borrowed from a financial institution	6.3	5.6	7.5
Borrowed from a financial institution, 2011	3.7	4.4	7.3
Borrowed from family or friends	21.5	30.7	33.1
Borrowed from a private informal lender	2.5	7.9	8.5
Borrowed any money	34.1	45.7	47.4
Borrowed for a farm or business	2.4	4.2	9.2
Borrowed for education or school fees	9.2	8.2	10.1
Outstanding mortgage at a financial institution	6.2	6.2	4.7

El Salvador

	Population, age 15+ (millions)	**4.4**	GNI per capita ($)	**3,720**

	Country data	Latin America & the Carib.	Lower middle income
Account (% age 15+)			
All adults	36.7	51.4	42.7
Women	31.9	48.6	36.3
Adults belonging to the poorest 40%	24.4	41.2	33.2
Young adults (% ages 15–24)	30.5	37.4	34.7
Adults living in rural areas	31.5	46.0	40.0
Financial Institution Account (% age 15+)			
All adults	34.6	51.1	41.8
All adults, 2011	13.8	39.3	28.7
Mobile Account (% age 15+)			
All adults	4.6	1.7	2.5
Access to Financial Institution Account (% age 15+)			
Has debit card	21.8	40.4	21.2
Has debit card, 2011	10.9	28.9	10.1
ATM is the main mode of withdrawal (% with an account)	66.5	71.1	42.4
ATM is the main mode of withdrawal (% with an account), 2011	70.2	57.0	28.1
Use of Account in the Past Year (% age 15+)			
Used an account to receive wages	15.1	18.0	5.6
Used an account to receive government transfers	4.4	9.0	3.3
Used a financial institution account to pay utility bills	3.9	6.3	3.1
Other Digital Payments in the Past Year (% age 15+)			
Used a debit card to make payments	12.9	27.7	9.6
Used a credit card to make payments	6.6	18.0	2.8
Used the Internet to pay bills or make purchases	4.0	6.9	2.6
Domestic Remittances in the Past Year (% age 15+)			
Sent remittances	7.9	9.5	14.2
Sent remittances via a financial institution (% senders)	..	..	30.9
Sent remittances via a mobile phone (% senders)	..	..	7.7
Sent remittances via a money transfer operator (% senders)	..	..	18.3
Received remittances	17.3	11.3	17.8
Received remittances via a financial institution (% recipients)	27.3	34.2	26.0
Received remittances via a mobile phone (% recipients)	12.4	4.3	5.7
Received remittances via a money transfer operator (% recipients)	19.6	28.4	16.6
Savings in the Past Year (% age 15+)			
Saved at a financial institution	14.0	13.5	14.8
Saved at a financial institution, 2011	12.9	9.6	11.1
Saved using a savings club or person outside the family	7.0	7.9	12.4
Saved any money	57.5	40.6	45.6
Saved for old age	14.8	10.6	12.6
Saved for a farm or business	14.8	10.6	11.8
Saved for education or school fees	30.1	17.2	20.0
Credit in the Past Year (% age 15+)			
Borrowed from a financial institution	17.2	11.3	7.5
Borrowed from a financial institution, 2011	3.9	7.9	7.3
Borrowed from family or friends	12.4	13.5	33.1
Borrowed from a private informal lender	6.2	4.7	8.5
Borrowed any money	44.0	32.7	47.4
Borrowed for a farm or business	10.8	6.1	9.2
Borrowed for education or school fees	10.6	8.3	10.1
Outstanding mortgage at a financial institution	12.1	9.6	4.7

Estonia

Population, age 15+ (millions)	**1.1**	GNI per capita ($)	**17,780**

	Country data	High income: OECD
Account (% age 15+)		
All adults	97.7	94.0
Women	97.5	93.8
Adults belonging to the poorest 40%	97.8	90.6
Young adults (% ages 15–24)	90.6	84.1
Adults living in rural areas	96.9	93.8
Financial Institution Account (% age 15+)		
All adults	97.7	94.0
All adults, 2011	96.8	90.0
Mobile Account (% age 15+)		
All adults	..	..
Access to Financial Institution Account (% age 15+)		
Has debit card	93.3	79.7
Has debit card, 2011	92.3	61.9
ATM is the main mode of withdrawal (% with an account)	94.8	..
ATM is the main mode of withdrawal (% with an account), 2011	92.7	68.5
Use of Account in the Past Year (% age 15+)		
Used an account to receive wages	58.7	44.3
Used an account to receive government transfers	31.5	17.2
Used a financial institution account to pay utility bills	68.0	61.1
Other Digital Payments in the Past Year (% age 15+)		
Used a debit card to make payments	88.8	65.3
Used a credit card to make payments	24.3	46.7
Used the Internet to pay bills or make purchases	63.6	54.1
Domestic Remittances in the Past Year (% age 15+)		
Sent remittances	19.3	..
Sent remittances via a financial institution (% senders)	67.5	..
Sent remittances via a mobile phone (% senders)	4.0	..
Sent remittances via a money transfer operator (% senders)	2.0	..
Received remittances	18.8	..
Received remittances via a financial institution (% recipients)	59.0	..
Received remittances via a mobile phone (% recipients)	4.6	..
Received remittances via a money transfer operator (% recipients)	5.4	..
Savings in the Past Year (% age 15+)		
Saved at a financial institution	31.6	51.6
Saved at a financial institution, 2011	28.9	45.3
Saved using a savings club or person outside the family	1.8	..
Saved any money	51.8	70.8
Saved for old age	28.1	39.7
Saved for a farm or business	9.5	9.0
Saved for education or school fees	10.3	25.0
Credit in the Past Year (% age 15+)		
Borrowed from a financial institution	14.3	18.4
Borrowed from a financial institution, 2011	7.7	14.2
Borrowed from family or friends	19.8	14.9
Borrowed from a private informal lender	1.1	0.9
Borrowed any money	36.7	39.8
Borrowed for a farm or business	1.5	2.6
Borrowed for education or school fees	3.3	5.6
Outstanding mortgage at a financial institution	26.8	26.1

Ethiopia

Sub-Saharan Africa **Low income**

Population, age 15+ (millions)	**53.9**	GNI per capita ($)	**470**

	Country data	Sub-Saharan Africa	Low income
Account (% age 15+)			
All adults	21.8	34.2	27.5
Women	21.0	29.9	23.9
Adults belonging to the poorest 40%	15.9	24.6	19.4
Young adults (% ages 15–24)	14.3	25.9	20.2
Adults living in rural areas	18.7	29.2	24.8
Financial Institution Account (% age 15+)			
All adults	21.8	28.9	22.3
All adults, 2011	..	23.9	21.1
Mobile Account (% age 15+)			
All adults	0.0	11.5	10.0
Access to Financial Institution Account (% age 15+)			
Has debit card	0.8	17.9	6.6
Has debit card, 2011	..	15.0	6.3
ATM is the main mode of withdrawal (% with an account)	0.9	53.8	20.2
ATM is the main mode of withdrawal (% with an account), 2011	..	51.7	19.7
Use of Account in the Past Year (% age 15+)			
Used an account to receive wages	0.7	7.3	3.2
Used an account to receive government transfers	0.3	3.8	1.0
Used a financial institution account to pay utility bills	0.1	2.8	0.9
Other Digital Payments in the Past Year (% age 15+)			
Used a debit card to make payments	0.0	8.7	2.1
Used a credit card to make payments	0.2	1.9	0.6
Used the Internet to pay bills or make purchases	0.4	2.4	1.2
Domestic Remittances in the Past Year (% age 15+)			
Sent remittances	9.9	28.7	18.3
Sent remittances via a financial institution (% senders)	..	31.0	15.4
Sent remittances via a mobile phone (% senders)	..	30.8	42.8
Sent remittances via a money transfer operator (% senders)	..	21.0	14.1
Received remittances	8.6	37.2	25.6
Received remittances via a financial institution (% recipients)	..	26.6	13.0
Received remittances via a mobile phone (% recipients)	..	27.6	33.8
Received remittances via a money transfer operator (% recipients)	..	22.1	14.8
Savings in the Past Year (% age 15+)			
Saved at a financial institution	13.6	15.9	9.9
Saved at a financial institution, 2011	..	14.3	11.5
Saved using a savings club or person outside the family	29.8	23.9	16.3
Saved any money	48.1	59.6	46.5
Saved for old age	8.0	9.8	8.3
Saved for a farm or business	14.9	22.7	16.7
Saved for education or school fees	8.3	22.9	16.6
Credit in the Past Year (% age 15+)			
Borrowed from a financial institution	7.4	6.3	8.6
Borrowed from a financial institution, 2011	..	4.8	11.7
Borrowed from family or friends	29.5	41.9	34.9
Borrowed from a private informal lender	1.1	4.7	6.5
Borrowed any money	43.5	54.5	52.5
Borrowed for a farm or business	11.5	12.8	12.2
Borrowed for education or school fees	4.2	12.3	10.9
Outstanding mortgage at a financial institution	2.0	5.2	4.1

Finland

High income: OECD		**High income**
Population, age 15+ (millions)	**4.5** GNI per capita ($)	**48,820**

	Country data	High income: OECD
Account (% age 15+)		
All adults	100.0	94.0
Women	100.0	93.8
Adults belonging to the poorest 40%	100.0	90.6
Young adults (% ages 15–24)	100.0	84.1
Adults living in rural areas	100.0	93.8
Financial Institution Account (% age 15+)		
All adults	100.0	94.0
All adults, 2011	99.7	90.0
Mobile Account (% age 15+)		
All adults	..	..
Access to Financial Institution Account (% age 15+)		
Has debit card	96.7	79.7
Has debit card, 2011	89.3	61.9
ATM is the main mode of withdrawal (% with an account)	..	..
ATM is the main mode of withdrawal (% with an account), 2011	86.8	68.5
Use of Account in the Past Year (% age 15+)		
Used an account to receive wages	58.1	44.3
Used an account to receive government transfers	37.0	17.2
Used a financial institution account to pay utility bills	79.2	61.1
Other Digital Payments in the Past Year (% age 15+)		
Used a debit card to make payments	91.6	65.3
Used a credit card to make payments	50.3	46.7
Used the Internet to pay bills or make purchases	75.0	54.1
Domestic Remittances in the Past Year (% age 15+)		
Sent remittances	..	..
Sent remittances via a financial institution (% senders)	..	..
Sent remittances via a mobile phone (% senders)	..	..
Sent remittances via a money transfer operator (% senders)	..	..
Received remittances	..	..
Received remittances via a financial institution (% recipients)	..	..
Received remittances via a mobile phone (% recipients)	..	..
Received remittances via a money transfer operator (% recipients)	..	..
Savings in the Past Year (% age 15+)		
Saved at a financial institution	57.0	51.6
Saved at a financial institution, 2011	56.1	45.3
Saved using a savings club or person outside the family	..	..
Saved any money	71.0	70.8
Saved for old age	32.7	39.7
Saved for a farm or business	5.4	9.0
Saved for education or school fees	10.1	25.0
Credit in the Past Year (% age 15+)		
Borrowed from a financial institution	21.6	18.4
Borrowed from a financial institution, 2011	23.9	14.2
Borrowed from family or friends	20.3	14.9
Borrowed from a private informal lender	0.1	0.9
Borrowed any money	46.4	39.8
Borrowed for a farm or business	2.1	2.6
Borrowed for education or school fees	6.0	5.6
Outstanding mortgage at a financial institution	30.6	26.1

France

High income: OECD		High income
Population, age 15+ (millions)	**53.9**	GNI per capita ($) **43,520**

	Country data	High income: OECD
Account (% age 15+)		
All adults	96.6	94.0
Women	95.5	93.8
Adults belonging to the poorest 40%	94.9	90.6
Young adults (% ages 15–24)	78.9	84.1
Adults living in rural areas	97.7	93.8
Financial Institution Account (% age 15+)		
All adults	96.6	94.0
All adults, 2011	97.0	90.0
Mobile Account (% age 15+)		
All adults	..	..
Access to Financial Institution Account (% age 15+)		
Has debit card	81.1	79.7
Has debit card, 2011	69.2	61.9
ATM is the main mode of withdrawal (% with an account)	..	..
ATM is the main mode of withdrawal (% with an account), 2011	77.7	68.5
Use of Account in the Past Year (% age 15+)		
Used an account to receive wages	48.3	44.3
Used an account to receive government transfers	16.4	17.2
Used a financial institution account to pay utility bills	70.7	61.1
Other Digital Payments in the Past Year (% age 15+)		
Used a debit card to make payments	76.0	65.3
Used a credit card to make payments	36.0	46.7
Used the Internet to pay bills or make purchases	44.5	54.1
Domestic Remittances in the Past Year (% age 15+)		
Sent remittances	..	..
Sent remittances via a financial institution (% senders)	..	..
Sent remittances via a mobile phone (% senders)	..	..
Sent remittances via a money transfer operator (% senders)	..	..
Received remittances	..	..
Received remittances via a financial institution (% recipients)	..	..
Received remittances via a mobile phone (% recipients)	..	..
Received remittances via a money transfer operator (% recipients)	..	..
Savings in the Past Year (% age 15+)		
Saved at a financial institution	52.2	51.6
Saved at a financial institution, 2011	49.5	45.3
Saved using a savings club or person outside the family	..	..
Saved any money	67.1	70.8
Saved for old age	29.5	39.7
Saved for a farm or business	7.3	9.0
Saved for education or school fees	17.9	25.0
Credit in the Past Year (% age 15+)		
Borrowed from a financial institution	15.1	18.4
Borrowed from a financial institution, 2011	18.6	14.2
Borrowed from family or friends	6.6	14.9
Borrowed from a private informal lender	0.2	0.9
Borrowed any money	28.3	39.8
Borrowed for a farm or business	2.1	2.6
Borrowed for education or school fees	3.2	5.6
Outstanding mortgage at a financial institution	25.9	26.1

Gabon

Sub-Saharan Africa			Upper middle income
Population, age 15+ (millions)	**1.0**	GNI per capita ($)	**10,650**

	Country data	Sub-Saharan Africa	Upper middle income
Account (% age 15+)			
All adults	33.0	34.2	70.5
Women	30.7	29.9	67.3
Adults belonging to the poorest 40%	20.4	24.6	62.7
Young adults (% ages 15–24)	23.1	25.9	58.1
Adults living in rural areas	26.3	29.2	68.8
Financial Institution Account (% age 15+)			
All adults	30.2	28.9	70.4
All adults, 2011	18.9	23.9	57.4
Mobile Account (% age 15+)			
All adults	6.6	11.5	0.7
Access to Financial Institution Account (% age 15+)			
Has debit card	18.5	17.9	45.9
Has debit card, 2011	8.6	15.0	38.5
ATM is the main mode of withdrawal (% with an account)	36.5	53.8	55.7
ATM is the main mode of withdrawal (% with an account), 2011	29.0	51.7	42.8
Use of Account in the Past Year (% age 15+)			
Used an account to receive wages	10.1	7.3	18.1
Used an account to receive government transfers	4.6	3.8	9.6
Used a financial institution account to pay utility bills	2.1	2.8	12.3
Other Digital Payments in the Past Year (% age 15+)			
Used a debit card to make payments	8.8	8.7	19.9
Used a credit card to make payments	4.8	1.9	14.4
Used the Internet to pay bills or make purchases	3.7	2.4	15.3
Domestic Remittances in the Past Year (% age 15+)			
Sent remittances	27.1	28.7	15.4
Sent remittances via a financial institution (% senders)	24.9	31.0	37.2
Sent remittances via a mobile phone (% senders)	9.7	30.8	8.8
Sent remittances via a money transfer operator (% senders)	67.0	21.0	19.7
Received remittances	36.8	37.2	17.8
Received remittances via a financial institution (% recipients)	14.6	26.6	29.8
Received remittances via a mobile phone (% recipients)	6.2	27.6	5.6
Received remittances via a money transfer operator (% recipients)	46.3	22.1	17.9
Savings in the Past Year (% age 15+)			
Saved at a financial institution	18.0	15.9	32.2
Saved at a financial institution, 2011	8.7	14.3	25.1
Saved using a savings club or person outside the family	24.7	23.9	4.9
Saved any money	56.0	59.6	62.7
Saved for old age	16.5	9.8	30.6
Saved for a farm or business	18.5	22.7	17.6
Saved for education or school fees	29.0	22.9	25.4
Credit in the Past Year (% age 15+)			
Borrowed from a financial institution	4.3	6.3	10.4
Borrowed from a financial institution, 2011	2.3	4.8	7.9
Borrowed from family or friends	28.0	41.9	24.0
Borrowed from a private informal lender	9.0	4.7	2.6
Borrowed any money	37.8	54.5	37.7
Borrowed for a farm or business	5.8	12.8	6.6
Borrowed for education or school fees	7.1	12.3	6.1
Outstanding mortgage at a financial institution	6.0	5.2	9.1

Georgia

Europe & Central Asia	Lower middle income

Population, age 15+ (millions)	**3.7**	GNI per capita ($)	**3,560**

	Country data	Europe & Central Asia	Lower middle income
Account (% age 15+)			
All adults	39.7	51.4	42.7
Women	39.8	47.4	36.3
Adults belonging to the poorest 40%	28.6	44.2	33.2
Young adults (% ages 15–24)	9.9	35.6	34.7
Adults living in rural areas	40.1	45.7	40.0
Financial Institution Account (% age 15+)			
All adults	39.7	51.4	41.8
All adults, 2011	33.0	43.3	28.7
Mobile Account (% age 15+)			
All adults	..	0.3	2.5
Access to Financial Institution Account (% age 15+)			
Has debit card	29.6	36.9	21.2
Has debit card, 2011	20.2	36.4	10.1
ATM is the main mode of withdrawal (% with an account)	36.2	66.7	42.4
ATM is the main mode of withdrawal (% with an account), 2011	40.0	72.5	28.1
Use of Account in the Past Year (% age 15+)			
Used an account to receive wages	14.5	22.5	5.6
Used an account to receive government transfers	4.9	7.3	3.3
Used a financial institution account to pay utility bills	2.2	12.5	3.1
Other Digital Payments in the Past Year (% age 15+)			
Used a debit card to make payments	7.1	22.9	9.6
Used a credit card to make payments	13.2	14.9	2.8
Used the Internet to pay bills or make purchases	5.0	11.9	2.6
Domestic Remittances in the Past Year (% age 15+)			
Sent remittances	10.1	12.9	14.2
Sent remittances via a financial institution (% senders)	15.9	31.5	30.9
Sent remittances via a mobile phone (% senders)	0.0	2.5	7.7
Sent remittances via a money transfer operator (% senders)	25.0	11.8	18.3
Received remittances	22.1	15.5	17.8
Received remittances via a financial institution (% recipients)	10.0	22.1	26.0
Received remittances via a mobile phone (% recipients)	0.0	1.0	5.7
Received remittances via a money transfer operator (% recipients)	35.6	15.6	16.6
Savings in the Past Year (% age 15+)			
Saved at a financial institution	1.0	8.4	14.8
Saved at a financial institution, 2011	1.0	4.9	11.1
Saved using a savings club or person outside the family	1.2	6.6	12.4
Saved any money	13.3	38.5	45.6
Saved for old age	0.9	11.8	12.6
Saved for a farm or business	3.1	5.1	11.8
Saved for education or school fees	4.3	12.1	20.0
Credit in the Past Year (% age 15+)			
Borrowed from a financial institution	13.7	12.4	7.5
Borrowed from a financial institution, 2011	11.0	7.8	7.3
Borrowed from family or friends	16.2	23.6	33.1
Borrowed from a private informal lender	2.7	2.1	8.5
Borrowed any money	33.1	39.5	47.4
Borrowed for a farm or business	2.7	2.8	9.2
Borrowed for education or school fees	2.0	6.2	10.1
Outstanding mortgage at a financial institution	14.6	10.2	4.7

Germany

Population, age 15+ (millions)	**70.1**	GNI per capita ($) **47,250**

	Country data	High Income: OECD
Account (% age 15+)		
All adults	98.8	94.0
Women	99.4	93.8
Adults belonging to the poorest 40%	97.1	90.6
Young adults (% ages 15–24)	93.7	84.1
Adults living in rural areas	98.8	93.8
Financial Institution Account (% age 15+)		
All adults	98.8	94.0
All adults, 2011	98.1	90.0
Mobile Account (% age 15+)		
All adults	..	..
Access to Financial Institution Account (% age 15+)		
Has debit card	92.0	79.7
Has debit card, 2011	88.0	61.9
ATM is the main mode of withdrawal (% with an account)	..	..
ATM is the main mode of withdrawal (% with an account), 2011	79.2	68.5
Use of Account in the Past Year (% age 15+)		
Used an account to receive wages	47.2	44.3
Used an account to receive government transfers	11.4	17.2
Used a financial institution account to pay utility bills	72.8	61.1
Other Digital Payments in the Past Year (% age 15+)		
Used a debit card to make payments	79.2	65.3
Used a credit card to make payments	36.4	46.7
Used the Internet to pay bills or make purchases	56.4	54.1
Domestic Remittances in the Past Year (% age 15+)		
Sent remittances	..	..
Sent remittances via a financial institution (% senders)	..	..
Sent remittances via a mobile phone (% senders)	..	..
Sent remittances via a money transfer operator (% senders)	..	..
Received remittances	..	..
Received remittances via a financial institution (% recipients)	..	..
Received remittances via a mobile phone (% recipients)	..	..
Received remittances via a money transfer operator (% recipients)	..	..
Savings in the Past Year (% age 15+)		
Saved at a financial institution	57.9	51.6
Saved at a financial institution, 2011	55.9	45.3
Saved using a savings club or person outside the family	..	..
Saved any money	79.8	70.8
Saved for old age	55.1	39.7
Saved for a farm or business	10.7	9.0
Saved for education or school fees	17.1	25.0
Credit in the Past Year (% age 15+)		
Borrowed from a financial institution	18.6	18.4
Borrowed from a financial institution, 2011	12.5	14.2
Borrowed from family or friends	9.8	14.9
Borrowed from a private informal lender	0.2	0.9
Borrowed any money	31.8	39.8
Borrowed for a farm or business	3.6	2.6
Borrowed for education or school fees	2.2	5.6
Outstanding mortgage at a financial institution	21.1	26.1

Ghana

Sub-Saharan Africa			Lower middle income

Population, age 15+ (millions)	**15.9**	GNI per capita ($)	**1,770**

	Country data	Sub-Saharan Africa	Lower middle income
Account (% age 15+)			
All adults	40.5	34.2	42.7
Women	39.4	29.9	36.3
Adults belonging to the poorest 40%	30.0	24.6	33.2
Young adults (% ages 15–24)	36.4	25.9	34.7
Adults living in rural areas	34.5	29.2	40.0
Financial Institution Account (% age 15+)			
All adults	34.6	28.9	41.8
All adults, 2011	29.4	23.9	28.7
Mobile Account (% age 15+)			
All adults	13.0	11.5	2.5
Access to Financial Institution Account (% age 15+)			
Has debit card	9.8	17.9	21.2
Has debit card, 2011	11.4	15.0	10.1
ATM is the main mode of withdrawal (% with an account)	19.9	53.8	42.4
ATM is the main mode of withdrawal (% with an account), 2011	24.3	51.7	28.1
Use of Account in the Past Year (% age 15+)			
Used an account to receive wages	5.8	7.3	5.6
Used an account to receive government transfers	2.0	3.8	3.3
Used a financial institution account to pay utility bills	0.7	2.8	3.1
Other Digital Payments in the Past Year (% age 15+)			
Used a debit card to make payments	4.4	8.7	9.6
Used a credit card to make payments	0.6	1.9	2.8
Used the Internet to pay bills or make purchases	2.7	2.4	2.6
Domestic Remittances in the Past Year (% age 15+)			
Sent remittances	26.5	28.7	14.2
Sent remittances via a financial institution (% senders)	16.8	31.0	30.9
Sent remittances via a mobile phone (% senders)	38.9	30.8	7.7
Sent remittances via a money transfer operator (% senders)	17.2	21.0	18.3
Received remittances	36.9	37.2	17.8
Received remittances via a financial institution (% recipients)	16.2	26.6	26.0
Received remittances via a mobile phone (% recipients)	34.6	27.6	5.7
Received remittances via a money transfer operator (% recipients)	13.0	22.1	16.6
Savings in the Past Year (% age 15+)			
Saved at a financial institution	18.6	15.9	14.8
Saved at a financial institution, 2011	16.1	14.3	11.1
Saved using a savings club or person outside the family	21.5	23.9	12.4
Saved any money	55.3	59.6	45.6
Saved for old age	13.9	9.8	12.6
Saved for a farm or business	24.5	22.7	11.8
Saved for education or school fees	28.7	22.9	20.0
Credit in the Past Year (% age 15+)			
Borrowed from a financial institution	8.1	6.3	7.5
Borrowed from a financial institution, 2011	5.8	4.8	7.3
Borrowed from family or friends	21.6	41.9	33.1
Borrowed from a private informal lender	4.3	4.7	8.5
Borrowed any money	36.4	54.5	47.4
Borrowed for a farm or business	10.2	12.8	9.2
Borrowed for education or school fees	10.7	12.3	10.1
Outstanding mortgage at a financial institution	12.0	5.2	4.7

Greece

High income: OECD		**High income**
Population, age 15+ (millions)	**9.4**	GNI per capita ($)	**22,690**

	Country data	High income: OECD
Account (% age 15+)		
All adults	87.5	94.0
Women	86.6	93.8
Adults belonging to the poorest 40%	81.5	90.6
Young adults (% ages 15–24)	47.0	84.1
Adults living in rural areas	86.6	93.8
Financial Institution Account (% age 15+)		
All adults	87.5	94.0
All adults, 2011	77.9	90.0
Mobile Account (% age 15+)		
All adults	..	..
Access to Financial Institution Account (% age 15+)		
Has debit card	55.1	79.7
Has debit card, 2011	34.0	61.9
ATM is the main mode of withdrawal (% with an account)	57.5	..
ATM is the main mode of withdrawal (% with an account), 2011	52.8	68.5
Use of Account in the Past Year (% age 15+)		
Used an account to receive wages	22.1	44.3
Used an account to receive government transfers	30.3	17.2
Used a financial institution account to pay utility bills	5.9	61.1
Other Digital Payments in the Past Year (% age 15+)		
Used a debit card to make payments	14.8	65.3
Used a credit card to make payments	8.3	46.7
Used the Internet to pay bills or make purchases	11.1	54.1
Domestic Remittances in the Past Year (% age 15+)		
Sent remittances	13.6	..
Sent remittances via a financial institution (% senders)	37.5	..
Sent remittances via a mobile phone (% senders)	0.0	..
Sent remittances via a money transfer operator (% senders)	1.0	..
Received remittances	15.1	..
Received remittances via a financial institution (% recipients)	28.9	..
Received remittances via a mobile phone (% recipients)	0.0	..
Received remittances via a money transfer operator (% recipients)	4.2	..
Savings in the Past Year (% age 15+)		
Saved at a financial institution	12.6	51.6
Saved at a financial institution, 2011	19.9	45.3
Saved using a savings club or person outside the family	0.7	..
Saved any money	23.7	70.8
Saved for old age	9.3	39.7
Saved for a farm or business	1.2	9.0
Saved for education or school fees	4.3	25.0
Credit in the Past Year (% age 15+)		
Borrowed from a financial institution	10.2	18.4
Borrowed from a financial institution, 2011	7.9	14.2
Borrowed from family or friends	14.1	14.9
Borrowed from a private informal lender	0.1	0.9
Borrowed any money	27.5	39.8
Borrowed for a farm or business	1.1	2.6
Borrowed for education or school fees	1.3	5.6
Outstanding mortgage at a financial institution	14.1	26.1

Guatemala

Latin America & Caribbean			Lower middle income

Population, age 15+ (millions)	**9.2**	GNI per capita ($)	**3,340**

	Country data	Latin America & the Carib.	Lower middle income
Account (% age 15+)			
All adults	41.3	51.4	42.7
Women	34.7	48.6	36.3
Adults belonging to the poorest 40%	27.2	41.2	33.2
Young adults (% ages 15–24)	36.9	37.4	34.7
Adults living in rural areas	40.9	46.0	40.0
Financial Institution Account (% age 15+)			
All adults	40.8	51.1	41.8
All adults, 2011	22.3	39.3	28.7
Mobile Account (% age 15+)			
All adults	1.8	1.7	2.5
Access to Financial Institution Account (% age 15+)			
Has debit card	16.2	40.4	21.2
Has debit card, 2011	13.0	28.9	10.1
ATM is the main mode of withdrawal (% with an account)	36.8	71.1	42.4
ATM is the main mode of withdrawal (% with an account), 2011	26.2	57.0	28.1
Use of Account in the Past Year (% age 15+)			
Used an account to receive wages	9.9	18.0	5.6
Used an account to receive government transfers	3.9	9.0	3.3
Used a financial institution account to pay utility bills	4.7	6.3	3.1
Other Digital Payments in the Past Year (% age 15+)			
Used a debit card to make payments	10.0	27.7	9.6
Used a credit card to make payments	4.9	18.0	2.8
Used the Internet to pay bills or make purchases	4.3	6.9	2.6
Domestic Remittances in the Past Year (% age 15+)			
Sent remittances	9.6	9.5	14.2
Sent remittances via a financial institution (% senders)	..	..	30.9
Sent remittances via a mobile phone (% senders)	..	..	7.7
Sent remittances via a money transfer operator (% senders)	..	..	18.3
Received remittances	13.6	11.3	17.8
Received remittances via a financial institution (% recipients)	31.8	34.2	26.0
Received remittances via a mobile phone (% recipients)	3.7	4.3	5.7
Received remittances via a money transfer operator (% recipients)	12.3	28.4	16.6
Savings in the Past Year (% age 15+)			
Saved at a financial institution	15.1	13.5	14.8
Saved at a financial institution, 2011	10.2	9.6	11.1
Saved using a savings club or person outside the family	11.8	7.9	12.4
Saved any money	55.7	40.6	45.6
Saved for old age	15.7	10.6	12.6
Saved for a farm or business	18.0	10.6	11.8
Saved for education or school fees	37.3	17.2	20.0
Credit in the Past Year (% age 15+)			
Borrowed from a financial institution	12.3	11.3	7.5
Borrowed from a financial institution, 2011	13.7	7.9	7.3
Borrowed from family or friends	19.5	13.5	33.1
Borrowed from a private informal lender	2.6	4.7	8.5
Borrowed any money	43.5	32.7	47.4
Borrowed for a farm or business	8.7	6.1	9.2
Borrowed for education or school fees	15.0	8.3	10.1
Outstanding mortgage at a financial institution	7.8	9.6	4.7

Guinea

Sub-Saharan Africa **Low income**

| Population, age 15+ (millions) | 6.8 | GNI per capita ($) | 460 |

	Country data	Sub-Saharan Africa	Low income
Account (% age 15+)			
All adults	7.0	34.2	27.5
Women	4.1	29.9	23.9
Adults belonging to the poorest 40%	2.2	24.6	19.4
Young adults (% ages 15–24)	4.3	25.9	20.2
Adults living in rural areas	4.7	29.2	24.8
Financial Institution Account (% age 15+)			
All adults	6.2	28.9	22.3
All adults, 2011	3.7	23.9	21.1
Mobile Account (% age 15+)			
All adults	1.5	11.5	10.0
Access to Financial Institution Account (% age 15+)			
Has debit card	3.7	17.9	6.6
Has debit card, 2011	2.3	15.0	6.3
ATM is the main mode of withdrawal (% with an account)	..	53.8	20.2
ATM is the main mode of withdrawal (% with an account), 2011	..	51.7	19.7
Use of Account in the Past Year (% age 15+)			
Used an account to receive wages	2.3	7.3	3.2
Used an account to receive government transfers	1.0	3.8	1.0
Used a financial institution account to pay utility bills	0.4	2.8	0.9
Other Digital Payments in the Past Year (% age 15+)			
Used a debit card to make payments	1.2	8.7	2.1
Used a credit card to make payments	1.0	1.9	0.6
Used the Internet to pay bills or make purchases	1.8	2.4	1.2
Domestic Remittances in the Past Year (% age 15+)			
Sent remittances	20.0	28.7	18.3
Sent remittances via a financial institution (% senders)	10.2	31.0	15.4
Sent remittances via a mobile phone (% senders)	5.4	30.8	42.8
Sent remittances via a money transfer operator (% senders)	25.3	21.0	14.1
Received remittances	34.2	37.2	25.6
Received remittances via a financial institution (% recipients)	7.9	26.6	13.0
Received remittances via a mobile phone (% recipients)	2.8	27.6	33.8
Received remittances via a money transfer operator (% recipients)	20.6	22.1	14.8
Savings in the Past Year (% age 15+)			
Saved at a financial institution	2.9	15.9	9.9
Saved at a financial institution, 2011	2.0	14.3	11.5
Saved using a savings club or person outside the family	18.7	23.9	16.3
Saved any money	45.2	59.6	46.5
Saved for old age	4.8	9.8	8.3
Saved for a farm or business	18.9	22.7	16.7
Saved for education or school fees	11.0	22.9	16.6
Credit in the Past Year (% age 15+)			
Borrowed from a financial institution	2.0	6.3	8.6
Borrowed from a financial institution, 2011	2.4	4.8	11.7
Borrowed from family or friends	37.1	41.9	34.9
Borrowed from a private informal lender	3.6	4.7	6.5
Borrowed any money	52.2	54.5	52.5
Borrowed for a farm or business	16.6	12.8	12.2
Borrowed for education or school fees	12.3	12.3	10.9
Outstanding mortgage at a financial institution	4.1	5.2	4.1

Haiti

Latin America & Caribbean			**Low income**
Population, age 15+ (millions)	6.7	GNI per capita ($)	810

	Country data	Latin America & the Carib.	Low income
Account (% age 15+)			
All adults	18.9	51.4	27.5
Women	16.1	48.6	23.9
Adults belonging to the poorest 40%	14.5	41.2	19.4
Young adults (% ages 15–24)	14.7	37.4	20.2
Adults living in rural areas	17.6	46.0	24.8
Financial Institution Account (% age 15+)			
All adults	17.5	51.1	22.3
All adults, 2011	22.0	39.3	21.1
Mobile Account (% age 15+)			
All adults	3.8	1.7	10.0
Access to Financial Institution Account (% age 15+)			
Has debit card	4.1	40.4	6.6
Has debit card, 2011	2.7	28.9	6.3
ATM is the main mode of withdrawal (% with an account)	7.3	71.1	20.2
ATM is the main mode of withdrawal (% with an account), 2011	5.9	57.0	19.7
Use of Account in the Past Year (% age 15+)			
Used an account to receive wages	2.2	18.0	3.2
Used an account to receive government transfers	3.5	9.0	1.0
Used a financial institution account to pay utility bills	0.8	6.3	0.9
Other Digital Payments in the Past Year (% age 15+)			
Used a debit card to make payments	1.8	27.7	2.1
Used a credit card to make payments	1.6	18.0	0.6
Used the Internet to pay bills or make purchases	2.7	6.9	1.2
Domestic Remittances in the Past Year (% age 15+)			
Sent remittances	13.4	9.5	18.3
Sent remittances via a financial institution (% senders)	14.6	..	15.4
Sent remittances via a mobile phone (% senders)	12.4	..	42.8
Sent remittances via a money transfer operator (% senders)	21.2	..	14.1
Received remittances	19.5	11.3	25.6
Received remittances via a financial institution (% recipients)	7.7	34.2	13.0
Received remittances via a mobile phone (% recipients)	8.6	4.3	33.8
Received remittances via a money transfer operator (% recipients)	48.6	28.4	14.8
Savings in the Past Year (% age 15+)			
Saved at a financial institution	9.4	13.5	9.9
Saved at a financial institution, 2011	18.0	9.6	11.5
Saved using a savings club or person outside the family	4.9	7.9	16.3
Saved any money	44.8	40.6	46.5
Saved for old age	11.4	10.6	8.3
Saved for a farm or business	14.7	10.6	16.7
Saved for education or school fees	28.2	17.2	16.6
Credit in the Past Year (% age 15+)			
Borrowed from a financial institution	4.6	11.3	8.6
Borrowed from a financial institution, 2011	8.3	7.9	11.7
Borrowed from family or friends	27.0	13.5	34.9
Borrowed from a private informal lender	11.9	4.7	5.1
Borrowed any money	47.6	32.7	52.5
Borrowed for a farm or business	8.1	6.1	12.2
Borrowed for education or school fees	26.5	8.3	10.9
Outstanding mortgage at a financial institution	7.1	9.6	4.1

Honduras

Latin America & Caribbean			Lower middle income

Population, age 15+ (millions)	**5.2**	GNI per capita ($)	**2,180**

	Country data	Latin America & the Carib.	Lower middle income
Account (% age 15+)			
All adults	31.5	51.4	42.7
Women	27.0	48.6	36.3
Adults belonging to the poorest 40%	19.7	41.2	33.2
Young adults (% ages 15–24)	27.2	37.4	34.7
Adults living in rural areas	26.5	46.0	40.0
Financial Institution Account (% age 15+)			
All adults	30.0	51.1	41.8
All adults, 2011	20.5	39.3	28.7
Mobile Account (% age 15+)			
All adults	3.4	1.7	2.5
Access to Financial Institution Account (% age 15+)			
Has debit card	14.2	40.4	21.2
Has debit card, 2011	11.1	28.9	10.1
ATM is the main mode of withdrawal (% with an account)	23.7	71.1	42.4
ATM is the main mode of withdrawal (% with an account), 2011	26.1	57.0	28.1
Use of Account in the Past Year (% age 15+)			
Used an account to receive wages	5.8	18.0	5.6
Used an account to receive government transfers	1.6	9.0	3.3
Used a financial institution account to pay utility bills	4.6	6.3	3.1
Other Digital Payments in the Past Year (% age 15+)			
Used a debit card to make payments	8.9	27.7	9.6
Used a credit card to make payments	5.0	18.0	2.8
Used the Internet to pay bills or make purchases	3.0	6.9	2.6
Domestic Remittances in the Past Year (% age 15+)			
Sent remittances	10.9	9.5	14.2
Sent remittances via a financial institution (% senders)	42.8	..	30.9
Sent remittances via a mobile phone (% senders)	11.3	..	7.7
Sent remittances via a money transfer operator (% senders)	26.8	..	18.3
Received remittances	16.1	11.3	17.8
Received remittances via a financial institution (% recipients)	43.7	34.2	26.0
Received remittances via a mobile phone (% recipients)	12.5	4.3	5.7
Received remittances via a money transfer operator (% recipients)	28.1	28.4	16.6
Savings in the Past Year (% age 15+)			
Saved at a financial institution	14.5	13.5	14.8
Saved at a financial institution, 2011	8.5	9.6	11.1
Saved using a savings club or person outside the family	5.4	7.9	12.4
Saved any money	39.7	40.6	45.6
Saved for old age	10.6	10.6	12.6
Saved for a farm or business	10.6	10.6	11.8
Saved for education or school fees	22.0	17.2	20.0
Credit in the Past Year (% age 15+)			
Borrowed from a financial institution	9.7	11.3	7.5
Borrowed from a financial institution, 2011	7.1	7.9	7.3
Borrowed from family or friends	18.3	13.5	33.1
Borrowed from a private informal lender	3.6	4.7	8.5
Borrowed any money	40.6	32.7	47.4
Borrowed for a farm or business	8.0	6.1	9.2
Borrowed for education or school fees	15.9	8.3	10.1
Outstanding mortgage at a financial institution	7.1	9.6	4.7

Hong Kong SAR, China

High income

Population, age 15+ (millions)	6.3	GNI per capita ($)	38,420

	Country data	High income: OECD
Account (% age 15+)		
All adults	96.1	94.0
Women	96.3	93.8
Adults belonging to the poorest 40%	94.8	90.6
Young adults (% ages 15–24)	89.0	84.1
Adults living in rural areas	89.9	93.8
Financial Institution Account (% age 15+)		
All adults	96.1	94.0
All adults, 2011	88.7	90.0
Mobile Account (% age 15+)		
All adults	..	..
Access to Financial Institution Account (% age 15+)		
Has debit card	69.9	79.7
Has debit card, 2011	75.8	61.9
ATM is the main mode of withdrawal (% with an account)	..	68.5
ATM is the main mode of withdrawal (% with an account), 2011	76.4	68.5
Use of Account in the Past Year (% age 15+)		
Used an account to receive wages	43.0	44.3
Used an account to receive government transfers	11.8	17.2
Used a financial institution account to pay utility bills	39.8	61.1
Other Digital Payments in the Past Year (% age 15+)		
Used a debit card to make payments	50.8	65.3
Used a credit card to make payments	59.3	46.7
Used the Internet to pay bills or make purchases	36.3	54.1
Domestic Remittances in the Past Year (% age 15+)		
Sent remittances	..	..
Sent remittances via a financial institution (% senders)	..	..
Sent remittances via a mobile phone (% senders)	..	..
Sent remittances via a money transfer operator (% senders)	..	..
Received remittances	..	..
Received remittances via a financial institution (% recipients)	..	..
Received remittances via a mobile phone (% recipients)	..	..
Received remittances via a money transfer operator (% recipients)	..	..
Savings in the Past Year (% age 15+)		
Saved at a financial institution	50.0	51.6
Saved at a financial institution, 2011	42.8	45.3
Saved using a savings club or person outside the family	..	..
Saved any money	67.4	70.8
Saved for old age	39.3	39.7
Saved for a farm or business	9.1	9.0
Saved for education or school fees	28.4	25.0
Credit in the Past Year (% age 15+)		
Borrowed from a financial institution	8.2	18.4
Borrowed from a financial institution, 2011	7.9	14.2
Borrowed from family or friends	8.3	14.0
Borrowed from a private informal lender	0.2	0.9
Borrowed any money	25.8	39.8
Borrowed for a farm or business	1.1	2.6
Borrowed for education or school fees	5.4	5.6
Outstanding mortgage at a financial institution	10.4	26.1

Hungary

	Country data	Europe & Central Asia	Upper middle income
Europe & Central Asia		**Upper middle income**	

Europe & Central Asia   **Upper middle income**

Population, age 15+ (millions)   **8.4**   GNI per capita ($)   **13,260**

	Country data	Europe & Central Asia	Upper middle income
Account (% age 15+)			
All adults	72.3	51.4	70.5
Women	72.5	47.4	67.3
Adults belonging to the poorest 40%	70.8	44.2	62.7
Young adults (% ages 15–24)	50.7	35.6	58.1
Adults living in rural areas	70.8	45.7	68.8
Financial Institution Account (% age 15+)			
All adults	72.3	51.4	70.4
All adults, 2011	72.7	43.3	57.4
Mobile Account (% age 15+)			
All adults	..	0.3	0.7
Access to Financial Institution Account (% age 15+)			
Has debit card	59.9	36.9	45.9
Has debit card, 2011	62.4	36.4	38.5
ATM is the main mode of withdrawal (% with an account)	82.7	66.7	55.7
ATM is the main mode of withdrawal (% with an account), 2011	80.9	72.5	42.8
Use of Account in the Past Year (% age 15+)			
Used an account to receive wages	35.9	22.5	18.1
Used an account to receive government transfers	11.1	7.3	9.6
Used a financial institution account to pay utility bills	31.9	12.5	12.3
Other Digital Payments in the Past Year (% age 15+)			
Used a debit card to make payments	47.1	22.9	19.9
Used a credit card to make payments	8.9	14.9	14.4
Used the Internet to pay bills or make purchases	22.2	11.9	15.3
Domestic Remittances in the Past Year (% age 15+)			
Sent remittances	9.4	12.9	15.4
Sent remittances via a financial institution (% senders)	..	31.5	37.2
Sent remittances via a mobile phone (% senders)	..	2.5	8.8
Sent remittances via a money transfer operator (% senders)	..	11.8	19.7
Received remittances	12.0	15.5	17.8
Received remittances via a financial institution (% recipients)	17.1	22.1	29.8
Received remittances via a mobile phone (% recipients)	0.0	1.0	5.6
Received remittances via a money transfer operator (% recipients)	11.9	15.6	17.9
Savings in the Past Year (% age 15+)			
Saved at a financial institution	19.3	8.4	32.2
Saved at a financial institution, 2011	17.3	4.9	25.1
Saved using a savings club or person outside the family	2.3	6.6	4.9
Saved any money	38.2	38.5	62.7
Saved for old age	17.6	11.8	30.6
Saved for a farm or business	4.0	5.1	17.6
Saved for education or school fees	5.8	12.1	25.4
Credit in the Past Year (% age 15+)			
Borrowed from a financial institution	8.7	12.4	10.4
Borrowed from a financial institution, 2011	9.4	7.8	7.9
Borrowed from family or friends	14.9	23.6	24.0
Borrowed from a private informal lender	0.7	2.1	2.6
Borrowed any money	31.4	39.5	37.7
Borrowed for a farm or business	1.1	2.8	6.6
Borrowed for education or school fees	2.0	6.2	6.1
Outstanding mortgage at a financial institution	17.4	10.2	9.1

India

South Asia			**Lower middle income**
Population, age 15+ (millions)	**887.9**	GNI per capita ($)	**1,570**

	Country data	South Asia	Lower middle income
Account (% age 15+)			
All adults	53.1	46.4	42.7
Women	-43.1	37.4	36.3
Adults belonging to the poorest 40%	43.9	38.1	33.2
Young adults (% ages 15–24)	43.2	36.7	34.7
Adults living in rural areas	50.1	43.5	40.0
Financial Institution Account (% age 15+)			
All adults	52.8	45.5	41.8
All adults, 2011	35.2	32.3	28.7
Mobile Account (% age 15+)			
All adults	2.4	2.6	2.5
Access to Financial Institution Account (% age 15+)			
Has debit card	22.1	18.0	21.2
Has debit card, 2011	8.4	7.2	10.1
ATM is the main mode of withdrawal (% with an account)	33.1	31.1	42.4
ATM is the main mode of withdrawal (% with an account), 2011	18.4	16.9	28.1
Use of Account in the Past Year (% age 15+)			
Used an account to receive wages	4.0	3.5	5.6
Used an account to receive government transfers	3.6	3.1	3.3
Used a financial institution account to pay utility bills	3.4	2.7	3.1
Other Digital Payments in the Past Year (% age 15+)			
Used a debit card to make payments	10.7	8.5	9.6
Used a credit card to make payments	3.4	2.6	2.8
Used the Internet to pay bills or make purchases	1.2	1.2	2.6
Domestic Remittances in the Past Year (% age 15+)			
Sent remittances	9.9	10.7	14.2
Sent remittances via a financial institution (% senders)	..	20.1	30.9
Sent remittances via a mobile phone (% senders)	..	7.7	7.7
Sent remittances via a money transfer operator (% senders)	..	13.7	18.3
Received remittances	9.8	12.2	17.8
Received remittances via a financial institution (% recipients)	..	15.8	26.0
Received remittances via a mobile phone (% recipients)	..	4.7	5.7
Received remittances via a money transfer operator (% recipients)	..	9.8	16.6
Savings in the Past Year (% age 15+)			
Saved at a financial institution	14.4	12.7	14.8
Saved at a financial institution, 2011	11.6	11.1	11.1
Saved using a savings club or person outside the family	8.8	8.8	12.4
Saved any money	38.3	36.2	45.6
Saved for old age	9.9	9.1	12.6
Saved for a farm or business	7.0	7.3	11.8
Saved for education or school fees	16.0	14.6	20.0
Credit in the Past Year (% age 15+)			
Borrowed from a financial institution	6.4	6.4	7.5
Borrowed from a financial institution, 2011	7.7	8.7	7.3
Borrowed from family or friends	32.3	31.4	33.1
Borrowed from a private informal lender	12.6	10.9	8.5
Borrowed any money	46.3	46.7	47.4
Borrowed for a farm or business	9.0	8.6	9.2
Borrowed for education or school fees	9.7	8.9	10.1
Outstanding mortgage at a financial institution	3.7	3.8	4.7

Indonesia

East Asia & Pacific			Lower middle income
Population, age 15+ (millions)	**177.7**	GNI per capita ($)	**3,580**

	Country data	East Asia & Pacific	Lower middle income
Account (% age 15+)			
All adults	36.1	69.0	42.7
Women	37.5	67.0	36.3
Adults belonging to the poorest 40%	22.2	60.9	33.2
Young adults (% ages 15-24)	35.2	60.7	34.7
Adults living in rural areas	28.7	64.5	40.0
Financial Institution Account (% age 15+)			
All adults	35.9	68.8	41.8
All adults, 2011	19.6	55.1	28.7
Mobile Account (% age 15+)			
All adults	0.4	0.4	2.5
Access to Financial Institution Account (% age 15+)			
Has debit card	25.9	42.9	21.2
Has debit card, 2011	10.5	34.7	10.1
ATM is the main mode of withdrawal (% with an account)	70.9	53.3	42.4
ATM is the main mode of withdrawal (% with an account), 2011	51.1	37.0	28.1
Use of Account in the Past Year (% age 15+)			
Used an account to receive wages	6.6	15.1	5.6
Used an account to receive government transfers	3.0	8.1	3.3
Used a financial institution account to pay utility bills	2.9	11.8	3.1
Other Digital Payments in the Past Year (% age 15+)			
Used a debit card to make payments	8.5	14.8	9.6
Used a credit card to make payments	1.1	10.8	2.8
Used the Internet to pay bills or make purchases	5.1	15.6	2.6
Domestic Remittances in the Past Year (% age 15+)			
Sent remittances	17.9	16.6	14.2
Sent remittances via a financial institution (% senders)	52.4	36.9	30.9
Sent remittances via a mobile phone (% senders)	3.6	8.7	7.7
Sent remittances via a money transfer operator (% senders)	8.7	18.5	18.3
Received remittances	31.0	20.6	17.8
Received remittances via a financial institution (% recipients)	36.3	29.0	26.0
Received remittances via a mobile phone (% recipients)	0.2	4.9	5.7
Received remittances via a money transfer operator (% recipients)	7.9	15.8	16.6
Savings in the Past Year (% age 15+)			
Saved at a financial institution	26.6	36.5	14.8
Saved at a financial institution, 2011	15.3	28.5	11.1
Saved using a savings club or person outside the family	25.2	6.0	12.4
Saved any money	69.3	71.0	45.6
Saved for old age	27.1	36.5	12.6
Saved for a farm or business	22.6	21.3	11.8
Saved for education or school fees	33.3	30.7	20.0
Credit in the Past Year (% age 15+)			
Borrowed from a financial institution	13.1	11.0	7.5
Borrowed from a financial institution, 2011	8.5	8.6	7.3
Borrowed from family or friends	41.5	28.3	33.1
Borrowed from a private informal lender	2.9	2.5	8.5
Borrowed any money	56.6	41.2	47.4
Borrowed for a farm or business	11.7	8.3	9.2
Borrowed for education or school fees	12.2	7.1	10.1
Outstanding mortgage at a financial institution	5.5	8.0	4.7

Iran, Islamic Rep.

		Upper middle income
Population, age 15+ (millions)	**59.0**	GNI per capita ($) **5,780**

	Country data	Upper middle income
Account (% age 15+)		
All adults	92.3	70.5
Women	87.3	67.3
Adults belonging to the poorest 40%	91.1	62.7
Young adults (% ages 15–24)	88.6	58.1
Adults living in rural areas	90.4	68.8
Financial Institution Account (% age 15+)		
All adults	92.2	70.4
All adults, 2011	73.7	57.4
Mobile Account (% age 15+)		
All adults	4.5	0.7
Access to Financial Institution Account (% age 15+)		
Has debit card	75.1	45.9
Has debit card, 2011	58.3	38.5
ATM is the main mode of withdrawal (% with an account)	76.7	55.7
ATM is the main mode of withdrawal (% with an account), 2011	67.7	42.8
Use of Account in the Past Year (% age 15+)		
Used an account to receive wages	16.8	18.1
Used an account to receive government transfers	61.6	9.6
Used a financial institution account to pay utility bills	34.9	12.3
Other Digital Payments in the Past Year (% age 15+)		
Used a debit card to make payments	55.3	19.9
Used a credit card to make payments	8.8	14.4
Used the Internet to pay bills or make purchases	17.8	15.3
Domestic Remittances in the Past Year (% age 15+)		
Sent remittances	25.1	15.4
Sent remittances via a financial institution (% senders)	60.7	37.2
Sent remittances via a mobile phone (% senders)	0.0	8.8
Sent remittances via a money transfer operator (% senders)	11.0	19.7
Received remittances	35.4	17.8
Received remittances via a financial institution (% recipients)	46.9	29.8
Received remittances via a mobile phone (% recipients)	0.0	5.6
Received remittances via a money transfer operator (% recipients)	10.9	17.9
Savings in the Past Year (% age 15+)		
Saved at a financial institution	21.6	32.2
Saved at a financial institution, 2011	19.7	25.1
Saved using a savings club or person outside the family	6.5	4.9
Saved any money	42.2	62.7
Saved for old age	8.3	30.6
Saved for a farm or business	10.4	17.6
Saved for education or school fees	16.4	25.4
Credit in the Past Year (% age 15+)		
Borrowed from a financial institution	31.6	10.4
Borrowed from a financial institution, 2011	30.7	7.9
Borrowed from family or friends	48.7	24.0
Borrowed from a private informal lender	9.1	2.6
Borrowed any money	80.1	37.7
Borrowed for a farm or business	7.1	6.6
Borrowed for education or school fees	8.3	6.1
Outstanding mortgage at a financial institution	21.2	9.1

Iraq

Population, age 15+ (millions)	**20.0**	GNI per capita ($)	**6,720**

	Country data	Middle East	Upper middle income
Account (% age 15+)			
All adults	11.0	14.2	70.5
Women	7.4	9.2	67.3
Adults belonging to the poorest 40%	8.0	7.3	62.7
Young adults (% ages 15–24)	8.6	7.6	58.1
Adults living in rural areas	11.3	10.7	68.8
Financial Institution Account (% age 15+)			
All adults	11.0	14.0	70.4
All adults, 2011	10.6	10.9	57.4
Mobile Account (% age 15+)			
All adults	..	0.7	0.7
Access to Financial Institution Account (% age 15+)			
Has debit card	3.5	8.5	45.9
Has debit card, 2011	3.3	5.5	38.5
ATM is the main mode of withdrawal (% with an account)	..	44.9	55.7
ATM is the main mode of withdrawal (% with an account), 2011	5.5	42.4	42.8
Use of Account in the Past Year (% age 15+)			
Used an account to receive wages	0.8	3.3	18.1
Used an account to receive government transfers	0.9	0.9	9.6
Used a financial institution account to pay utility bills	0.4	0.2	12.3
Other Digital Payments in the Past Year (% age 15+)			
Used a debit card to make payments	1.4	3.3	19.9
Used a credit card to make payments	1.0	1.5	14.4
Used the Internet to pay bills or make purchases	5.0	2.1	15.3
Domestic Remittances in the Past Year (% age 15+)			
Sent remittances	20.7	9.3	15.4
Sent remittances via a financial institution (% senders)	6.8	..	37.2
Sent remittances via a mobile phone (% senders)	1.8	..	8.8
Sent remittances via a money transfer operator (% senders)	16.5	..	19.7
Received remittances	15.0	11.3	17.8
Received remittances via a financial institution (% recipients)	10.6	9.8	29.8
Received remittances via a mobile phone (% recipients)	0.6	0.2	5.6
Received remittances via a money transfer operator (% recipients)	18.1	15.6	17.9
Savings in the Past Year (% age 15+)			
Saved at a financial institution	3.5	4.0	32.2
Saved at a financial institution, 2011	5.4	2.7	25.1
Saved using a savings club or person outside the family	16.9	11.5	4.9
Saved any money	48.6	30.5	62.7
Saved for old age	16.1	5.0	30.6
Saved for a farm or business	13.0	5.1	17.6
Saved for education or school fees	17.1	9.1	25.4
Credit in the Past Year (% age 15+)			
Borrowed from a financial institution	4.2	5.6	10.4
Borrowed from a financial institution, 2011	8.0	4.4	7.9
Borrowed from family or friends	48.2	30.7	24.0
Borrowed from a private informal lender	19.8	7.9	2.6
Borrowed any money	69.4	45.7	37.7
Borrowed for a farm or business	9.9	4.2	6.6
Borrowed for education or school fees	10.8	8.2	6.1
Outstanding mortgage at a financial institution	6.2	6.2	9.1

Ireland

High income: OECD			**High income**
Population, age 15+ (millions)	**3.6**	GNI per capita ($)	**43,090**

	Country data	High income: OECD
Account (% age 15+)		
All adults	94.7	94.0
Women	94.8	93.8
Adults belonging to the poorest 40%	90.9	90.6
Young adults (% ages 15–24)	90.9	84.1
Adults living in rural areas	94.5	93.8
Financial Institution Account (% age 15+)		
All adults	94.7	94.0
All adults, 2011	93.9	90.0
Mobile Account (% age 15+)		
All adults	..	..
Access to Financial Institution Account (% age 15+)		
Has debit card	86.0	79.7
Has debit card, 2011	70.5	61.9
ATM is the main mode of withdrawal (% with an account)	..	..
ATM is the main mode of withdrawal (% with an account), 2011	74.4	68.5
Use of Account in the Past Year (% age 15+)		
Used an account to receive wages	37.9	44.3
Used an account to receive government transfers	23.5	17.2
Used a financial institution account to pay utility bills	56.3	61.1
Other Digital Payments in the Past Year (% age 15+)		
Used a debit card to make payments	75.8	65.3
Used a credit card to make payments	39.2	46.7
Used the Internet to pay bills or make purchases	54.1	54.1
Domestic Remittances in the Past Year (% age 15+)		
Sent remittances	..	..
Sent remittances via a financial institution (% senders)	..	..
Sent remittances via a mobile phone (% senders)	..	..
Sent remittances via a money transfer operator (% senders)	..	..
Received remittances	..	..
Received remittances via a financial institution (% recipients)	..	..
Received remittances via a mobile phone (% recipients)	..	..
Received remittances via a money transfer operator (% recipients)	..	..
Savings in the Past Year (% age 15+)		
Saved at a financial institution	49.4	51.6
Saved at a financial institution, 2011	51.3	45.3
Saved using a savings club or person outside the family	..	..
Saved any money	69.7	70.8
Saved for old age	30.8	39.7
Saved for a farm or business	10.9	9.0
Saved for education or school fees	25.9	25.0
Credit in the Past Year (% age 15+)		
Borrowed from a financial institution	18.3	18.4
Borrowed from a financial institution, 2011	15.7	14.2
Borrowed from family or friends	16.2	14.9
Borrowed from a private informal lender	0.8	0.9
Borrowed any money	36.1	39.8
Borrowed for a farm or business	3.3	2.6
Borrowed for education or school fees	8.4	5.6
Outstanding mortgage at a financial institution	26.3	26.1

Israel

High income: OECD			High income
Population, age 15+ (millions)	**5.8**	GNI per capita ($)	**33,930**

	Country data	High income: OECD
Account (% age 15+)		
All adults	90.0	94.0
Women	90.0	93.8
Adults belonging to the poorest 40%	83.9	90.6
Young adults (% ages 15–24)	67.3	84.1
Adults living in rural areas	88.4	93.8
Financial Institution Account (% age 15+)		
All adults	90.0	94.0
All adults, 2011	90.5	90.0
Mobile Account (% age 15+)		
All adults	..	..
Access to Financial Institution Account (% age 15+)		
Has debit card	32.4	79.7
Has debit card, 2011	7.5	61.9
ATM is the main mode of withdrawal (% with an account)	80.0	..
ATM is the main mode of withdrawal (% with an account), 2011	67.8	68.5
Use of Account in the Past Year (% age 15+)		
Used an account to receive wages	53.2	44.3
Used an account to receive government transfers	28.9	17.2
Used a financial institution account to pay utility bills	43.5	61.1
Other Digital Payments in the Past Year (% age 15+)		
Used a debit card to make payments	20.4	65.3
Used a credit card to make payments	75.1	46.7
Used the Internet to pay bills or make purchases	35.7	54.1
Domestic Remittances in the Past Year (% age 15+)		
Sent remittances	18.2	..
Sent remittances via a financial institution (% senders)	43.7	..
Sent remittances via a mobile phone (% senders)	5.8	..
Sent remittances via a money transfer operator (% senders)	16.7	..
Received remittances	21.6	..
Received remittances via a financial institution (% recipients)	37.3	..
Received remittances via a mobile phone (% recipients)	2.3	..
Received remittances via a money transfer operator (% recipients)	8.8	..
Savings in the Past Year (% age 15+)		
Saved at a financial institution	53.5	51.6
Saved at a financial institution, 2011	24.8	45.3
Saved using a savings club or person outside the family	4.7	..
Saved any money	62.1	70.8
Saved for old age	28.6	39.7
Saved for a farm or business	10.9	9.0
Saved for education or school fees	17.1	25.0
Credit in the Past Year (% age 15+)		
Borrowed from a financial institution	40.5	18.4
Borrowed from a financial institution, 2011	16.7	14.2
Borrowed from family or friends	17.1	14.9
Borrowed from a private informal lender	1.6	0.9
Borrowed any money	64.2	39.8
Borrowed for a farm or business	5.9	2.6
Borrowed for education or school fees	10.3	5.6
Outstanding mortgage at a financial institution	34.3	26.1

Italy

Population, age 15+ (millions)	**51.8**	GNI per capita ($)	**35,620**

	Country data	High income: OECD
Account (% age 15+)		
All adults	87.3	94.0
Women	83.2	93.8
Adults belonging to the poorest 40%	83.4	90.6
Young adults (% ages 15–24)	60.8	84.1
Adults living in rural areas	85.8	93.8
Financial Institution Account (% age 15+)		
All adults	87.3	94.0
All adults, 2011	71.0	90.0
Mobile Account (% age 15+)		
All adults	..	..
Access to Financial Institution Account (% age 15+)		
Has debit card	64.5	79.7
Has debit card, 2011	35.2	61.9
ATM is the main mode of withdrawal (% with an account)	..	..
ATM is the main mode of withdrawal (% with an account), 2011	56.4	68.5
Use of Account in the Past Year (% age 15+)		
Used an account to receive wages	32.3	44.3
Used an account to receive government transfers	6.8	17.2
Used a financial institution account to pay utility bills	44.4	61.1
Other Digital Payments in the Past Year (% age 15+)		
Used a debit card to make payments	52.6	65.3
Used a credit card to make payments	32.3	46.7
Used the Internet to pay bills or make purchases	39.0	54.1
Domestic Remittances in the Past Year (% age 15+)		
Sent remittances	..	..
Sent remittances via a financial institution (% senders)	..	..
Sent remittances via a mobile phone (% senders)	..	..
Sent remittances via a money transfer operator (% senders)	..	..
Received remittances	..	..
Received remittances via a financial institution (% recipients)	..	..
Received remittances via a mobile phone (% recipients)	..	..
Received remittances via a money transfer operator (% recipients)	..	..
Savings in the Past Year (% age 15+)		
Saved at a financial institution	34.0	51.6
Saved at a financial institution, 2011	15.5	45.3
Saved using a savings club or person outside the family	..	..
Saved any money	56.6	70.8
Saved for old age	25.1	39.7
Saved for a farm or business	2.4	9.0
Saved for education or school fees	23.7	25.0
Credit in the Past Year (% age 15+)		
Borrowed from a financial institution	13.5	18.4
Borrowed from a financial institution, 2011	4.6	14.2
Borrowed from family or friends	23.1	14.9
Borrowed from a private informal lender	0.4	0.9
Borrowed any money	43.5	39.8
Borrowed for a farm or business	1.1	2.6
Borrowed for education or school fees	6.5	5.6
Outstanding mortgage at a financial institution	11.2	26.1

Jamaica

Latin America & Caribbean			Upper middle income
Population, age 15+ (millions)	**2.0**	GNI per capita ($)	**5,220**

	Country data	Latin America & the Carib.	Upper middle income
Account (% age 15+)			
All adults	78.5	51.4	70.5
Women	77.8	48.6	67.3
Adults belonging to the poorest 40%	69.5	41.2	62.7
Young adults (% ages 15–24)	73.4	37.4	58.1
Adults living in rural areas	76.2	46.0	68.8
Financial Institution Account (% age 15+)			
All adults	78.3	51.1	70.4
All adults, 2011	71.0	39.3	57.4
Mobile Account (% age 15+)			
All adults	0.9	1.7	0.7
Access to Financial Institution Account (% age 15+)			
Has debit card	45.0	40.4	45.9
Has debit card, 2011	41.1	28.9	38.5
ATM is the main mode of withdrawal (% with an account)	49.7	71.1	55.7
ATM is the main mode of withdrawal (% with an account), 2011	46.8	57.0	42.8
Use of Account in the Past Year (% age 15+)			
Used an account to receive wages	12.6	18.0	18.1
Used an account to receive government transfers	2.8	9.0	9.6
Used a financial institution account to pay utility bills	7.8	6.3	12.3
Other Digital Payments in the Past Year (% age 15+)			
Used a debit card to make payments	24.6	27.7	19.9
Used a credit card to make payments	9.8	18.0	14.4
Used the Internet to pay bills or make purchases	10.5	6.9	15.3
Domestic Remittances in the Past Year (% age 15+)			
Sent remittances	27.8	9.5	15.4
Sent remittances via a financial institution (% senders)	26.8	..	37.2
Sent remittances via a mobile phone (% senders)	0.0	..	8.8
Sent remittances via a money transfer operator (% senders)	36.0	..	19.7
Received remittances	33.1	11.3	17.8
Received remittances via a financial institution (% recipients)	38.5	34.2	29.8
Received remittances via a mobile phone (% recipients)	2.9	4.3	5.6
Received remittances via a money transfer operator (% recipients)	49.3	28.4	17.9
Savings in the Past Year (% age 15+)			
Saved at a financial institution	29.7	13.5	32.2
Saved at a financial institution, 2011	30.4	9.6	25.1
Saved using a savings club or person outside the family	27.2	7.9	4.9
Saved any money	74.3	40.6	62.7
Saved for old age	32.2	10.6	30.6
Saved for a farm or business	25.1	10.6	17.6
Saved for education or school fees	37.9	17.2	25.4
Credit in the Past Year (% age 15+)			
Borrowed from a financial institution	11.1	11.3	10.4
Borrowed from a financial institution, 2011	7.9	7.9	7.9
Borrowed from family or friends	29.6	13.5	24.0
Borrowed from a private informal lender	1.7	4.7	2.6
Borrowed any money	45.4	32.7	37.7
Borrowed for a farm or business	6.6	6.1	6.6
Borrowed for education or school fees	10.3	8.3	6.1
Outstanding mortgage at a financial institution	6.9	9.6	9.1

Japan

High income: OECD		**High income**
Population, age 15+ (millions)	**110.7**	GNI per capita ($) **46,330**

	Country data	High income: OECD
Account (% age 15+)		
All adults	96.6	94.0
Women	97.0	93.8
Adults belonging to the poorest 40%	95.4	90.6
Young adults (% ages 15–24)	81.5	84.1
Adults living in rural areas	96.4	93.8
Financial Institution Account (% age 15+)		
All adults	96.6	94.0
All adults, 2011	96.4	90.0
Mobile Account (% age 15+)		
All adults	..	..
Access to Financial Institution Account (% age 15+)		
Has debit card	88.1	79.7
Has debit card, 2011	13.0	61.9
ATM is the main mode of withdrawal (% with an account)	..	68.5
ATM is the main mode of withdrawal (% with an account), 2011	83.2	68.5
Use of Account in the Past Year (% age 15+)		
Used an account to receive wages	43.1	44.3
Used an account to receive government transfers	10.6	17.2
Used a financial institution account to pay utility bills	65.6	61.1
Other Digital Payments in the Past Year (% age 15+)		
Used a debit card to make payments	39.3	65.3
Used a credit card to make payments	52.1	46.7
Used the internet to pay bills or make purchases	36.1	54.1
Domestic Remittances in the Past Year (% age 15+)		
Sent remittances	..	..
Sent remittances via a financial institution (% senders)	..	..
Sent remittances via a mobile phone (% senders)	..	..
Sent remittances via a money transfer operator (% senders)	..	..
Received remittances	..	..
Received remittances via a financial institution (% recipients)	..	..
Received remittances via a mobile phone (% recipients)	..	..
Received remittances via a money transfer operator (% recipients)	..	..
Savings in the Past Year (% age 15+)		
Saved at a financial institution	60.4	51.6
Saved at a financial institution, 2011	51.3	45.3
Saved using a savings club or person outside the family	..	..
Saved any money	71.9	70.8
Saved for old age	43.5	39.7
Saved for a farm or business	4.9	9.0
Saved for education or school fees	28.4	25.0
Credit in the Past Year (% age 15+)		
Borrowed from a financial institution	7.9	18.4
Borrowed from a financial institution, 2011	6.1	14.2
Borrowed from family or friends	6.0	14.9
Borrowed from a private informal lender	0.3	0.9
Borrowed any money	23.1	39.8
Borrowed for a farm or business	1.1	2.6
Borrowed for education or school fees	2.2	5.6
Outstanding mortgage at a financial institution	19.1	26.1

Jordan

Middle East			**Upper middle income**
Population, age 15+ (millions)	**4.3**	GNI per capita ($)	**4,950**

	Country data	Middle East	Upper middle income
Account (% age 15+)			
All adults	24.6	14.2	70.5
Women	15.5	9.2	67.3
Adults belonging to the poorest 40%	16.4	7.3	62.7
Young adults (% ages 15–24)	12.4	7.6	58.1
Adults living in rural areas	25.4	10.7	68.8
Financial Institution Account (% age 15+)			
All adults	24.6	14.0	70.4
All adults, 2011	25.5	10.9	57.4
Mobile Account (% age 15+)			
All adults	0.5	0.7	0.7
Access to Financial Institution Account (% age 15+)			
Has debit card	19.1	8.5	45.9
Has debit card, 2011	14.7	5.5	38.5
ATM is the main mode of withdrawal (% with an account)	67.3	44.9	55.7
ATM is the main mode of withdrawal (% with an account), 2011	55.1	42.4	42.8
Use of Account in the Past Year (% age 15+)			
Used an account to receive wages	7.9	3.3	18.1
Used an account to receive government transfers	0.7	0.9	9.6
Used a financial institution account to pay utility bills	0.1	0.2	12.3
Other Digital Payments in the Past Year (% age 15+)			
Used a debit card to make payments	6.4	3.3	19.9
Used a credit card to make payments	1.8	1.5	14.4
Used the Internet to pay bills or make purchases	2.5	2.1	15.3
Domestic Remittances in the Past Year (% age 15+)			
Sent remittances	11.4	9.3	15.4
Sent remittances via a financial institution (% senders)	9.4	..	37.2
Sent remittances via a mobile phone (% senders)	1.9	..	8.8
Sent remittances via a money transfer operator (% senders)	4.1	..	19.7
Received remittances	9.5	11.3	17.8
Received remittances via a financial institution (% recipients)	..	9.8	29.8
Received remittances via a mobile phone (% recipients)	..	0.2	5.6
Received remittances via a money transfer operator (% recipients)	..	15.6	17.9
Savings in the Past Year (% age 15+)			
Saved at a financial institution	3.8	4.0	32.2
Saved at a financial institution, 2011	8.3	2.7	25.1
Saved using a savings club or person outside the family	15.2	11.5	4.9
Saved any money	29.2	30.5	62.7
Saved for old age	1.9	5.0	30.6
Saved for a farm or business	3.2	5.1	17.6
Saved for education or school fees	5.5	9.1	25.4
Credit in the Past Year (% age 15+)			
Borrowed from a financial institution	13.6	5.6	10.4
Borrowed from a financial institution, 2011	4.5	4.4	7.9
Borrowed from family or friends	17.4	30.7	24.0
Borrowed from a private informal lender	1.1	7.9	2.6
Borrowed any money	32.2	45.7	37.7
Borrowed for a farm or business	2.8	4.2	6.6
Borrowed for education or school fees	4.1	8.2	6.1
Outstanding mortgage at a financial institution	14.9	6.2	9.1

Kazakhstan

Europe & Central Asia		Upper middle income	

Population, age 15+ (millions)	**12.6**	GNI per capita ($)	**11,550**

	Country data	Europe & Central Asia	Upper middle income
Account (% age 15+)			
All adults	53.9	51.4	70.5
Women	55.6	47.4	67.3
Adults belonging to the poorest 40%	46.0	44.2	62.7
Young adults (% ages 15–24)	31.6	35.6	58.1
Adults living in rural areas	47.9	45.7	68.8
Financial Institution Account (% age 15+)			
All adults	53.9	51.4	70.4
All adults, 2011	42.1	43.3	57.4
Mobile Account (% age 15+)			
All adults	..	0.3	0.7
Access to Financial Institution Account (% age 15+)			
Has debit card	32.0	36.9	45.9
Has debit card, 2011	31.3	36.4	38.5
ATM is the main mode of withdrawal (% with an account)	69.4	66.7	55.7
ATM is the main mode of withdrawal (% with an account), 2011	55.5	72.5	42.8
Use of Account in the Past Year (% age 15+)			
Used an account to receive wages	29.9	22.5	18.1
Used an account to receive government transfers	10.4	7.3	9.6
Used a financial institution account to pay utility bills	2.6	12.5	12.3
Other Digital Payments in the Past Year (% age 15+)			
Used a debit card to make payments	12.7	22.9	19.9
Used a credit card to make payments	5.2	14.9	14.4
Used the Internet to pay bills or make purchases	0.9	11.9	15.3
Domestic Remittances in the Past Year (% age 15+)			
Sent remittances	13.5	12.9	15.4
Sent remittances via a financial institution (% senders)	36.7	31.5	37.2
Sent remittances via a mobile phone (% senders)	1.8	2.5	8.8
Sent remittances via a money transfer operator (% senders)	17.3	11.8	19.7
Received remittances	12.4	15.5	17.8
Received remittances via a financial institution (% recipients)	19.9	22.1	29.8
Received remittances via a mobile phone (% recipients)	0.0	1.0	5.6
Received remittances via a money transfer operator (% recipients)	25.0	15.6	17.9
Savings in the Past Year (% age 15+)			
Saved at a financial institution	8.0	8.4	32.2
Saved at a financial institution, 2011	6.7	4.9	25.1
Saved using a savings club or person outside the family	2.6	6.6	4.9
Saved any money	30.3	38.5	62.7
Saved for old age	6.3	11.8	30.6
Saved for a farm or business	2.8	5.1	17.6
Saved for education or school fees	8.5	12.1	25.4
Credit in the Past Year (% age 15+)			
Borrowed from a financial institution	16.5	12.4	10.4
Borrowed from a financial institution, 2011	13.1	7.8	7.9
Borrowed from family or friends	23.9	23.6	24.0
Borrowed from a private informal lender	2.1	2.1	2.6
Borrowed any money	43.4	39.5	37.7
Borrowed for a farm or business	1.5	2.8	6.6
Borrowed for education or school fees	5.6	6.2	6.1
Outstanding mortgage at a financial institution	15.2	10.2	9.1

Kenya

Sub-Saharan Africa   **Low income**

Population, age 15+ (millions)	25.6	GNI per capita ($)	1,160

	Country data	Sub-Saharan Africa	Low income
Account (% age 15+)			
All adults	74.7	34.2	27.5
Women	71.1	29.9	23.9
Adults belonging to the poorest 40%	63.4	24.6	19.4
Young adults (% ages 15–24)	66.4	25.9	20.2
Adults living in rural areas	73.0	29.2	24.8
Financial Institution Account (% age 15+)			
All adults	55.2	28.9	22.3
All adults, 2011	42.3	23.9	21.1
Mobile Account (% age 15+)			
All adults	58.4	11.5	10.0
Access to Financial Institution Account (% age 15+)			
Has debit card	34.7	17.9	6.6
Has debit card, 2011	29.9	15.0	6.3
ATM is the main mode of withdrawal (% with an account)	52.7	53.8	20.2
ATM is the main mode of withdrawal (% with an account), 2011	69.2	51.7	19.7
Use of Account in the Past Year (% age 15+)			
Used an account to receive wages	18.0	7.3	3.2
Used an account to receive government transfers	6.4	3.8	1.0
Used a financial institution account to pay utility bills	5.8	2.8	0.9
Other Digital Payments in the Past Year (% age 15+)			
Used a debit card to make payments	11.2	8.7	2.1
Used a credit card to make payments	2.7	1.9	0.6
Used the Internet to pay bills or make purchases	4.7	2.4	1.2
Domestic Remittances in the Past Year (% age 15+)			
Sent remittances	53.0	28.7	18.3
Sent remittances via a financial institution (% senders)	16.2	31.0	15.4
Sent remittances via a mobile phone (% senders)	92.0	30.8	42.8
Sent remittances via a money transfer operator (% senders)	8.9	21.0	14.1
Received remittances	61.0	37.2	25.6
Received remittances via a financial institution (% recipients)	14.2	26.6	13.0
Received remittances via a mobile phone (% recipients)	88.8	27.6	33.8
Received remittances via a money transfer operator (% recipients)	9.9	22.1	14.8
Savings in the Past Year (% age 15+)			
Saved at a financial institution	30.2	15.9	9.9
Saved at a financial institution, 2011	23.3	14.3	11.5
Saved using a savings club or person outside the family	39.9	23.9	16.3
Saved any money	76.1	59.6	46.5
Saved for old age	17.9	9.8	8.3
Saved for a farm or business	36.2	22.7	16.7
Saved for education or school fees	39.3	22.9	16.6
Credit in the Past Year (% age 15+)			
Borrowed from a financial institution	14.9	6.3	8.6
Borrowed from a financial institution, 2011	9.7	4.8	11.7
Borrowed from family or friends	60.5	41.9	34.9
Borrowed from a private informal lender	7.3	4.7	6.5
Borrowed any money	79.2	54.5	52.5
Borrowed for a farm or business	24.3	12.8	12.2
Borrowed for education or school fees	33.5	12.3	10.9
Outstanding mortgage at a financial institution	12.1	5.2	4.1

Korea, Rep.

High income: OECD		High income
Population, age 15+ (millions)	**42.7**	GNI per capita ($)	**25,920**

	Country data	High income: OECD
Account (% age 15+)		
All adults	94.4	94.0
Women	93.4	93.8
Adults belonging to the poorest 40%	92.4	90.6
Young adults (% ages 15–24)	86.1	84.1
Adults living in rural areas	92.9	93.8
Financial Institution Account (% age 15+)		
All adults	94.4	94.0
All adults, 2011	93.0	90.0
Mobile Account (% age 15+)		
All adults	..	..
Access to Financial Institution Account (% age 15+)		
Has debit card	66.8	79.7
Has debit card, 2011	57.9	61.9
ATM is the main mode of withdrawal (% with an account)	..	..
ATM is the main mode of withdrawal (% with an account), 2011	77.0	68.5
Use of Account in the Past Year (% age 15+)		
Used an account to receive wages	37.9	44.3
Used an account to receive government transfers	14.7	17.2
Used a financial institution account to pay utility bills	52.3	61.1
Other Digital Payments in the Past Year (% age 15+)		
Used a debit card to make payments	56.1	65.3
Used a credit card to make payments	53.9	46.7
Used the Internet to pay bills or make purchases	52.5	54.1
Domestic Remittances in the Past Year (% age 15+)		
Sent remittances	..	..
Sent remittances via a financial institution (% senders)	..	..
Sent remittances via a mobile phone (% senders)	..	..
Sent remittances via a money transfer operator (% senders)	..	..
Received remittances	..	..
Received remittances via a financial institution (% recipients)	..	..
Received remittances via a mobile phone (% recipients)	..	..
Received remittances via a money transfer operator (% recipients)	..	..
Savings in the Past Year (% age 15+)		
Saved at a financial institution	52.7	51.6
Saved at a financial institution, 2011	46.9	45.3
Saved using a savings club or person outside the family	..	..
Saved any money	73.9	70.8
Saved for old age	41.6	39.7
Saved for a farm or business	25.4	9.0
Saved for education or school fees	33.9	25.0
Credit in the Past Year (% age 15+)		
Borrowed from a financial institution	18.2	18.4
Borrowed from a financial institution, 2011	16.6	14.2
Borrowed from family or friends	17.1	14.9
Borrowed from a private informal lender	0.7	0.9
Borrowed any money	39.4	39.8
Borrowed for a farm or business	4.6	2.6
Borrowed for education or school fees	6.9	5.6
Outstanding mortgage at a financial institution	18.9	26.1

Kosovo

Population, age 15+ (millions)	**1.3**	GNI per capita ($)	**3,940**

	Country data	Europe & Central Asia	Lower middle income
Account (% age 15+)			
All adults	47.8	51.4	42.7
Women	36.3	47.4	36.3
Adults belonging to the poorest 40%	42.3	44.2	33.2
Young adults (% ages 15–24)	41.1	35.6	34.7
Adults living in rural areas	46.0	45.7	40.0
Financial Institution Account (% age 15+)			
All adults	47.8	51.4	41.8
All adults, 2011	44.3	43.3	28.7
Mobile Account (% age 15+)			
All adults	..	0.3	2.5
Access to Financial Institution Account (% age 15+)			
Has debit card	33.9	36.9	21.2
Has debit card, 2011	29.0	36.4	10.1
ATM is the main mode of withdrawal (% with an account)	51.7	66.7	42.4
ATM is the main mode of withdrawal (% with an account), 2011	48.5	72.5	28.1
Use of Account in the Past Year (% age 15+)			
Used an account to receive wages	13.4	22.5	5.6
Used an account to receive government transfers	4.4	7.3	3.3
Used a financial institution account to pay utility bills	1.4	12.5	3.1
Other Digital Payments in the Past Year (% age 15+)			
Used a debit card to make payments	17.8	22.9	9.6
Used a credit card to make payments	9.4	14.9	2.8
Used the Internet to pay bills or make purchases	5.2	11.9	2.6
Domestic Remittances in the Past Year (% age 15+)			
Sent remittances	12.4	12.9	14.2
Sent remittances via a financial institution (% senders)	14.6	31.5	30.9
Sent remittances via a mobile phone (% senders)	2.7	2.5	7.7
Sent remittances via a money transfer operator (% senders)	4.6	11.8	18.3
Received remittances	20.7	15.5	17.8
Received remittances via a financial institution (% recipients)	10.6	22.1	26.0
Received remittances via a mobile phone (% recipients)	2.9	1.0	5.7
Received remittances via a money transfer operator (% recipients)	8.0	15.6	16.6
Savings in the Past Year (% age 15+)			
Saved at a financial institution	7.2	8.4	14.8
Saved at a financial institution, 2011	4.9	4.9	11.1
Saved using a savings club or person outside the family	3.0	6.6	12.4
Saved any money	35.6	38.5	45.6
Saved for old age	16.2	11.8	12.6
Saved for a farm or business	6.5	5.1	11.8
Saved for education or school fees	9.2	12.1	20.0
Credit in the Past Year (% age 15+)			
Borrowed from a financial institution	9.2	12.4	7.5
Borrowed from a financial institution, 2011	6.1	7.8	7.3
Borrowed from family or friends	16.7	23.6	33.1
Borrowed from a private informal lender	1.7	2.1	8.5
Borrowed any money	36.4	39.5	47.4
Borrowed for a farm or business	3.4	2.8	9.2
Borrowed for education or school fees	6.3	6.2	10.1
Outstanding mortgage at a financial institution	8.9	10.2	4.7

Kuwait

Population, age 15+ (millions)	2.5	GNI per capita ($)	45,130

	Country data	High income: OCED
Account (% age 15+)		
All adults	72.9	94.0
Women	64.0	93.8
Adults belonging to the poorest 40%	65.6	90.6
Young adults (% ages 15–24)	62.9	84.1
Adults living in rural areas	78.9	93.8
Financial Institution Account (% age 15+)		
All adults	72.9	94.0
All adults, 2011	86.8	90.0
Mobile Account (% age 15+)		
All adults	..	..
Access to Financial Institution Account (% age 15+)		
Has debit card	70.3	79.7
Has debit card, 2011	83.9	61.9
ATM is the main mode of withdrawal (% with an account)	..	..
ATM is the main mode of withdrawal (% with an account), 2011	85.0	68.5
Use of Account in the Past Year (% age 15+)		
Used an account to receive wages	28.3	44.3
Used an account to receive government transfers	2.4	17.2
Used a financial institution account to pay utility bills	7.2	61.1
Other Digital Payments in the Past Year (% age 15+)		
Used a debit card to make payments	55.1	65.3
Used a credit card to make payments	22.8	46.7
Used the Internet to pay bills or make purchases	25.9	54.1
Domestic Remittances in the Past Year (% age 15+)		
Sent remittances	..	..
Sent remittances via a financial institution (% senders)	..	..
Sent remittances via a mobile phone (% senders)	..	..
Sent remittances via a money transfer operator (% senders)	..	..
Received remittances	..	..
Received remittances via a financial institution (% recipients)	..	..
Received remittances via a mobile phone (% recipients)	..	..
Received remittances via a money transfer operator (% recipients)	..	..
Savings in the Past Year (% age 15+)		
Saved at a financial institution	25.5	51.6
Saved at a financial institution, 2011	40.3	45.3
Saved using a savings club or person outside the family	..	..
Saved any money	61.5	70.8
Saved for old age	17.6	39.7
Saved for a farm or business	18.4	9.0
Saved for education or school fees	23.6	25.0
Credit in the Past Year (% age 15+)		
Borrowed from a financial institution	14.1	18.4
Borrowed from a financial institution, 2011	20.8	14.2
Borrowed from family or friends	30.2	14.9
Borrowed from a private informal lender	12.0	0.9
Borrowed any money	53.8	39.8
Borrowed for a farm or business	6.7	2.6
Borrowed for education or school fees	8.9	5.6
Outstanding mortgage at a financial institution	16.7	26.1

Kyrgyz Republic

Europe & Central Asia			**Lower middle income**

Population, age 15+ (millions)	**4.0**	GNI per capita ($)		**1,210**

	Country data	Europe & Central Asia	Lower middle income
Account (% age 15+)			
All adults	18.5	51.4	42.7
Women	18.9	47.4	36.3
Adults belonging to the poorest 40%	14.8	44.2	33.2
Young adults (% ages 15–24)	11.6	35.6	34.7
Adults living in rural areas	15.1	45.7	40.0
Financial Institution Account (% age 15+)			
All adults	18.5	51.4	41.8
All adults, 2011	3.8	43.3	28.7
Mobile Account (% age 15+)			
All adults	..	0.3	2.5
Access to Financial Institution Account (% age 15+)			
Has debit card	6.4	36.9	21.2
Has debit card, 2011	1.7	36.4	10.1
ATM is the main mode of withdrawal (% with an account)	57.6	66.7	42.4
ATM is the main mode of withdrawal (% with an account), 2011	..	72.5	28.1
Use of Account in the Past Year (% age 15+)			
Used an account to receive wages	5.2	22.5	5.6
Used an account to receive government transfers	1.8	7.3	3.3
Used a financial institution account to pay utility bills	4.0	12.5	3.1
Other Digital Payments in the Past Year (% age 15+)			
Used a debit card to make payments	3.1	22.9	9.6
Used a credit card to make payments	1.7	14.9	2.8
Used the Internet to pay bills or make purchases	3.6	11.9	2.6
Domestic Remittances in the Past Year (% age 15+)			
Sent remittances	13.2	12.9	14.2
Sent remittances via a financial institution (% senders)	37.6	31.5	30.9
Sent remittances via a mobile phone (% senders)	0.0	2.5	7.7
Sent remittances via a money transfer operator (% senders)	38.8	11.8	18.3
Received remittances	21.8	15.5	17.8
Received remittances via a financial institution (% recipients)	48.2	22.1	26.0
Received remittances via a mobile phone (% recipients)	0.4	1.0	5.7
Received remittances via a money transfer operator (% recipients)	48.1	15.6	16.6
Savings in the Past Year (% age 15+)			
Saved at a financial institution	4.9	8.4	14.8
Saved at a financial institution, 2011	0.9	4.9	11.1
Saved using a savings club or person outside the family	9.9	6.6	12.4
Saved any money	36.2	38.5	45.6
Saved for old age	4.6	11.8	12.6
Saved for a farm or business	9.3	5.1	11.8
Saved for education or school fees	14.4	12.1	20.0
Credit in the Past Year (% age 15+)			
Borrowed from a financial institution	13.5	12.4	7.5
Borrowed from a financial institution, 2011	11.3	7.8	7.3
Borrowed from family or friends	21.0	23.6	33.1
Borrowed from a private informal lender	3.7	2.1	8.5
Borrowed any money	37.4	39.5	47.4
Borrowed for a farm or business	6.4	2.8	9.2
Borrowed for education or school fees	4.4	6.2	10.1
Outstanding mortgage at a financial institution	5.9	10.2	4.7

Latvia

Population, age 15+ (millions)	1.7	GNI per capita ($)	15,290

	Country data	High income: OECD
Account (% age 15+)		
All adults	90.2	94.0
Women	90.2	93.8
Adults belonging to the poorest 40%	85.5	90.6
Young adults (% ages 15–24)	81.3	84.1
Adults living in rural areas	87.1	93.8
Financial Institution Account (% age 15+)		
All adults	90.2	94.0
All adults, 2011	89.7	90.0
Mobile Account (% age 15+)		
All adults	..	..
Access to Financial Institution Account (% age 15+)		
Has debit card	84.5	79.7
Has debit card, 2011	77.8	61.9
ATM is the main mode of withdrawal (% with an account)	91.3	..
ATM is the main mode of withdrawal (% with an account), 2011	84.2	68.5
Use of Account in the Past Year (% age 15+)		
Used an account to receive wages	54.2	44.3
Used an account to receive government transfers	31.9	17.2
Used a financial institution account to pay utility bills	45.3	61.1
Other Digital Payments in the Past Year (% age 15+)		
Used a debit card to make payments	77.8	65.3
Used a credit card to make payments	18.4	46.7
Used the Internet to pay bills or make purchases	48.2	54.1
Domestic Remittances in the Past Year (% age 15+)		
Sent remittances	23.9	..
Sent remittances via a financial institution (% senders)	47.2	..
Sent remittances via a mobile phone (% senders)	1.5	..
Sent remittances via a money transfer operator (% senders)	7.0	..
Received remittances	24.2	..
Received remittances via a financial institution (% recipients)	43.3	..
Received remittances via a mobile phone (% recipients)	0.3	..
Received remittances via a money transfer operator (% recipients)	8.7	..
Savings in the Past Year (% age 15+)		
Saved at a financial institution	25.3	51.6
Saved at a financial institution, 2011	13.3	45.3
Saved using a savings club or person outside the family	4.6	..
Saved any money	44.3	70.8
Saved for old age	16.0	39.7
Saved for a farm or business	4.2	9.0
Saved for education or school fees	9.0	25.0
Credit in the Past Year (% age 15+)		
Borrowed from a financial institution	16.8	18.4
Borrowed from a financial institution, 2011	6.8	14.2
Borrowed from family or friends	20.0	14.9
Borrowed from a private informal lender	1.8	0.9
Borrowed any money	37.3	39.8
Borrowed for a farm or business	1.9	2.6
Borrowed for education or school fees	3.4	5.6
Outstanding mortgage at a financial institution	16.6	26.1

Lebanon

Population, age 15+ (millions)	**3.5**	GNI per capita ($)	**9,870**

	Country data	Middle East	Upper middle income
Account (% age 15+)			
All adults	46.9	14.2	70.5
Women	32.9	9.2	67.3
Adults belonging to the poorest 40%	27.2	7.3	62.7
Young adults (% ages 15–24)	29.8	7.6	58.1
Adults living in rural areas	42.3	10.7	68.8
Financial Institution Account (% age 15+)			
All adults	46.9	14.0	70.4
All adults, 2011	37.0	10.9	57.4
Mobile Account (% age 15+)			
All adults	0.7	0.7	0.7
Access to Financial Institution Account (% age 15+)			
Has debit card	33.4	8.5	45.9
Has debit card, 2011	21.4	5.5	38.5
ATM is the main mode of withdrawal (% with an account)	60.9	44.9	55.7
ATM is the main mode of withdrawal (% with an account), 2011	50.1	42.4	42.8
Use of Account in the Past Year (% age 15+)			
Used an account to receive wages	19.0	3.3	18.1
Used an account to receive government transfers	4.6	0.9	9.6
Used a financial institution account to pay utility bills	0.6	0.2	12.3
Other Digital Payments in the Past Year (% age 15+)			
Used a debit card to make payments	19.6	3.3	19.9
Used a credit card to make payments	9.1	1.5	14.4
Used the Internet to pay bills or make purchases	4.4	2.1	15.3
Domestic Remittances in the Past Year (% age 15+)			
Sent remittances	14.2	9.3	15.4
Sent remittances via a financial institution (% senders)	5.2	..	37.2
Sent remittances via a mobile phone (% senders)	2.8	..	8.8
Sent remittances via a money transfer operator (% senders)	12.1	..	19.7
Received remittances	15.5	11.3	17.8
Received remittances via a financial institution (% recipients)	11.6	9.8	29.8
Received remittances via a mobile phone (% recipients)	1.2	0.2	5.6
Received remittances via a money transfer operator (% recipients)	19.6	15.6	17.9
Savings in the Past Year (% age 15+)			
Saved at a financial institution	17.5	4.0	32.2
Saved at a financial institution, 2011	17.1	2.7	25.1
Saved using a savings club or person outside the family	3.6	11.5	4.9
Saved any money	47.1	30.5	62.7
Saved for old age	6.5	5.0	30.6
Saved for a farm or business	8.4	5.1	17.6
Saved for education or school fees	10.0	9.1	25.4
Credit in the Past Year (% age 15+)			
Borrowed from a financial institution	15.6	5.6	10.4
Borrowed from a financial institution, 2011	11.3	4.4	7.9
Borrowed from family or friends	12.9	30.7	24.0
Borrowed from a private informal lender	4.4	7.9	2.6
Borrowed any money	34.8	45.7	37.7
Borrowed for a farm or business	5.9	4.2	6.6
Borrowed for education or school fees	3.4	8.2	6.1
Outstanding mortgage at a financial institution	18.0	6.2	9.1

Lithuania

High income

Population, age 15+ (millions)	**2.5**	GNI per capita ($)	**14,900**

	Country data	High income: OECD
Account (% age 15+)		
All adults	77.9	94.0
Women	77.9	93.8
Adults belonging to the poorest 40%	66.7	90.6
Young adults (% ages 15–24)	33.4	84.1
Adults living in rural areas	76.8	93.8
Financial Institution Account (% age 15+)		
All adults	77.9	94.0
All adults, 2011	73.8	90.0
Mobile Account (% age 15+)		
All adults	..	..
Access to Financial Institution Account (% age 15+)		
Has debit card	64.8	79.7
Has debit card, 2011	61.3	61.9
ATM is the main mode of withdrawal (% with an account)	87.5	..
ATM is the main mode of withdrawal (% with an account), 2011	83.2	68.5
Use of Account in the Past Year (% age 15+)		
Used an account to receive wages	44.1	44.3
Used an account to receive government transfers	24.6	17.2
Used a financial institution account to pay utility bills	23.4	61.1
Other Digital Payments in the Past Year (% age 15+)		
Used a debit card to make payments	52.2	65.3
Used a credit card to make payments	7.3	46.7
Used the Internet to pay bills or make purchases	31.2	54.1
Domestic Remittances in the Past Year (% age 15+)		
Sent remittances	13.3	..
Sent remittances via a financial institution (% senders)	25.3	..
Sent remittances via a mobile phone (% senders)	5.0	..
Sent remittances via a money transfer operator (% senders)	12.4	..
Received remittances	20.1	..
Received remittances via a financial institution (% recipients)	24.1	..
Received remittances via a mobile phone (% recipients)	1.5	..
Received remittances via a money transfer operator (% recipients)	10.2	..
Savings in the Past Year (% age 15+)		
Saved at a financial institution	28.3	51.6
Saved at a financial institution, 2011	20.5	45.3
Saved using a savings club or person outside the family	3.7	..
Saved any money	53.7	70.8
Saved for old age	26.8	39.7
Saved for a farm or business	5.2	9.0
Saved for education or school fees	8.9	25.0
Credit in the Past Year (% age 15+)		
Borrowed from a financial institution	10.4	18.4
Borrowed from a financial institution, 2011	5.6	14.2
Borrowed from family or friends	20.9	14.9
Borrowed from a private informal lender	0.2	0.9
Borrowed any money	35.2	39.8
Borrowed for a farm or business	2.7	2.6
Borrowed for education or school fees	2.5	5.6
Outstanding mortgage at a financial institution	9.8	26.1

Luxembourg

High income: OECD		High income
Population, age 15+ (thousands)	**448**	GNI per capita ($) **69,880**

	Country data	High income: OECD
Account (% age 15+)		
All adults	96.2	94.0
Women	96.7	93.8
Adults belonging to the poorest 40%	93.8	90.6
Young adults (% ages 15–24)	86.5	84.1
Adults living in rural areas	95.3	93.8
Financial Institution Account (% age 15+)		
All adults	96.2	94.0
All adults, 2011	94.6	90.0
Mobile Account (% age 15+)		
All adults	..	..
Access to Financial Institution Account (% age 15+)		
Has debit card	84.8	79.7
Has debit card, 2011	73.2	61.9
ATM is the main mode of withdrawal (% with an account)	..	..
ATM is the main mode of withdrawal (% with an account), 2011	67.9	68.5
Use of Account in the Past Year (% age 15+)		
Used an account to receive wages	49.9	44.3
Used an account to receive government transfers	23.4	17.2
Used a financial institution account to pay utility bills	68.7	61.1
Other Digital Payments in the Past Year (% age 15+)		
Used a debit card to make payments	79.3	65.3
Used a credit card to make payments	62.7	46.7
Used the Internet to pay bills or make purchases	56.3	54.1
Domestic Remittances in the Past Year (% age 15+)		
Sent remittances	..	..
Sent remittances via a financial institution (% senders)	..	..
Sent remittances via a mobile phone (% senders)	..	..
Sent remittances via a money transfer operator (% senders)	..	..
Received remittances	..	..
Received remittances via a financial institution (% recipients)	..	..
Received remittances via a mobile phone (% recipients)	..	..
Received remittances via a money transfer operator (% recipients)	..	..
Savings in the Past Year (% age 15+)		
Saved at a financial institution	59.9	51.6
Saved at a financial institution, 2011	52.0	45.3
Saved using a savings club or person outside the family	..	..
Saved any money	77.8	70.8
Saved for old age	36.4	39.7
Saved for a farm or business	8.6	9.0
Saved for education or school fees	25.2	25.0
Credit in the Past Year (% age 15+)		
Borrowed from a financial institution	18.2	18.4
Borrowed from a financial institution, 2011	17.4	14.2
Borrowed from family or friends	7.9	14.9
Borrowed from a private informal lender	1.0	0.9
Borrowed any money	38.1	39.8
Borrowed for a farm or business	2.5	2.6
Borrowed for education or school fees	5.9	5.6
Outstanding mortgage at a financial institution	31.9	26.1

Macedonia, FYR

Europe & Central Asia			Upper middle income
Population, age 15+ (millions)	1.8	GNI per capita ($)	4,870

	Country data	Europe & Central Asia	Upper middle income
Account (% age 15+)			
All adults	71.8	51.4	70.5
Women	64.0	47.4	67.3
Adults belonging to the poorest 40%	61.6	44.2	62.7
Young adults (% ages 15–24)	46.7	35.6	58.1
Adults living in rural areas	73.0	45.7	68.8
Financial Institution Account (% age 15+)			
All adults	71.8	51.4	70.4
All adults, 2011	73.7	43.3	57.4
Mobile Account (% age 15+)			
All adults	..	0.3	0.7
Access to Financial Institution Account (% age 15+)			
Has debit card	52.7	36.9	45.9
Has debit card, 2011	36.3	36.4	38.5
ATM is the main mode of withdrawal (% with an account)	63.4	66.7	55.7
ATM is the main mode of withdrawal (% with an account), 2011	33.2	72.5	42.8
Use of Account in the Past Year (% age 15+)			
Used an account to receive wages	30.3	22.5	18.1
Used an account to receive government transfers	12.6	7.3	9.6
Used a financial institution account to pay utility bills	10.8	12.5	12.3
Other Digital Payments in the Past Year (% age 15+)			
Used a debit card to make payments	35.7	22.9	19.9
Used a credit card to make payments	18.8	14.9	14.4
Used the Internet to pay bills or make purchases	11.1	11.9	15.3
Domestic Remittances in the Past Year (% age 15+)			
Sent remittances	9.3	12.9	15.4
Sent remittances via a financial institution (% senders)	..	31.5	37.2
Sent remittances via a mobile phone (% senders)	..	2.5	8.8
Sent remittances via a money transfer operator (% senders)	..	11.8	19.7
Received remittances	12.2	15.5	17.8
Received remittances via a financial institution (% recipients)	27.7	22.1	29.8
Received remittances via a mobile phone (% recipients)	1.5	1.0	5.6
Received remittances via a money transfer operator (% recipients)	6.5	15.6	17.9
Savings in the Past Year (% age 15+)			
Saved at a financial institution	13.7	8.4	32.2
Saved at a financial institution, 2011	7.8	4.9	25.1
Saved using a savings club or person outside the family	5.2	6.6	4.9
Saved any money	39.2	38.5	62.7
Saved for old age	13.4	11.8	30.6
Saved for a farm or business	5.6	5.1	17.6
Saved for education or school fees	13.2	12.1	25.4
Credit in the Past Year (% age 15+)			
Borrowed from a financial institution	13.2	12.4	10.4
Borrowed from a financial institution, 2011	10.6	7.8	7.9
Borrowed from family or friends	20.1	23.6	24.0
Borrowed from a private informal lender	0.9	2.1	2.6
Borrowed any money	40.0	39.5	37.7
Borrowed for a farm or business	2.0	2.8	6.6
Borrowed for education or school fees	5.0	6.2	6.1
Outstanding mortgage at a financial institution	12.3	10.2	9.1

Madagascar

Sub-Saharan Africa   **Low income**

Population, age 15+ (millions)	**13.2**	GNI per capita ($)	**440**

	Country data	Sub-Saharan Africa	Low income
Account (% age 15+)			
All adults	8.6	34.2	27.5
Women	8.4	29.9	23.9
Adults belonging to the poorest 40%	3.8	24.6	19.4
Young adults (% ages 15–24)	6.4	25.9	20.2
Adults living in rural areas	4.8	29.2	24.8
Financial Institution Account (% age 15+)			
All adults	5.7	28.9	22.3
All adults, 2011	5.5	23.9	21.1
Mobile Account (% age 15+)			
All adults	4.4	11.5	10.0
Access to Financial Institution Account (% age 15+)			
Has debit card	1.6	17.9	6.6
Has debit card, 2011	0.9	15.0	6.3
ATM is the main mode of withdrawal (% with an account)	..	53.8	20.2
ATM is the main mode of withdrawal (% with an account), 2011	..	51.7	19.7
Use of Account in the Past Year (% age 15+)			
Used an account to receive wages	0.6	7.3	3.2
Used an account to receive government transfers	0.1	3.8	1.0
Used a financial institution account to pay utility bills	0.1	2.8	0.9
Other Digital Payments in the Past Year (% age 15+)			
Used a debit card to make payments	0.5	8.7	2.1
Used a credit card to make payments	0.1	1.9	0.6
Used the Internet to pay bills or make purchases	0.0	2.4	1.2
Domestic Remittances in the Past Year (% age 15+)			
Sent remittances	21.5	28.7	18.3
Sent remittances via a financial institution (% senders)	1.4	31.0	15.4
Sent remittances via a mobile phone (% senders)	18.0	30.8	42.8
Sent remittances via a money transfer operator (% senders)	2.0	21.0	14.1
Received remittances	23.8	37.2	25.6
Received remittances via a financial institution (% recipients)	0.4	26.6	13.0
Received remittances via a mobile phone (% recipients)	15.0	27.6	33.8
Received remittances via a money transfer operator (% recipients)	0.5	22.1	14.8
Savings in the Past Year (% age 15+)			
Saved at a financial institution	3.3	15.9	9.9
Saved at a financial institution, 2011	1.4	14.3	11.5
Saved using a savings club or person outside the family	1.4	23.9	16.3
Saved any money	39.7	59.6	46.5
Saved for old age	5.9	9.8	8.3
Saved for a farm or business	12.4	22.7	16.7
Saved for education or school fees	16.4	22.9	16.6
Credit in the Past Year (% age 15+)			
Borrowed from a financial institution	2.0	6.3	8.6
Borrowed from a financial institution, 2011	2.3	4.8	11.7
Borrowed from family or friends	50.9	41.9	34.9
Borrowed from a private informal lender	3.4	4.7	6.5
Borrowed any money	57.3	54.5	52.5
Borrowed for a farm or business	12.6	12.8	12.2
Borrowed for education or school fees	9.5	12.3	10.9
Outstanding mortgage at a financial institution	1.8	5.2	4.1

Malawi

Sub-Saharan Africa   **Low income**

Population, age 15+ (millions)	**9.0**	GNI per capita ($)	**270**

	Country data	Sub-Saharan Africa	Low income
Account (% age 15+)			
All adults	18.1	34.2	27.5
Women	14.0	29.9	23.9
Adults belonging to the poorest 40%	10.5	24.6	19.4
Young adults (% ages 15–24)	12.1	25.9	20.2
Adults living in rural areas	16.1	29.2	24.8
Financial Institution Account (% age 15+)			
All adults	16.1	28.9	22.3
All adults, 2011	16.5	23.9	21.1
Mobile Account (% age 15+)			
All adults	3.8	11.5	10.0
Access to Financial Institution Account (% age 15+)			
Has debit card	11.7	17.9	6.6
Has debit card, 2011	9.4	15.0	6.3
ATM is the main mode of withdrawal (% with an account)	39.5	53.8	20.2
ATM is the main mode of withdrawal (% with an account), 2011	39.2	51.7	19.7
Use of Account in the Past Year (% age 15+)			
Used an account to receive wages	2.1	7.3	3.2
Used an account to receive government transfers	0.6	3.8	1.0
Used a financial institution account to pay utility bills	1.3	2.8	0.9
Other Digital Payments in the Past Year (% age 15+)			
Used a debit card to make payments	4.7	8.7	2.1
Used a credit card to make payments	1.1	1.9	0.6
Used the Internet to pay bills or make purchases	1.1	2.4	1.2
Domestic Remittances in the Past Year (% age 15+)			
Sent remittances	22.6	28.7	18.3
Sent remittances via a financial institution (% senders)	18.6	31.0	15.4
Sent remittances via a mobile phone (% senders)	12.3	30.8	42.8
Sent remittances via a money transfer operator (% senders)	9.2	21.0	14.1
Received remittances	26.4	37.2	25.6
Received remittances via a financial institution (% recipients)	16.6	26.6	13.0
Received remittances via a mobile phone (% recipients)	10.9	27.6	33.8
Received remittances via a money transfer operator (% recipients)	7.9	22.1	14.8
Savings in the Past Year (% age 15+)			
Saved at a financial institution	7.1	15.9	9.9
Saved at a financial institution, 2011	8.2	14.3	11.5
Saved using a savings club or person outside the family	28.0	23.9	16.3
Saved any money	59.7	59.6	46.5
Saved for old age	3.7	9.8	8.3
Saved for a farm or business	22.1	22.7	16.7
Saved for education or school fees	15.5	22.9	16.6
Credit in the Past Year (% age 15+)			
Borrowed from a financial institution	6.0	6.3	8.6
Borrowed from a financial institution, 2011	9.2	4.8	11.7
Borrowed from family or friends	46.1	41.9	34.9
Borrowed from a private informal lender	12.2	4.7	6.5
Borrowed any money	66.3	54.5	52.5
Borrowed for a farm or business	17.6	12.8	12.2
Borrowed for education or school fees	9.6	12.3	10.9
Outstanding mortgage at a financial institution	6.0	5.2	4.1

Malaysia

	Country data	East Asia & Pacific	Upper middle income
Population, age 15+ (millions) **22.0**	GNI per capita ($)		**10,430**

	Country data	East Asia & Pacific	Upper middle income
Account (% age 15+)			
All adults	80.7	69.0	70.5
Women	78.1	67.0	67.3
Adults belonging to the poorest 40%	75.6	60.9	62.7
Young adults (% ages 15–24)	76.2	60.7	58.1
Adults living in rural areas	73.7	64.5	68.8
Financial Institution Account (% age 15+)			
All adults	80.7	68.8	70.4
All adults, 2011	66.2	55.1	57.4
Mobile Account (% age 15+)			
All adults	2.8	0.4	0.7
Access to Financial Institution Account (% age 15+)			
Has debit card	41.2	42.9	45.9
Has debit card, 2011	23.1	34.7	38.5
ATM is the main mode of withdrawal (% with an account)	72.1	53.3	55.7
ATM is the main mode of withdrawal (% with an account), 2011	77.1	37.0	42.8
Use of Account in the Past Year (% age 15+)			
Used an account to receive wages	30.8	15.1	18.1
Used an account to receive government transfers	19.9	8.1	9.6
Used a financial institution account to pay utility bills	12.7	11.8	12.3
Other Digital Payments in the Past Year (% age 15+)			
Used a debit card to make payments	18.6	14.8	19.9
Used a credit card to make payments	16.9	10.8	14.4
Used the Internet to pay bills or make purchases	18.8	15.6	15.3
Domestic Remittances in the Past Year (% age 15+)			
Sent remittances	27.7	16.6	15.4
Sent remittances via a financial institution (% senders)	78.8	36.9	37.2
Sent remittances via a mobile phone (% senders)	7.5	8.7	8.8
Sent remittances via a money transfer operator (% senders)	39.8	18.5	19.7
Received remittances	25.5	20.6	17.8
Received remittances via a financial institution (% recipients)	64.8	29.0	29.8
Received remittances via a mobile phone (% recipients)	6.9	4.9	5.6
Received remittances via a money transfer operator (% recipients)	33.8	15.8	17.9
Savings in the Past Year (% age 15+)			
Saved at a financial institution	33.8	36.5	32.2
Saved at a financial institution, 2011	35.4	28.5	25.1
Saved using a savings club or person outside the family	9.9	6.0	4.9
Saved any money	81.6	71.0	62.7
Saved for old age	54.0	36.5	30.6
Saved for a farm or business	17.5	21.3	17.6
Saved for education or school fees	48.4	30.7	25.4
Credit in the Past Year (% age 15+)			
Borrowed from a financial institution	19.5	11.0	10.4
Borrowed from a financial institution, 2011	11.2	8.6	7.9
Borrowed from family or friends	39.0	28.3	24.0
Borrowed from a private informal lender	0.8	2.5	2.6
Borrowed any money	56.1	41.2	37.7
Borrowed for a farm or business	6.1	8.3	6.6
Borrowed for education or school fees	10.6	7.1	6.1
Outstanding mortgage at a financial institution	18.4	8.0	9.1

Sub-Saharan Africa			Low income
Population, age 15+ (millions)	**8.0**	GNI per capita ($)	**670**

	Country data	Sub-Saharan Africa	Low income
Account (% age 15+)			
All adults	20.1	34.2	27.5
Women	14.7	29.9	23.9
Adults belonging to the poorest 40%	13.0	24.6	19.4
Young adults (% ages 15–24)	15.7	25.9	20.2
Adults living in rural areas	19.3	29.2	24.8
Financial Institution Account (% age 15+)			
All adults	13.3	28.9	22.3
All adults, 2011	8.2	23.9	21.1
Mobile Account (% age 15+)			
All adults	11.6	11.5	10.0
Access to Financial Institution Account (% age 15+)			
Has debit card	4.0	17.9	6.6
Has debit card, 2011	1.8	15.0	6.3
ATM is the main mode of withdrawal (% with an account)	17.5	53.8	20.2
ATM is the main mode of withdrawal (% with an account), 2011	..	51.7	19.7
Use of Account in the Past Year (% age 15+)			
Used an account to receive wages	1.3	7.3	3.2
Used an account to receive government transfers	0.1	3.8	1.0
Used a financial institution account to pay utility bills	0.2	2.8	0.9
Other Digital Payments in the Past Year (% age 15+)			
Used a debit card to make payments	1.9	8.7	2.1
Used a credit card to make payments	0.5	1.9	0.6
Used the Internet to pay bills or make purchases	0.5	2.4	1.2
Domestic Remittances in the Past Year (% age 15+)			
Sent remittances	13.4	28.7	18.3
Sent remittances via a financial institution (% senders)	4.3	31.0	15.4
Sent remittances via a mobile phone (% senders)	37.3	30.8	42.8
Sent remittances via a money transfer operator (% senders)	14.9	21.0	14.1
Received remittances	30.7	37.2	25.6
Received remittances via a financial institution (% recipients)	4.9	26.6	13.0
Received remittances via a mobile phone (% recipients)	33.4	27.6	33.8
Received remittances via a money transfer operator (% recipients)	14.6	22.1	14.8
Savings in the Past Year (% age 15+)			
Saved at a financial institution	2.9	15.9	9.9
Saved at a financial institution, 2011	4.5	14.3	11.5
Saved using a savings club or person outside the family	23.5	23.9	16.3
Saved any money	44.9	59.6	46.5
Saved for old age	4.5	9.8	8.3
Saved for a farm or business	14.5	22.7	16.7
Saved for education or school fees	8.3	22.9	16.6
Credit in the Past Year (% age 15+)			
Borrowed from a financial institution	2.7	6.3	8.6
Borrowed from a financial institution, 2011	3.7	4.8	11.7
Borrowed from family or friends	32.9	41.9	34.9
Borrowed from a private informal lender	2.5	4.7	6.5
Borrowed any money	41.5	54.5	52.5
Borrowed for a farm or business	7.4	12.8	12.2
Borrowed for education or school fees	2.3	12.3	10.9
Outstanding mortgage at a financial institution	1.7	5.2	4.1

Malta

			High income
Population, age 15+ (thousands)	**361**	GNI per capita ($)	**20,980**

	Country data	High income: OECD
Account (% age 15+)		
All adults	96.3	94.0
Women	95.6	93.8
Adults belonging to the poorest 40%	93.8	90.6
Young adults (% ages 15–24)	87.3	84.1
Adults living in rural areas	97.0	93.8
Financial Institution Account (% age 15+)		
All adults	96.3	94.0
All adults, 2011	95.3	90.0
Mobile Account (% age 15+)		
All adults	..	..
Access to Financial Institution Account (% age 15+)		
Has debit card	78.5	79.7
Has debit card, 2011	71.2	61.9
ATM is the main mode of withdrawal (% with an account)	..	..
ATM is the main mode of withdrawal (% with an account), 2011	71.3	68.5
Use of Account in the Past Year (% age 15+)		
Used an account to receive wages	30.0	44.3
Used an account to receive government transfers	28.4	17.2
Used a financial institution account to pay utility bills	36.9	61.1
Other Digital Payments in the Past Year (% age 15+)		
Used a debit card to make payments	61.2	65.3
Used a credit card to make payments	33.5	46.7
Used the Internet to pay bills or make purchases	38.2	54.1
Domestic Remittances in the Past Year (% age 15+)		
Sent remittances	..	..
Sent remittances via a financial institution (% senders)	..	..
Sent remittances via a mobile phone (% senders)	..	..
Sent remittances via a money transfer operator (% senders)	..	..
Received remittances	..	..
Received remittances via a financial institution (% recipients)	..	..
Received remittances via a mobile phone (% recipients)	..	..
Received remittances via a money transfer operator (% recipients)	..	..
Savings in the Past Year (% age 15+)		
Saved at a financial institution	41.6	51.6
Saved at a financial institution, 2011	44.8	45.3
Saved using a savings club or person outside the family	..	..
Saved any money	71.4	70.8
Saved for old age	37.0	39.7
Saved for a farm or business	5.8	9.0
Saved for education or school fees	23.7	25.0
Credit in the Past Year (% age 15+)		
Borrowed from a financial institution	9.5	18.4
Borrowed from a financial institution, 2011	10.0	14.2
Borrowed from family or friends	8.4	14.9
Borrowed from a private informal lender	0.3	0.9
Borrowed any money	20.4	39.8
Borrowed for a farm or business	1.0	2.6
Borrowed for education or school fees	2.1	5.6
Outstanding mortgage at a financial institution	19.0	26.1

Mauritania

Population, age 15+ (millions)	**2.3**	GNI per capita ($)	**1,060**

	Country data	Sub-Saharan Africa	Lower middle income
Account (% age 15+)			
All adults	22.9	34.2	42.7
Women	21.0	29.9	36.3
Adults belonging to the poorest 40%	12.1	24.6	33.2
Young adults (% ages 15–24)	14.7	25.9	34.7
Adults living in rural areas	19.2	29.2	40.0
Financial Institution Account (% age 15+)			
All adults	20.4	28.9	41.8
All adults, 2011	17.5	23.9	28.7
Mobile Account (% age 15+)			
All adults	6.5	11.5	2.5
Access to Financial Institution Account (% age 15+)			
Has debit card	11.3	17.9	21.2
Has debit card, 2011	6.3	15.0	10.1
ATM is the main mode of withdrawal (% with an account)	33.2	53.8	42.4
ATM is the main mode of withdrawal (% with an account), 2011	6.5	51.7	28.1
Use of Account in the Past Year (% age 15+)			
Used an account to receive wages	10.8	7.3	5.6
Used an account to receive government transfers	4.7	3.8	3.3
Used a financial institution account to pay utility bills	1.9	2.8	3.1
Other Digital Payments in the Past Year (% age 15+)			
Used a debit card to make payments	3.8	8.7	9.6
Used a credit card to make payments	2.5	1.9	2.8
Used the Internet to pay bills or make purchases	4.0	2.4	2.6
Domestic Remittances in the Past Year (% age 15+)			
Sent remittances	19.7	28.7	14.2
Sent remittances via a financial institution (% senders)	13.6	31.0	30.9
Sent remittances via a mobile phone (% senders)	16.8	30.8	7.7
Sent remittances via a money transfer operator (% senders)	41.5	21.0	18.3
Received remittances	46.3	37.2	17.8
Received remittances via a financial institution (% recipients)	8.9	26.6	26.0
Received remittances via a mobile phone (% recipients)	9.7	27.6	5.7
Received remittances via a money transfer operator (% recipients)	38.1	22.1	16.6
Savings in the Past Year (% age 15+)			
Saved at a financial institution	10.6	15.9	14.8
Saved at a financial institution, 2011	6.4	14.3	11.1
Saved using a savings club or person outside the family	11.6	23.9	12.4
Saved any money	41.2	59.6	45.6
Saved for old age	10.0	9.8	12.6
Saved for a farm or business	12.4	22.7	11.8
Saved for education or school fees	14.3	22.9	20.0
Credit in the Past Year (% age 15+)			
Borrowed from a financial institution	7.7	6.3	7.5
Borrowed from a financial institution, 2011	7.9	4.8	7.3
Borrowed from family or friends	29.8	41.9	33.1
Borrowed from a private informal lender	5.1	4.7	8.5
Borrowed any money	46.6	54.5	47.4
Borrowed for a farm or business	8.2	12.8	9.2
Borrowed for education or school fees	8.4	12.3	10.1
Outstanding mortgage at a financial institution	8.3	5.2	4.7

Mauritius

Sub-Saharan Africa | **Upper middle income**

Population, age 15+ (millions)	**1.0**	GNI per capita ($)	**9,570**

	Country data	Sub-Saharan Africa	Upper middle income
Account (% age 15+)			
All adults	82.2	34.2	70.5
Women	80.0	29.9	67.3
Adults belonging to the poorest 40%	71.4	24.6	62.7
Young adults (% ages 15–24)	69.1	25.9	58.1
Adults living in rural areas	80.7	29.2	68.8
Financial Institution Account (% age 15+)			
All adults	82.2	28.9	70.4
All adults, 2011	80.1	23.9	57.4
Mobile Account (% age 15+)			
All adults	0.9	11.5	0.7
Access to Financial Institution Account (% age 15+)			
Has debit card	62.0	17.9	45.9
Has debit card, 2011	50.9	15.0	38.5
ATM is the main mode of withdrawal (% with an account)	66.9	53.8	55.7
ATM is the main mode of withdrawal (% with an account), 2011	56.7	51.7	42.8
Use of Account in the Past Year (% age 15+)			
Used an account to receive wages	29.5	7.3	18.1
Used an account to receive government transfers	9.5	3.8	9.6
Used a financial institution account to pay utility bills	3.4	2.8	12.3
Other Digital Payments in the Past Year (% age 15+)			
Used a debit card to make payments	33.1	8.7	19.9
Used a credit card to make payments	13.4	1.9	14.4
Used the Internet to pay bills or make purchases	4.3	2.4	15.3
Domestic Remittances in the Past Year (% age 15+)			
Sent remittances	4.3	28.7	15.4
Sent remittances via a financial institution (% senders)	..	31.0	37.2
Sent remittances via a mobile phone (% senders)	..	30.8	8.8
Sent remittances via a money transfer operator (% senders)	..	21.0	19.7
Received remittances	6.7	37.2	17.8
Received remittances via a financial institution (% recipients)	..	26.6	29.8
Received remittances via a mobile phone (% recipients)	..	27.6	5.6
Received remittances via a money transfer operator (% recipients)	..	22.1	17.9
Savings in the Past Year (% age 15+)			
Saved at a financial institution	35.5	15.9	32.2
Saved at a financial institution, 2011	30.8	14.3	25.1
Saved using a savings club or person outside the family	5.9	23.9	4.9
Saved any money	54.2	59.6	62.7
Saved for old age	22.8	9.8	30.6
Saved for a farm or business	3.7	22.7	17.6
Saved for education or school fees	16.7	22.9	25.4
Credit in the Past Year (% age 15+)			
Borrowed from a financial institution	17.1	6.3	10.4
Borrowed from a financial institution, 2011	14.3	4.8	7.9
Borrowed from family or friends	3.7	41.9	24.0
Borrowed from a private informal lender	0.0	4.7	2.6
Borrowed any money	28.8	54.5	37.7
Borrowed for a farm or business	1.8	12.8	6.6
Borrowed for education or school fees	2.7	12.3	6.1
Outstanding mortgage at a financial institution	15.2	5.2	9.1

Mexico

Latin America & Caribbean		Upper middle income

Population, age 15+ (millions)	87.5	GNI per capita ($)	9,940

	Country data	Latin America & the Carib.	Upper middle income
Account (% age 15+)			
All adults	39.1	51.4	70.5
Women	38.9	48.6	67.3
Adults belonging to the poorest 40%	29.3	41.2	62.7
Young adults (% ages 15–24)	32.1	37.4	58.1
Adults living in rural areas	28.7	46.0	68.8
Financial Institution Account (% age 15+)			
All adults	38.7	51.1	70.4
All adults, 2011	27.4	39.3	57.4
Mobile Account (% age 15+)			
All adults	3.4	1.7	0.7
Access to Financial Institution Account (% age 15+)			
Has debit card	26.8	40.4	45.9
Has debit card, 2011	22.3	28.9	38.5
ATM is the main mode of withdrawal (% with an account)	69.1	71.1	55.7
ATM is the main mode of withdrawal (% with an account), 2011	57.4	57.0	42.8
Use of Account in the Past Year (% age 15+)			
Used an account to receive wages	17.2	18.0	18.1
Used an account to receive government transfers	10.5	9.0	9.6
Used a financial institution account to pay utility bills	5.3	6.3	12.3
Other Digital Payments in the Past Year (% age 15+)			
Used a debit card to make payments	19.0	27.7	19.9
Used a credit card to make payments	11.1	18.0	14.4
Used the Internet to pay bills or make purchases	6.0	6.9	15.3
Domestic Remittances in the Past Year (% age 15+)			
Sent remittances	10.6	9.5	15.4
Sent remittances via a financial institution (% senders)	53.2	..	37.2
Sent remittances via a mobile phone (% senders)	21.3	..	8.8
Sent remittances via a money transfer operator (% senders)	34.6	..	19.7
Received remittances	11.7	11.3	17.8
Received remittances via a financial institution (% recipients)	56.9	34.2	29.8
Received remittances via a mobile phone (% recipients)	13.1	4.3	5.6
Received remittances via a money transfer operator (% recipients)	37.6	28.4	17.9
Savings in the Past Year (% age 15+)			
Saved at a financial institution	14.5	13.5	32.2
Saved at a financial institution, 2011	6.7	9.6	25.1
Saved using a savings club or person outside the family	17.6	7.9	4.9
Saved any money	58.4	40.6	62.7
Saved for old age	20.9	10.6	30.6
Saved for a farm or business	13.7	10.6	17.6
Saved for education or school fees	28.4	17.2	25.4
Credit in the Past Year (% age 15+)			
Borrowed from a financial institution	10.4	11.3	10.4
Borrowed from a financial institution, 2011	7.6	7.9	7.9
Borrowed from family or friends	26.0	13.5	24.0
Borrowed from a private informal lender	9.9	4.7	2.6
Borrowed any money	50.8	32.7	37.7
Borrowed for a farm or business	9.5	6.1	6.6
Borrowed for education or school fees	18.9	8.3	6.1
Outstanding mortgage at a financial institution	8.3	9.6	9.1

Moldova

Population, age 15+ (millions)	**3.0**	GNI per capita ($)	**2,470**

	Country data	Europe & Central Asia	Lower middle income
Account (% age 15+)			
All adults	17.8	51.4	42.7
Women	19.0	47.4	36.3
Adults belonging to the poorest 40%	12.4	44.2	33.2
Young adults (% ages 15-24)	12.2	35.6	34.7
Adults living in rural areas	15.2	45.7	40.0
Financial Institution Account (% age 15+)			
All adults	17.8	51.4	41.8
All adults, 2011	18.1	43.3	28.7
Mobile Account (% age 15+)			
All adults	..	0.3	2.5
Access to Financial Institution Account (% age 15+)			
Has debit card	15.8	36.9	21.2
Has debit card, 2011	16.0	36.4	10.1
ATM is the main mode of withdrawal (% with an account)	65.7	66.7	42.4
ATM is the main mode of withdrawal (% with an account), 2011	69.6	72.5	28.1
Use of Account in the Past Year (% age 15+)			
Used an account to receive wages	11.1	22.5	5.6
Used an account to receive government transfers	1.0	7.3	3.3
Used a financial institution account to pay utility bills	1.2	12.5	3.1
Other Digital Payments in the Past Year (% age 15+)			
Used a debit card to make payments	7.1	22.9	9.6
Used a credit card to make payments	5.5	14.9	2.8
Used the Internet to pay bills or make purchases	10.0	11.9	2.6
Domestic Remittances in the Past Year (% age 15+)			
Sent remittances	11.4	12.9	14.2
Sent remittances via a financial institution (% senders)	4.2	31.5	30.9
Sent remittances via a mobile phone (% senders)	0.0	2.5	7.7
Sent remittances via a money transfer operator (% senders)	6.7	11.8	18.3
Received remittances	20.0	15.5	17.8
Received remittances via a financial institution (% recipients)	8.4	22.1	26.0
Received remittances via a mobile phone (% recipients)	0.0	1.0	5.7
Received remittances via a money transfer operator (% recipients)	24.6	15.6	16.6
Savings in the Past Year (% age 15+)			
Saved at a financial institution	6.8	8.4	14.8
Saved at a financial institution, 2011	3.5	4.9	11.1
Saved using a savings club or person outside the family	5.2	6.6	12.4
Saved any money	44.1	38.5	45.6
Saved for old age	11.4	11.8	12.6
Saved for a farm or business	7.7	5.1	11.8
Saved for education or school fees	16.8	12.1	20.0
Credit in the Past Year (% age 15+)			
Borrowed from a financial institution	6.6	12.4	7.5
Borrowed from a financial institution, 2011	6.4	7.8	7.3
Borrowed from family or friends	39.1	23.6	33.1
Borrowed from a private informal lender	3.7	2.1	8.5
Borrowed any money	46.8	39.5	47.4
Borrowed for a farm or business	4.9	2.8	9.2
Borrowed for education or school fees	10.6	6.2	10.1
Outstanding mortgage at a financial institution	6.4	10.2	4.7

Mongolia

Population, age 15+ (millions)	2.1	GNI per capita ($)		3,770

	Country data	East Asia & Pacific	Lower middle income
Account (% age 15+)			
All adults	91.8	69.0	42.7
Women	93.2	67.0	36.3
Adults belonging to the poorest 40%	89.1	60.9	33.2
Young adults (% ages 15–24)	93.0	60.7	34.7
Adults living in rural areas	90.0	64.5	40.0
Financial Institution Account (% age 15+)			
All adults	91.8	68.8	41.8
All adults, 2011	77.7	55.1	28.7
Mobile Account (% age 15+)			
All adults	5.0	0.4	2.5
Access to Financial Institution Account (% age 15+)			
Has debit card	65.7	42.9	21.2
Has debit card, 2011	60.6	34.7	10.1
ATM is the main mode of withdrawal (% with an account)	46.9	53.3	42.4
ATM is the main mode of withdrawal (% with an account), 2011	45.8	37.0	28.1
Use of Account in the Past Year (% age 15+)			
Used an account to receive wages	25.6	15.1	5.6
Used an account to receive government transfers	25.2	8.1	3.3
Used a financial institution account to pay utility bills	6.1	11.8	3.1
Other Digital Payments in the Past Year (% age 15+)			
Used a debit card to make payments	36.6	14.8	9.6
Used a credit card to make payments	0.8	10.8	2.8
Used the Internet to pay bills or make purchases	6.8	15.6	2.6
Domestic Remittances in the Past Year (% age 15+)			
Sent remittances	34.0	16.6	14.2
Sent remittances via a financial institution (% senders)	65.7	36.9	30.9
Sent remittances via a mobile phone (% senders)	12.7	8.7	7.7
Sent remittances via a money transfer operator (% senders)	21.5	18.5	18.3
Received remittances	37.8	20.6	17.8
Received remittances via a financial institution (% recipients)	55.9	29.0	26.0
Received remittances via a mobile phone (% recipients)	6.2	4.9	5.7
Received remittances via a money transfer operator (% recipients)	19.1	15.8	16.6
Savings in the Past Year (% age 15+)			
Saved at a financial institution	33.2	36.5	14.8
Saved at a financial institution, 2011	23.2	28.5	11.1
Saved using a savings club or person outside the family	5.6	6.0	12.4
Saved any money	47.3	71.0	45.6
Saved for old age	8.0	36.5	12.6
Saved for a farm or business	8.8	21.3	11.8
Saved for education or school fees	21.6	30.7	20.0
Credit in the Past Year (% age 15+)			
Borrowed from a financial institution	35.7	11.0	7.5
Borrowed from a financial institution, 2011	24.8	8.6	7.3
Borrowed from family or friends	28.8	28.3	33.1
Borrowed from a private informal lender	3.1	2.5	8.5
Borrowed any money	53.9	41.2	47.4
Borrowed for a farm or business	8.7	8.3	9.2
Borrowed for education or school fees	7.6	7.1	10.1
Outstanding mortgage at a financial institution	17.3	8.0	4.7

Montenegro

Population, age 15+ (thousands)	**505**	GNI per capita ($)	**7,250**

	Country data	Europe & Central Asia	Upper middle income
Account (% age 15+)			
All adults	59.8	51.4	70.5
Women	57.9	47.4	67.3
Adults belonging to the poorest 40%	49.1	44.2	62.7
Young adults (% ages 15–24)	41.3	35.6	58.1
Adults living in rural areas	53.1	45.7	68.8
Financial Institution Account (% age 15+)			
All adults	59.8	51.4	70.4
All adults, 2011	50.4	43.3	57.4
Mobile Account (% age 15+)			
All adults	..	0.3	0.7
Access to Financial Institution Account (% age 15+)			
Has debit card	33.8	36.9	45.9
Has debit card, 2011	22.0	36.4	38.5
ATM is the main mode of withdrawal (% with an account)	33.2	66.7	55.7
ATM is the main mode of withdrawal (% with an account), 2011	35.9	72.5	42.8
Use of Account in the Past Year (% age 15+)			
Used an account to receive wages	26.5	22.5	18.1
Used an account to receive government transfers	5.6	7.3	9.6
Used a financial institution account to pay utility bills	2.9	12.5	12.3
Other Digital Payments in the Past Year (% age 15+)			
Used a debit card to make payments	22.8	22.9	19.9
Used a credit card to make payments	12.3	14.9	14.4
Used the Internet to pay bills or make purchases	7.3	11.9	15.3
Domestic Remittances in the Past Year (% age 15+)			
Sent remittances	12.3	12.9	15.4
Sent remittances via a financial institution (% senders)	26.9	31.5	37.2
Sent remittances via a mobile phone (% senders)	0.6	2.5	8.8
Sent remittances via a money transfer operator (% senders)	7.7	11.8	19.7
Received remittances	13.1	15.5	17.8
Received remittances via a financial institution (% recipients)	19.3	22.1	29.8
Received remittances via a mobile phone (% recipients)	1.1	1.0	5.6
Received remittances via a money transfer operator (% recipients)	8.0	15.6	17.9
Savings in the Past Year (% age 15+)			
Saved at a financial institution	5.3	8.4	32.2
Saved at a financial institution, 2011	3.4	4.9	25.1
Saved using a savings club or person outside the family	3.6	6.6	4.9
Saved any money	26.8	38.5	62.7
Saved for old age	6.8	11.8	30.6
Saved for a farm or business	2.9	5.1	17.6
Saved for education or school fees	8.6	12.1	25.4
Credit in the Past Year (% age 15+)			
Borrowed from a financial institution	23.5	12.4	10.4
Borrowed from a financial institution, 2011	21.8	7.8	7.9
Borrowed from family or friends	20.7	23.6	24.0
Borrowed from a private informal lender	0.5	2.1	2.6
Borrowed any money	50.1	39.5	37.7
Borrowed for a farm or business	3.6	2.8	6.6
Borrowed for education or school fees	8.0	6.2	6.1
Outstanding mortgage at a financial institution	23.9	10.2	9.1

Myanmar

East Asia & Pacific   **Low income**

Population, age 15+ (millions)	**40.0**	GNI per capita ($)	..

	Country data	East Asia & Pacific	Low income
Account (% age 15+)			
All adults	22.8	69.0	27.5
Women	17.4	67.0	23.9
Adults belonging to the poorest 40%	16.1	60.9	19.4
Young adults (% ages 15–24)	13.5	60.7	20.2
Adults living in rural areas	21.2	64.5	24.8
Financial Institution Account (% age 15+)			
All adults	22.6	68.8	22.3
All adults, 2011	..	55.1	21.1
Mobile Account (% age 15+)			
All adults	0.2	0.4	10.0
Access to Financial Institution Account (% age 15+)			
Has debit card	1.7	42.9	6.6
Has debit card, 2011	..	34.7	6.3
ATM is the main mode of withdrawal (% with an account)	4.8	53.3	20.2
ATM is the main mode of withdrawal (% with an account), 2011	..	37.0	19.7
Use of Account in the Past Year (% age 15+)			
Used an account to receive wages	0.4	15.1	3.2
Used an account to receive government transfers	0.4	8.1	1.0
Used a financial institution account to pay utility bills	0.0	11.8	0.9
Other Digital Payments in the Past Year (% age 15+)			
Used a debit card to make payments	0.4	14.8	2.1
Used a credit card to make payments	0.0	10.8	0.6
Used the Internet to pay bills or make purchases	0.2	15.6	1.2
Domestic Remittances in the Past Year (% age 15+)			
Sent remittances	6.8	16.6	18.3
Sent remittances via a financial institution (% senders)	..	36.9	15.4
Sent remittances via a mobile phone (% senders)	..	8.7	42.8
Sent remittances via a money transfer operator (% senders)	..	18.5	14.1
Received remittances	11.0	20.6	25.6
Received remittances via a financial institution (% recipients)	39.0	29.0	13.0
Received remittances via a mobile phone (% recipients)	0.0	4.9	33.8
Received remittances via a money transfer operator (% recipients)	11.6	15.8	14.8
Savings in the Past Year (% age 15+)			
Saved at a financial institution	12.8	36.5	9.9
Saved at a financial institution, 2011	..	28.5	11.5
Saved using a savings club or person outside the family	6.0	6.0	16.3
Saved any money	46.7	71.0	46.5
Saved for old age	15.8	36.5	8.3
Saved for a farm or business	19.0	21.3	16.7
Saved for education or school fees	16.5	30.7	16.6
Credit in the Past Year (% age 15+)			
Borrowed from a financial institution	15.5	11.0	8.6
Borrowed from a financial institution, 2011	..	8.6	11.7
Borrowed from family or friends	21.8	28.3	34.9
Borrowed from a private informal lender	16.3	2.5	6.5
Borrowed any money	42.8	41.2	52.5
Borrowed for a farm or business	22.4	8.3	12.2
Borrowed for education or school fees	5.7	7.1	10.9
Outstanding mortgage at a financial institution	0.7	8.0	4.1

Namibia

Sub-Saharan Africa			**Upper middle income**
Population, age 15+ (millions)	1.5	GNI per capita ($)	5,870

	Country data	Sub-Saharan Africa	Upper middle income
Account (% age 15+)			
All adults	58.8	34.2	70.5
Women	56.8	29.9	67.3
Adults belonging to the poorest 40%	41.9	24.6	62.7
Young adults (% ages 15–24)	42.1	25.9	58.1
Adults living in rural areas	53.9	29.2	68.8
Financial Institution Account (% age 15+)			
All adults	58.1	28.9	70.4
All adults, 2011	..	23.9	57.4
Mobile Account (% age 15+)			
All adults	10.4	11.5	0.7
Access to Financial Institution Account (% age 15+)			
Has debit card	48.8	17.9	45.9
Has debit card, 2011	..	15.0	38.5
ATM is the main mode of withdrawal (% with an account)	69.2	53.8	55.7
ATM is the main mode of withdrawal (% with an account), 2011	..	51.7	42.8
Use of Account in the Past Year (% age 15+)			
Used an account to receive wages	17.6	7.3	18.1
Used an account to receive government transfers	6.2	3.8	9.6
Used a financial institution account to pay utility bills	4.9	2.8	12.3
Other Digital Payments in the Past Year (% age 15+)			
Used a debit card to make payments	28.2	8.7	19.9
Used a credit card to make payments	6.9	1.9	14.4
Used the Internet to pay bills or make purchases	3.4	2.4	15.3
Domestic Remittances in the Past Year (% age 15+)			
Sent remittances	31.3	28.7	15.4
Sent remittances via a financial institution (% senders)	69.6	31.0	37.2
Sent remittances via a mobile phone (% senders)	21.6	30.8	8.8
Sent remittances via a money transfer operator (% senders)	16.7	21.0	19.7
Received remittances	34.9	37.2	17.8
Received remittances via a financial institution (% recipients)	59.8	26.6	29.8
Received remittances via a mobile phone (% recipients)	31.6	27.6	5.6
Received remittances via a money transfer operator (% recipients)	20.0	22.1	17.9
Savings in the Past Year (% age 15+)			
Saved at a financial institution	26.7	15.9	32.2
Saved at a financial institution, 2011	..	14.3	25.1
Saved using a savings club or person outside the family	9.5	23.9	4.9
Saved any money	56.9	59.6	62.7
Saved for old age	15.6	9.8	30.6
Saved for a farm or business	15.4	22.7	17.6
Saved for education or school fees	34.0	22.9	25.4
Credit in the Past Year (% age 15+)			
Borrowed from a financial institution	6.9	6.3	10.4
Borrowed from a financial institution, 2011	..	4.8	7.9
Borrowed from family or friends	30.0	41.9	24.0
Borrowed from a private informal lender	2.4	4.7	2.6
Borrowed any money	46.0	54.5	37.7
Borrowed for a farm or business	4.5	12.8	6.6
Borrowed for education or school fees	19.7	12.3	6.1
Outstanding mortgage at a financial institution	5.1	5.2	9.1

Nepal

South Asia   **Low income**

Population, age 15+ (millions)	**18.2**	GNI per capita ($)	**730**

	Country data	South Asia	Low income
Account (% age 15+)			
All adults	33.8	46.4	27.5
Women	31.3	37.4	23.9
Adults belonging to the poorest 40%	23.7	38.1	19.4
Young adults (% ages 15–24)	25.4	36.7	20.2
Adults living in rural areas	32.1	43.5	24.8
Financial Institution Account (% age 15+)			
All adults	33.8	45.5	22.3
All adults, 2011	25.3	32.3	21.1
Mobile Account (% age 15+)			
All adults	0.3	2.6	10.0
Access to Financial Institution Account (% age 15+)			
Has debit card	6.7	18.0	6.6
Has debit card, 2011	3.7	7.2	6.3
ATM is the main mode of withdrawal (% with an account)	13.9	31.1	20.2
ATM is the main mode of withdrawal (% with an account), 2011	11.8	16.9	19.7
Use of Account in the Past Year (% age 15+)			
Used an account to receive wages	2.4	3.5	3.2
Used an account to receive government transfers	0.5	3.1	1.0
Used a financial institution account to pay utility bills	0.0	2.7	0.9
Other Digital Payments in the Past Year (% age 15+)			
Used a debit card to make payments	2.6	8.5	2.1
Used a credit card to make payments	0.1	2.6	0.6
Used the Internet to pay bills or make purchases	0.4	1.2	1.2
Domestic Remittances in the Past Year (% age 15+)			
Sent remittances	12.5	10.7	18.3
Sent remittances via a financial institution (% senders)	20.5	20.1	15.4
Sent remittances via a mobile phone (% senders)	0.0	7.7	42.8
Sent remittances via a money transfer operator (% senders)	20.9	13.7	14.1
Received remittances	24.1	12.2	25.6
Received remittances via a financial institution (% recipients)	17.4	15.8	13.0
Received remittances via a mobile phone (% recipients)	0.0	4.7	33.8
Received remittances via a money transfer operator (% recipients)	17.9	9.8	14.8
Savings in the Past Year (% age 15+)			
Saved at a financial institution	16.4	12.7	9.9
Saved at a financial institution, 2011	9.9	11.1	11.5
Saved using a savings club or person outside the family	14.4	8.8	16.3
Saved any money	44.7	36.2	46.5
Saved for old age	9.2	9.1	8.3
Saved for a farm or business	12.4	7.3	16.7
Saved for education or school fees	18.1	14.6	16.6
Credit in the Past Year (% age 15+)			
Borrowed from a financial institution	11.9	6.4	8.6
Borrowed from a financial institution, 2011	10.8	8.7	11.7
Borrowed from family or friends	35.1	31.4	34.9
Borrowed from a private informal lender	17.8	10.9	6.5
Borrowed any money	59.0	46.7	52.5
Borrowed for a farm or business	8.5	8.6	12.2
Borrowed for education or school fees	12.7	8.9	10.9
Outstanding mortgage at a financial institution	8.0	3.8	4.1

Netherlands

			High income
High income: OECD			**High income**
Population, age 15+ (millions)	**13.9**	GNI per capita ($)	**51,060**

	Country data	High income: OECD
Account (% age 15+)		
All adults	99.3	94.0
Women	99.2	93.8
Adults belonging to the poorest 40%	98.7	90.6
Young adults (% ages 15–24)	99.1	84.1
Adults living in rural areas	99.4	93.8
Financial Institution Account (% age 15+)		
All adults	99.3	94.0
All adults, 2011	98.7	90.0
Mobile Account (% age 15+)		
All adults	..	..
Access to Financial Institution Account (% age 15+)		
Has debit card	98.4	79.7
Has debit card, 2011	97.6	61.9
ATM is the main mode of withdrawal (% with an account)	..	..
ATM is the main mode of withdrawal (% with an account), 2011	85.0	68.5
Use of Account in the Past Year (% age 15+)		
Used an account to receive wages	60.6	44.3
Used an account to receive government transfers	32.4	17.2
Used a financial institution account to pay utility bills	63.4	61.1
Other Digital Payments in the Past Year (% age 15+)		
Used a debit card to make payments	94.0	65.3
Used a credit card to make payments	26.0	46.7
Used the Internet to pay bills or make purchases	68.1	54.1
Domestic Remittances in the Past Year (% age 15+)		
Sent remittances	..	..
Sent remittances via a financial institution (% senders)	..	..
Sent remittances via a mobile phone (% senders)	..	..
Sent remittances via a money transfer operator (% senders)	..	..
Received remittances	..	..
Received remittances via a financial institution (% recipients)	..	..
Received remittances via a mobile phone (% recipients)	..	..
Received remittances via a money transfer operator (% recipients)	..	..
Savings in the Past Year (% age 15+)		
Saved at a financial institution	58.9	51.6
Saved at a financial institution, 2011	57.8	45.3
Saved using a savings club or person outside the family	..	..
Saved any money	74.5	70.8
Saved for old age	31.0	39.7
Saved for a farm or business	4.9	9.0
Saved for education or school fees	23.9	25.0
Credit in the Past Year (% age 15+)		
Borrowed from a financial institution	12.6	18.4
Borrowed from a financial institution, 2011	12.6	14.2
Borrowed from family or friends	13.2	14.9
Borrowed from a private informal lender	0.0	0.9
Borrowed any money	27.0	39.8
Borrowed for a farm or business	1.1	2.6
Borrowed for education or school fees	4.1	5.6
Outstanding mortgage at a financial institution	38.9	26.1

New Zealand

Population, age 15+ (millions)	**3.5**	GNI per capita ($)	**35,760**

	Country data	High income: OECD
Account (% age 15+)		
All adults	99.5	94.0
Women	99.2	93.8
Adults belonging to the poorest 40%	99.0	90.6
Young adults (% ages 15–24)	99.1	84.1
Adults living in rural areas	100.0	93.8
Financial Institution Account (% age 15+)		
All adults	99.5	94.0
All adults, 2011	99.4	90.0
Mobile Account (% age 15+)		
All adults	..	..
Access to Financial Institution Account (% age 15+)		
Has debit card	95.5	79.7
Has debit card, 2011	93.8	61.9
ATM is the main mode of withdrawal (% with an account)	..	..
ATM is the main mode of withdrawal (% with an account), 2011	71.9	68.5
Use of Account in the Past Year (% age 15+)		
Used an account to receive wages	58.9	44.3
Used an account to receive government transfers	34.6	17.2
Used a financial institution account to pay utility bills	68.6	61.1
Other Digital Payments in the Past Year (% age 15+)		
Used a debit card to make payments	91.9	65.3
Used a credit card to make payments	58.3	46.7
Used the Internet to pay bills or make purchases	71.7	54.1
Domestic Remittances in the Past Year (% age 15+)		
Sent remittances	..	..
Sent remittances via a financial institution (% senders)	..	..
Sent remittances via a mobile phone (% senders)	..	..
Sent remittances via a money transfer operator (% senders)	..	..
Received remittances	..	..
Received remittances via a financial institution (% recipients)	..	..
Received remittances via a mobile phone (% recipients)	..	..
Received remittances via a money transfer operator (% recipients)	..	..
Savings in the Past Year (% age 15+)		
Saved at a financial institution	70.6	51.6
Saved at a financial institution, 2011	60.4	45.3
Saved using a savings club or person outside the family	..	..
Saved any money	86.9	70.8
Saved for old age	51.5	39.7
Saved for a farm or business	12.0	9.0
Saved for education or school fees	32.1	25.0
Credit in the Past Year (% age 15+)		
Borrowed from a financial institution	32.5	18.4
Borrowed from a financial institution, 2011	26.6	14.2
Borrowed from family or friends	15.6	14.9
Borrowed from a private informal lender	0.9	0.9
Borrowed any money	54.3	39.8
Borrowed for a farm or business	6.7	2.6
Borrowed for education or school fees	8.8	5.6
Outstanding mortgage at a financial institution	39.2	26.1

Nicaragua

Latin America & Caribbean			Lower middle income

Population, age 15+ (millions)	**4.1**	GNI per capita ($)	**1,790**

	Country data	Latin America & the Carib.	Lower middle income
Account (% age 15+)			
All adults	19.4	51.4	42.7
Women	14.4	48.6	36.3
Adults belonging to the poorest 40%	8.5	41.2	33.2
Young adults (% ages 15–24)	11.1	37.4	34.7
Adults living in rural areas	16.3	46.0	40.0
Financial Institution Account (% age 15+)			
All adults	18.9	51.1	41.8
All adults, 2011	14.2	39.3	28.7
Mobile Account (% age 15+)			
All adults	1.1	1.7	2.5
Access to Financial Institution Account (% age 15+)			
Has debit card	11.3	40.4	21.2
Has debit card, 2011	8.3	28.9	10.1
ATM is the main mode of withdrawal (% with an account)	57.9	71.1	42.4
ATM is the main mode of withdrawal (% with an account), 2011	35.2	57.0	28.1
Use of Account in the Past Year (% age 15+)			
Used an account to receive wages	7.9	18.0	5.6
Used an account to receive government transfers	1.2	9.0	3.3
Used a financial institution account to pay utility bills	1.6	6.3	3.1
Other Digital Payments in the Past Year (% age 15+)			
Used a debit card to make payments	4.8	27.7	9.6
Used a credit card to make payments	1.9	18.0	2.8
Used the Internet to pay bills or make purchases	2.3	6.9	2.6
Domestic Remittances in the Past Year (% age 15+)			
Sent remittances	8.8	9.5	14.2
Sent remittances via a financial institution (% senders)	..	..	30.9
Sent remittances via a mobile phone (% senders)	..	..	7.7
Sent remittances via a money transfer operator (% senders)	..	..	18.3
Received remittances	15.8	11.3	17.8
Received remittances via a financial institution (% recipients)	20.7	34.2	26.0
Received remittances via a mobile phone (% recipients)	3.8	4.3	5.7
Received remittances via a money transfer operator (% recipients)	30.5	28.4	16.6
Savings in the Past Year (% age 15+)			
Saved at a financial institution	8.1	13.5	14.8
Saved at a financial institution, 2011	6.5	9.6	11.1
Saved using a savings club or person outside the family	9.8	7.9	12.4
Saved any money	51.4	40.6	45.6
Saved for old age	10.2	10.6	12.6
Saved for a farm or business	15.0	10.6	11.8
Saved for education or school fees	31.1	17.2	20.0
Credit in the Past Year (% age 15+)			
Borrowed from a financial institution	14.3	11.3	7.5
Borrowed from a financial institution, 2011	7.6	7.9	7.3
Borrowed from family or friends	16.7	13.5	33.1
Borrowed from a private informal lender	6.3	4.7	8.5
Borrowed any money	42.5	32.7	47.4
Borrowed for a farm or business	8.9	6.1	9.2
Borrowed for education or school fees	12.5	8.3	10.1
Outstanding mortgage at a financial institution	6.7	9.6	4.7

Niger

Sub-Saharan Africa			Low income
Population, age 15+ (millions)	**8.9**	GNI per capita ($)	**400**

	Country data	Sub-Saharan Africa	Low income
Account (% age 15+)			
All adults	6.7	34.2	27.5
Women	4.3	29.9	23.9
Adults belonging to the poorest 40%	6.0	24.6	19.4
Young adults (% ages 15–24)	6.2	25.9	20.2
Adults living in rural areas	7.0	29.2	24.8
Financial Institution Account (% age 15+)			
All adults	3.5	28.9	22.3
All adults, 2011	1.5	23.9	21.1
Mobile Account (% age 15+)			
All adults	3.9	11.5	10.0
Access to Financial Institution Account (% age 15+)			
Has debit card	0.5	17.9	6.6
Has debit card, 2011	0.8	15.0	6.3
ATM is the main mode of withdrawal (% with an account)	..	53.8	20.2
ATM is the main mode of withdrawal (% with an account), 2011	..	51.7	19.7
Use of Account in the Past Year (% age 15+)			
Used an account to receive wages	0.9	7.3	3.2
Used an account to receive government transfers	0.8	3.8	1.0
Used a financial institution account to pay utility bills	0.0	2.8	0.9
Other Digital Payments in the Past Year (% age 15+)			
Used a debit card to make payments	0.1	8.7	2.1
Used a credit card to make payments	1.2	1.9	0.6
Used the Internet to pay bills or make purchases	1.0	2.4	1.2
Domestic Remittances in the Past Year (% age 15+)			
Sent remittances	19.8	28.7	18.3
Sent remittances via a financial institution (% senders)	4.2	31.0	15.4
Sent remittances via a mobile phone (% senders)	3.9	30.8	42.8
Sent remittances via a money transfer operator (% senders)	14.1	21.0	14.1
Received remittances	47.5	37.2	25.6
Received remittances via a financial institution (% recipients)	1.2	26.6	13.0
Received remittances via a mobile phone (% recipients)	3.7	27.6	33.8
Received remittances via a money transfer operator (% recipients)	16.3	22.1	14.8
Savings in the Past Year (% age 15+)			
Saved at a financial institution	2.0	15.9	9.9
Saved at a financial institution, 2011	1.2	14.3	11.5
Saved using a savings club or person outside the family	27.9	23.9	16.3
Saved any money	61.0	59.6	46.5
Saved for old age	0.9	9.8	8.3
Saved for a farm or business	24.6	22.7	16.7
Saved for education or school fees	6.1	22.9	16.6
Credit in the Past Year (% age 15+)			
Borrowed from a financial institution	1.4	6.3	8.6
Borrowed from a financial institution, 2011	1.3	4.8	11.7
Borrowed from family or friends	56.0	41.9	34.9
Borrowed from a private informal lender	1.5	4.7	6.5
Borrowed any money	70.7	54.5	52.5
Borrowed for a farm or business	17.5	12.8	12.2
Borrowed for education or school fees	6.0	12.3	10.9
Outstanding mortgage at a financial institution	1.9	5.2	4.1

Nigeria

Population, age 15+ (millions)	**96.6**	GNI per capita ($)	**2,710**

	Country data	Sub-Saharan Africa	Lower middle income
Account (% age 15+)			
All adults	44.4	34.2	42.7
Women	34.0	29.9	36.3
Adults belonging to the poorest 40%	34.4	24.6	33.2
Young adults (% ages 15–24)	35.7	25.9	34.7
Adults living in rural areas	39.4	29.2	40.0
Financial Institution Account (% age 15+)			
All adults	44.2	28.9	41.8
All adults, 2011	29.7	23.9	28.7
Mobile Account (% age 15+)			
All adults	2.3	11.5	2.5
Access to Financial Institution Account (% age 15+)			
Has debit card	35.6	17.9	21.2
Has debit card, 2011	18.6	15.0	10.1
ATM is the main mode of withdrawal (% with an account)	70.5	53.8	42.4
ATM is the main mode of withdrawal (% with an account), 2011	40.8	51.7	28.1
Use of Account in the Past Year (% age 15+)			
Used an account to receive wages	8.8	7.3	5.6
Used an account to receive government transfers	3.0	3.8	3.3
Used a financial institution account to pay utility bills	5.2	2.8	3.1
Other Digital Payments in the Past Year (% age 15+)			
Used a debit card to make payments	14.1	8.7	9.6
Used a credit card to make payments	1.9	1.9	2.8
Used the Internet to pay bills or make purchases	3.3	2.4	2.6
Domestic Remittances in the Past Year (% age 15+)			
Sent remittances	39.3	28.7	14.2
Sent remittances via a financial institution (% senders)	53.2	31.0	30.9
Sent remittances via a mobile phone (% senders)	4.6	30.8	7.7
Sent remittances via a money transfer operator (% senders)	8.9	21.0	18.3
Received remittances	45.3	37.2	17.8
Received remittances via a financial institution (% recipients)	51.7	26.6	26.0
Received remittances via a mobile phone (% recipients)	5.8	27.6	5.7
Received remittances via a money transfer operator (% recipients)	10.1	22.1	16.6
Savings in the Past Year (% age 15+)			
Saved at a financial institution	27.1	15.9	14.8
Saved at a financial institution, 2011	23.6	14.3	11.1
Saved using a savings club or person outside the family	23.0	23.9	12.4
Saved any money	69.0	59.6	45.6
Saved for old age	16.3	9.8	12.6
Saved for a farm or business	31.7	22.7	11.8
Saved for education or school fees	32.5	22.9	20.0
Credit in the Past Year (% age 15+)			
Borrowed from a financial institution	5.3	6.3	7.5
Borrowed from a financial institution, 2011	2.1	4.8	7.3
Borrowed from family or friends	37.5	41.9	33.1
Borrowed from a private informal lender	1.7	4.7	8.5
Borrowed any money	44.8	54.5	47.4
Borrowed for a farm or business	12.7	12.8	9.2
Borrowed for education or school fees	7.1	12.3	10.1
Outstanding mortgage at a financial institution	6.3	5.2	4.7

Norway

High income: OECD			High income
Population, age 15+ (millions)	**4.1**	GNI per capita ($)	**102,700**

	Country data	High income: OECD
Account (% age 15+)		
All adults	100.0	94.0
Women	100.0	93.8
Adults belonging to the poorest 40%	100.0	90.6
Young adults (% ages 15–24)	100.0	84.1
Adults living in rural areas	100.0	93.8
Financial Institution Account (% age 15+)		
All adults	100.0	94.0
All adults, 2011	..	90.0
Mobile Account (% age 15+)		
All adults	..	..
Access to Financial Institution Account (% age 15+)		
Has debit card	98.6	79.7
Has debit card, 2011	..	61.9
ATM is the main mode of withdrawal (% with an account)	..	..
ATM is the main mode of withdrawal (% with an account), 2011	..	68.5
Use of Account in the Past Year (% age 15+)		
Used an account to receive wages	66.7	44.3
Used an account to receive government transfers	41.5	17.2
Used a financial institution account to pay utility bills	74.7	61.1
Other Digital Payments in the Past Year (% age 15+)		
Used a debit card to make payments	95.9	65.3
Used a credit card to make payments	54.2	46.7
Used the Internet to pay bills or make purchases	79.0	54.1
Domestic Remittances in the Past Year (% age 15+)		
Sent remittances	..	..
Sent remittances via a financial institution (% senders)	..	..
Sent remittances via a mobile phone (% senders)	..	..
Sent remittances via a money transfer operator (% senders)	..	..
Received remittances	..	..
Received remittances via a financial institution (% recipients)	..	..
Received remittances via a mobile phone (% recipients)	..	..
Received remittances via a money transfer operator (% recipients)	..	..
Savings in the Past Year (% age 15+)		
Saved at a financial institution	78.4	51.6
Saved at a financial institution, 2011	..	45.3
Saved using a savings club or person outside the family	..	..
Saved any money	89.8	70.8
Saved for old age	40.5	39.7
Saved for a farm or business	8.2	9.0
Saved for education or school fees	16.5	25.0
Credit in the Past Year (% age 15+)		
Borrowed from a financial institution	29.4	18.4
Borrowed from a financial institution, 2011	..	14.2
Borrowed from family or friends	13.0	14.9
Borrowed from a private informal lender	0.1	0.9
Borrowed any money	47.3	39.8
Borrowed for a farm or business	2.5	2.6
Borrowed for education or school fees	6.9	5.6
Outstanding mortgage at a financial institution	49.5	26.1

Pakistan

South Asia			Lower middle income
Population, age 15+ (millions)	**120.5**	GNI per capita ($)	**1,360**

	Country data	South Asia	Lower middle income
Account (% age 15+)			
All adults	13.0	46.4	42.7
Women	4.8	37.4	36.3
Adults belonging to the poorest 40%	11.2	38.1	33.2
Young adults (% ages 15–24)	13.2	36.7	34.7
Adults living in rural areas	12.4	43.5	40.0
Financial Institution Account (% age 15+)			
All adults	8.7	45.5	41.8
All adults, 2011	10.3	32.3	28.7
Mobile Account (% age 15+)			
All adults	5.8	2.6	2.5
Access to Financial Institution Account (% age 15+)			
Has debit card	2.9	18.0	21.2
Has debit card, 2011	2.9	7.2	10.1
ATM is the main mode of withdrawal (% with an account)	..	31.1	42.4
ATM is the main mode of withdrawal (% with an account), 2011	32.4	16.9	28.1
Use of Account in the Past Year (% age 15+)			
Used an account to receive wages	1.4	3.5	5.6
Used an account to receive government transfers	1.8	3.1	3.3
Used a financial institution account to pay utility bills	0.4	2.7	3.1
Other Digital Payments in the Past Year (% age 15+)			
Used a debit card to make payments	1.0	8.5	9.6
Used a credit card to make payments	0.1	2.6	2.8
Used the Internet to pay bills or make purchases	1.8	1.2	2.6
Domestic Remittances in the Past Year (% age 15+)			
Sent remittances	15.7	10.7	14.2
Sent remittances via a financial institution (% senders)	4.8	20.1	30.9
Sent remittances via a mobile phone (% senders)	5.7	7.7	7.7
Sent remittances via a money transfer operator (% senders)	12.5	13.7	18.3
Received remittances	24.8	12.2	17.8
Received remittances via a financial institution (% recipients)	4.6	15.8	26.0
Received remittances via a mobile phone (% recipients)	4.3	4.7	5.7
Received remittances via a money transfer operator (% recipients)	11.2	9.8	16.6
Savings in the Past Year (% age 15+)			
Saved at a financial institution	3.3	12.7	14.8
Saved at a financial institution, 2011	1.4	11.1	11.1
Saved using a savings club or person outside the family	11.4	8.8	12.4
Saved any money	31.6	36.2	45.6
Saved for old age	5.0	9.1	12.6
Saved for a farm or business	12.3	7.3	11.8
Saved for education or school fees	10.8	14.6	20.0
Credit in the Past Year (% age 15+)			
Borrowed from a financial institution	1.5	6.4	7.5
Borrowed from a financial institution, 2011	1.6	8.7	7.3
Borrowed from family or friends	34.0	31.4	33.1
Borrowed from a private informal lender	5.3	10.9	8.5
Borrowed any money	49.8	46.7	47.4
Borrowed for a farm or business	10.7	8.6	9.2
Borrowed for education or school fees	6.3	8.9	10.1
Outstanding mortgage at a financial institution	4.4	3.8	4.7

Panama

Latin America & Caribbean		Upper middle income	
Population, age 15+ (millions)	2.8	GNI per capita ($)	10,700

	Country data	Latin America & the Carib.	Upper middle income
Account (% age 15+)			
All adults	43.7	51.4	70.5
Women	40.3	48.6	67.3
Adults belonging to the poorest 40%	32.4	41.2	62.7
Young adults (% ages 15-24)	30.7	37.4	58.1
Adults living in rural areas	35.8	46.0	68.8
Financial Institution Account (% age 15+)			
All adults	43.4	51.1	70.4
All adults, 2011	24.9	39.3	57.4
Mobile Account (% age 15+)			
All adults	1.6	1.7	0.7
Access to Financial Institution Account (% age 15+)			
Has debit card	25.3	40.4	45.9
Has debit card, 2011	11.3	28.9	38.5
ATM is the main mode of withdrawal (% with an account)	63.5	71.1	55.7
ATM is the main mode of withdrawal (% with an account), 2011	39.1	57.0	42.8
Use of Account in the Past Year (% age 15+)			
Used an account to receive wages	15.3	18.0	18.1
Used an account to receive government transfers	5.5	9.0	9.6
Used a financial institution account to pay utility bills	2.5	6.3	12.3
Other Digital Payments in the Past Year (% age 15+)			
Used a debit card to make payments	18.1	27.7	19.9
Used a credit card to make payments	8.1	18.0	14.4
Used the Internet to pay bills or make purchases	6.2	6.9	15.3
Domestic Remittances in the Past Year (% age 15+)			
Sent remittances	17.5	9.5	15.4
Sent remittances via a financial institution (% senders)	31.5	..	37.2
Sent remittances via a mobile phone (% senders)	2.7	..	8.8
Sent remittances via a money transfer operator (% senders)	48.0	..	19.7
Received remittances	21.2	11.3	17.8
Received remittances via a financial institution (% recipients)	20.1	34.2	29.8
Received remittances via a mobile phone (% recipients)	1.3	4.3	5.6
Received remittances via a money transfer operator (% recipients)	50.1	28.4	17.9
Savings in the Past Year (% age 15+)			
Saved at a financial institution	20.4	13.5	32.2
Saved at a financial institution, 2011	12.5	9.6	25.1
Saved using a savings club or person outside the family	19.1	7.9	4.9
Saved any money	62.5	40.6	62.7
Saved for old age	16.5	10.6	30.6
Saved for a farm or business	12.7	10.6	17.6
Saved for education or school fees	34.3	17.2	25.4
Credit in the Past Year (% age 15+)			
Borrowed from a financial institution	11.8	11.3	10.4
Borrowed from a financial institution, 2011	9.8	7.9	7.9
Borrowed from family or friends	22.6	13.5	24.0
Borrowed from a private informal lender	16.5	4.7	2.6
Borrowed any money	47.7	32.7	37.7
Borrowed for a farm or business	6.8	6.1	6.6
Borrowed for education or school fees	14.5	8.3	6.1
Outstanding mortgage at a financial institution	13.7	9.6	9.1

Peru

	Latin America & Caribbean		Upper middle income
Population, age 15+ (millions)	21.6	GNI per capita ($)	6,270

	Country data	Latin America & the Carib.	Upper middle income
Account (% age 15+)			
All adults	29.0	51.4	70.5
Women	22.5	48.6	67.3
Adults belonging to the poorest 40%	18.4	41.2	62.7
Young adults (% ages 15–24)	19.5	37.4	58.1
Adults living in rural areas	23.2	46.0	68.8
Financial Institution Account (% age 15+)			
All adults	29.0	51.1	70.4
All adults, 2011	20.5	39.3	57.4
Mobile Account (% age 15+)			
All adults	0.0	1.7	0.7
Access to Financial Institution Account (% age 15+)			
Has debit card	21.4	40.4	45.9
Has debit card, 2011	14.1	28.9	38.5
ATM is the main mode of withdrawal (% with an account)	51.8	71.1	55.7
ATM is the main mode of withdrawal (% with an account), 2011	43.6	57.0	42.8
Use of Account in the Past Year (% age 15+)			
Used an account to receive wages	11.9	18.0	18.1
Used an account to receive government transfers	1.2	9.0	9.6
Used a financial institution account to pay utility bills	1.1	6.3	12.3
Other Digital Payments in the Past Year (% age 15+)			
Used a debit card to make payments	11.9	27.7	19.9
Used a credit card to make payments	10.0	18.0	14.4
Used the Internet to pay bills or make purchases	2.8	6.9	15.3
Domestic Remittances in the Past Year (% age 15+)			
Sent remittances	10.9	9.5	15.4
Sent remittances via a financial institution (% senders)	61.8	..	37.2
Sent remittances via a mobile phone (% senders)	0.0	..	8.8
Sent remittances via a money transfer operator (% senders)	17.9	..	19.7
Received remittances	15.9	11.3	17.8
Received remittances via a financial institution (% recipients)	42.2	34.2	29.8
Received remittances via a mobile phone (% recipients)	0.0	4.3	5.6
Received remittances via a money transfer operator (% recipients)	15.2	28.4	17.9
Savings in the Past Year (% age 15+)			
Saved at a financial institution	12.3	13.5	32.2
Saved at a financial institution, 2011	8.6	9.6	25.1
Saved using a savings club or person outside the family	6.5	7.9	4.9
Saved any money	39.3	40.6	62.7
Saved for old age	9.9	10.6	30.6
Saved for a farm or business	12.8	10.6	17.6
Saved for education or school fees	21.6	17.2	25.4
Credit in the Past Year (% age 15+)			
Borrowed from a financial institution	11.2	11.3	10.4
Borrowed from a financial institution, 2011	12.7	7.9	7.9
Borrowed from family or friends	10.4	13.5	24.0
Borrowed from a private informal lender	2.3	4.7	2.6
Borrowed any money	27.5	32.7	37.7
Borrowed for a farm or business	6.8	6.1	6.6
Borrowed for education or school fees	7.0	8.3	6.1
Outstanding mortgage at a financial institution	9.8	9.6	9.1

Philippines

	Country data	East Asia & Pacific	Lower middle income
East Asia & Pacific		**Lower middle income**	

Population, age 15+ (millions)	**64.8**	GNI per capita ($)	**3,270**

	Country data	East Asia & Pacific	Lower middle income
Account (% age 15+)			
All adults	31.3	69.0	42.7
Women	37.9	67.0	36.3
Adults belonging to the poorest 40%	17.8	60.9	33.2
Young adults (% ages 15–24)	19.0	60.7	34.7
Adults living in rural areas	27.5	64.5	40.0
Financial Institution Account (% age 15+)			
All adults	28.1	68.8	41.8
All adults, 2011	26.6	55.1	28.7
Mobile Account (% age 15+)			
All adults	4.2	0.4	2.5
Access to Financial Institution Account (% age 15+)			
Has debit card	20.5	42.9	21.2
Has debit card, 2011	13.2	34.7	10.1
ATM is the main mode of withdrawal (% with an account)	67.1	53.3	42.4
ATM is the main mode of withdrawal (% with an account), 2011	62.5	37.0	28.1
Use of Account in the Past Year (% age 15+)			
Used an account to receive wages	6.3	15.1	5.6
Used an account to receive government transfers	4.0	8.1	3.3
Used a financial institution account to pay utility bills	1.0	11.8	3.1
Other Digital Payments in the Past Year (% age 15+)			
Used a debit card to make payments	11.9	14.8	9.6
Used a credit card to make payments	2.2	10.8	2.8
Used the Internet to pay bills or make purchases	3.5	15.6	2.6
Domestic Remittances in the Past Year (% age 15+)			
Sent remittances	21.3	16.6	14.2
Sent remittances via a financial institution (% senders)	17.0	36.9	30.9
Sent remittances via a mobile phone (% senders)	16.2	8.7	7.7
Sent remittances via a money transfer operator (% senders)	70.5	18.5	18.3
Received remittances	34.1	20.6	17.8
Received remittances via a financial institution (% recipients)	12.1	29.0	26.0
Received remittances via a mobile phone (% recipients)	10.8	4.9	5.7
Received remittances via a money transfer operator (% recipients)	58.0	15.8	16.6
Savings in the Past Year (% age 15+)			
Saved at a financial institution	14.8	36.5	14.8
Saved at a financial institution, 2011	14.7	28.5	11.1
Saved using a savings club or person outside the family	9.3	6.0	12.4
Saved any money	67.3	71.0	45.6
Saved for old age	24.5	36.5	12.6
Saved for a farm or business	22.9	21.3	11.8
Saved for education or school fees	41.9	30.7	20.0
Credit in the Past Year (% age 15+)			
Borrowed from a financial institution	11.8	11.0	7.5
Borrowed from a financial institution, 2011	10.5	8.6	7.3
Borrowed from family or friends	48.7	28.3	33.1
Borrowed from a private informal lender	13.5	2.5	8.5
Borrowed any money	69.7	41.2	47.4
Borrowed for a farm or business	13.6	8.3	9.2
Borrowed for education or school fees	29.9	7.1	10.1
Outstanding mortgage at a financial institution	4.9	8.0	4.7

Poland

High income: OECD			High income
Population, age 15+ (millions)	32.8	GNI per capita ($)	13,240

	Country data	High income: OECD
Account (% age 15+)		
All adults	77.9	94.0
Women	73.0	93.8
Adults belonging to the poorest 40%	70.5	90.6
Young adults (% ages 15–24)	63.7	84.1
Adults living in rural areas	74.8	93.8
Financial Institution Account (% age 15+)		
All adults	77.9	94.0
All adults, 2011	70.2	90.0
Mobile Account (% age 15+)		
All adults	..	..
Access to Financial Institution Account (% age 15+)		
Has debit card	49.5	79.7
Has debit card, 2011	37.3	61.9
ATM is the main mode of withdrawal (% with an account)	68.2	..
ATM is the main mode of withdrawal (% with an account), 2011	60.6	68.5
Use of Account in the Past Year (% age 15+)		
Used an account to receive wages	35.5	44.3
Used an account to receive government transfers	7.9	17.2
Used a financial institution account to pay utility bills	31.9	61.1
Other Digital Payments in the Past Year (% age 15+)		
Used a debit card to make payments	39.6	65.3
Used a credit card to make payments	13.6	46.7
Used the Internet to pay bills or make purchases	42.7	54.1
Domestic Remittances in the Past Year (% age 15+)		
Sent remittances	12.8	..
Sent remittances via a financial institution (% senders)	56.2	..
Sent remittances via a mobile phone (% senders)	3.7	..
Sent remittances via a money transfer operator (% senders)	14.7	..
Received remittances	10.5	..
Received remittances via a financial institution (% recipients)	41.4	..
Received remittances via a mobile phone (% recipients)	0.8	..
Received remittances via a money transfer operator (% recipients)	13.4	..
Savings in the Past Year (% age 15+)		
Saved at a financial institution	20.8	51.6
Saved at a financial institution, 2011	18.0	45.3
Saved using a savings club or person outside the family	2.5	..
Saved any money	46.6	70.8
Saved for old age	15.8	39.7
Saved for a farm or business	8.3	9.0
Saved for education or school fees	11.6	25.0
Credit in the Past Year (% age 15+)		
Borrowed from a financial institution	18.9	18.4
Borrowed from a financial institution, 2011	9.6	14.2
Borrowed from family or friends	12.1	14.9
Borrowed from a private informal lender	0.6	0.9
Borrowed any money	35.4	39.8
Borrowed for a farm or business	1.4	2.6
Borrowed for education or school fees	1.8	5.6
Outstanding mortgage at a financial institution	14.6	26.1

Portugal

Population, age 15+ (millions)	**8.9**	GNI per capita ($)	**21,270**

	Country data	High income: OECD
Account (% age 15+)		
All adults	87.4	94.0
Women	86.1	93.8
Adults belonging to the poorest 40%	78.7	90.6
Young adults (% ages 15–24)	85.7	84.1
Adults living in rural areas	85.1	93.8
Financial Institution Account (% age 15+)		
All adults	87.4	94.0
All adults, 2011	81.2	90.0
Mobile Account (% age 15+)		
All adults	..	..
Access to Financial Institution Account (% age 15+)		
Has debit card	66.7	79.7
Has debit card, 2011	68.2	61.9
ATM is the main mode of withdrawal (% with an account)	..	..
ATM is the main mode of withdrawal (% with an account), 2011	79.0	68.5
Use of Account in the Past Year (% age 15+)		
Used an account to receive wages	31.0	44.3
Used an account to receive government transfers	15.8	17.2
Used a financial institution account to pay utility bills	53.5	61.1
Other Digital Payments in the Past Year (% age 15+)		
Used a debit card to make payments	56.8	65.3
Used a credit card to make payments	20.7	46.7
Used the Internet to pay bills or make purchases	24.8	54.1
Domestic Remittances in the Past Year (% age 15+)		
Sent remittances	..	..
Sent remittances via a financial institution (% senders)	..	..
Sent remittances via a mobile phone (% senders)	..	..
Sent remittances via a money transfer operator (% senders)	..	..
Received remittances	..	..
Received remittances via a financial institution (% recipients)	..	..
Received remittances via a mobile phone (% recipients)	..	..
Received remittances via a money transfer operator (% recipients)	..	..
Savings in the Past Year (% age 15+)		
Saved at a financial institution	24.9	51.6
Saved at a financial institution, 2011	25.6	45.3
Saved using a savings club or person outside the family	..	..
Saved any money	53.3	70.8
Saved for old age	27.7	39.7
Saved for a farm or business	7.2	9.0
Saved for education or school fees	19.8	25.0
Credit in the Past Year (% age 15+)		
Borrowed from a financial institution	9.5	18.4
Borrowed from a financial institution, 2011	8.3	14.2
Borrowed from family or friends	15.6	14.9
Borrowed from a private informal lender	0.4	0.9
Borrowed any money	31.0	39.8
Borrowed for a farm or business	0.6	2.6
Borrowed for education or school fees	3.1	5.6
Outstanding mortgage at a financial institution	22.8	26.1

Puerto Rico

Population, age 15+ (millions)	2.9	GNI per capita ($)	19,210

	Country data	High income: OECD
Account (% age 15+)		
All adults	69.7	94.0
Women	66.1	93.8
Adults belonging to the poorest 40%	56.0	90.6
Young adults (% ages 15–24)	45.0	84.1
Adults living in rural areas	..	93.8
Financial Institution Account (% age 15+)		
All adults	69.7	94.0
All adults, 2011	..	90.0
Mobile Account (% age 15+)		
All adults	..	..
Access to Financial Institution Account (% age 15+)		
Has debit card	58.5	79.7
Has debit card, 2011	..	61.9
ATM is the main mode of withdrawal (% with an account)	76.4	..
ATM is the main mode of withdrawal (% with an account), 2011	..	68.5
Use of Account in the Past Year (% age 15+)		
Used an account to receive wages	18.5	44.3
Used an account to receive government transfers	11.8	17.2
Used a financial institution account to pay utility bills	23.9	61.1
Other Digital Payments in the Past Year (% age 15+)		
Used a debit card to make payments	51.3	65.3
Used a credit card to make payments	20.1	46.7
Used the Internet to pay bills or make purchases	20.1	54.1
Domestic Remittances in the Past Year (% age 15+)		
Sent remittances	13.0	..
Sent remittances via a financial institution (% senders)	19.2	..
Sent remittances via a mobile phone (% senders)	0.9	..
Sent remittances via a money transfer operator (% senders)	31.5	..
Received remittances	12.3	..
Received remittances via a financial institution (% recipients)	23.6	..
Received remittances via a mobile phone (% recipients)	3.7	..
Received remittances via a money transfer operator (% recipients)	25.8	..
Savings in the Past Year (% age 15+)		
Saved at a financial institution	23.5	51.6
Saved at a financial institution, 2011	..	45.3
Saved using a savings club or person outside the family	9.6	..
Saved any money	44.2	70.8
Saved for old age	19.5	39.7
Saved for a farm or business	3.9	9.0
Saved for education or school fees	17.4	25.0
Credit in the Past Year (% age 15+)		
Borrowed from a financial institution	11.4	18.4
Borrowed from a financial institution, 2011	..	14.2
Borrowed from family or friends	10.8	14.9
Borrowed from a private informal lender	1.0	0.9
Borrowed any money	26.2	39.8
Borrowed for a farm or business	0.5	2.6
Borrowed for education or school fees	5.9	5.6
Outstanding mortgage at a financial institution	15.9	26.1

Romania

Population, age 15+ (millions)		**17.0**	GNI per capita ($)	**9,050**

	Country data	Europe & Central Asia	Upper middle income
Account (% age 15+)			
All adults	60.8	51.4	70.5
Women	56.9	47.4	67.3
Adults belonging to the poorest 40%	46.1	44.2	62.7
Young adults (% ages 15–24)	55.0	35.6	58.1
Adults living in rural areas	56.4	45.7	68.8
Financial Institution Account (% age 15+)			
All adults	60.8	51.4	70.4
All adults, 2011	44.6	43.3	57.4
Mobile Account (% age 15+)			
All adults	0.5	0.3	0.7
Access to Financial Institution Account (% age 15+)			
Has debit card	45.8	36.9	45.9
Has debit card, 2011	27.7	36.4	38.5
ATM is the main mode of withdrawal (% with an account)	75.3	66.7	55.7
ATM is the main mode of withdrawal (% with an account), 2011	72.2	72.5	42.8
Use of Account in the Past Year (% age 15+)			
Used an account to receive wages	24.2	22.5	18.1
Used an account to receive government transfers	5.2	7.3	9.6
Used a financial institution account to pay utility bills	6.9	12.5	12.3
Other Digital Payments in the Past Year (% age 15+)			
Used a debit card to make payments	24.4	22.9	19.9
Used a credit card to make payments	9.8	14.9	14.4
Used the Internet to pay bills or make purchases	11.5	11.9	15.3
Domestic Remittances in the Past Year (% age 15+)			
Sent remittances	11.1	12.9	15.4
Sent remittances via a financial institution (% senders)	32.3	31.5	37.2
Sent remittances via a mobile phone (% senders)	0.0	2.5	8.8
Sent remittances via a money transfer operator (% senders)	27.0	11.8	19.7
Received remittances	13.8	15.5	17.8
Received remittances via a financial institution (% recipients)	35.9	22.1	29.8
Received remittances via a mobile phone (% recipients)	0.0	1.0	5.6
Received remittances via a money transfer operator (% recipients)	42.2	15.6	17.9
Savings in the Past Year (% age 15+)			
Saved at a financial institution	13.3	8.4	32.2
Saved at a financial institution, 2011	8.7	4.9	25.1
Saved using a savings club or person outside the family	6.6	6.6	4.9
Saved any money	36.5	38.5	62.7
Saved for old age	15.1	11.8	30.6
Saved for a farm or business	4.6	5.1	17.6
Saved for education or school fees	9.4	12.1	25.4
Credit in the Past Year (% age 15+)			
Borrowed from a financial institution	11.8	12.4	10.4
Borrowed from a financial institution, 2011	8.4	7.8	7.9
Borrowed from family or friends	31.7	23.6	24.0
Borrowed from a private informal lender	1.6	2.1	2.6
Borrowed any money	45.7	39.5	37.7
Borrowed for a farm or business	2.0	2.8	6.6
Borrowed for education or school fees	5.4	6.2	6.1
Outstanding mortgage at a financial institution	10.3	10.2	9.1

Russian Federation

High income

Population, age 15+ (millions)	**120.8**	GNI per capita ($)	**13,850**

	Country data	High income: OECD
Account (% age 15+)		
All adults	67.4	94.0
Women	70.2	93.8
Adults belonging to the poorest 40%	61.8	90.6
Young adults (% ages 15–24)	54.4	84.1
Adults living in rural areas	61.2	93.8
Financial Institution Account (% age 15+)		
All adults	67.4	94.0
All adults, 2011	48.2	90.0
Mobile Account (% age 15+)		
All adults	..	..
Access to Financial Institution Account (% age 15+)		
Has debit card	44.3	79.7
Has debit card, 2011	37.0	61.9
ATM is the main mode of withdrawal (% with an account)	67.9	..
ATM is the main mode of withdrawal (% with an account), 2011	65.2	68.5
Use of Account in the Past Year (% age 15+)		
Used an account to receive wages	37.9	44.3
Used an account to receive government transfers	14.1	17.2
Used a financial institution account to pay utility bills	12.2	61.1
Other Digital Payments in the Past Year (% age 15+)		
Used a debit card to make payments	35.0	65.3
Used a credit card to make payments	16.6	46.7
Used the Internet to pay bills or make purchases	17.5	54.1
Domestic Remittances in the Past Year (% age 15+)		
Sent remittances	12.9	..
Sent remittances via a financial institution (% senders)	48.5	..
Sent remittances via a mobile phone (% senders)	8.0	..
Sent remittances via a money transfer operator (% senders)	28.0	..
Received remittances	12.0	..
Received remittances via a financial institution (% recipients)	36.2	..
Received remittances via a mobile phone (% recipients)	6.9	..
Received remittances via a money transfer operator (% recipients)	19.1	..
Savings in the Past Year (% age 15+)		
Saved at a financial institution	15.5	51.6
Saved at a financial institution, 2011	10.9	45.3
Saved using a savings club or person outside the family	1.6	..
Saved any money	40.7	70.8
Saved for old age	14.6	39.7
Saved for a farm or business	3.6	9.0
Saved for education or school fees	7.8	25.0
Credit in the Past Year (% age 15+)		
Borrowed from a financial institution	10.3	18.4
Borrowed from a financial institution, 2011	7.7	14.2
Borrowed from family or friends	17.0	14.9
Borrowed from a private informal lender	0.9	0.9
Borrowed any money	30.2	39.8
Borrowed for a farm or business	1.3	2.6
Borrowed for education or school fees	2.1	5.6
Outstanding mortgage at a financial institution	18.4	26.1

Rwanda

Population, age 15+ (millions)	6.7	GNI per capita ($)	630

	Country data	Sub-Saharan Africa	Low income
Account (% age 15+)			
All adults	42.1	34.2	27.5
Women	35.3	29.9	23.9
Adults belonging to the poorest 40%	18.3	24.6	19.4
Young adults (% ages 15–24)	23.3	25.9	20.2
Adults living in rural areas	37.9	29.2	24.8
Financial Institution Account (% age 15+)			
All adults	38.1	28.9	22.3
All adults, 2011	32.8	23.9	21.1
Mobile Account (% age 15+)			
All adults	18.1	11.5	10.0
Access to Financial Institution Account (% age 15+)			
Has debit card	4.5	17.9	6.6
Has debit card, 2011	5.3	15.0	6.3
ATM is the main mode of withdrawal (% with an account)	2.6	53.8	20.2
ATM is the main mode of withdrawal (% with an account), 2011	2.5	51.7	19.7
Use of Account in the Past Year (% age 15+)			
Used an account to receive wages	6.8	7.3	3.2
Used an account to receive government transfers	1.9	3.8	1.0
Used a financial institution account to pay utility bills	1.3	2.8	0.9
Other Digital Payments in the Past Year (% age 15+)			
Used a debit card to make payments	1.8	8.7	2.1
Used a credit card to make payments	0.3	1.9	0.6
Used the Internet to pay bills or make purchases	1.7	2.4	1.2
Domestic Remittances in the Past Year (% age 15+)			
Sent remittances	26.5	28.7	18.3
Sent remittances via a financial institution (% senders)	24.6	31.0	15.4
Sent remittances via a mobile phone (% senders)	59.5	30.8	42.8
Sent remittances via a money transfer operator (% senders)	9.9	21.0	14.1
Received remittances	36.0	37.2	25.6
Received remittances via a financial institution (% recipients)	17.0	26.6	13.0
Received remittances via a mobile phone (% recipients)	44.5	27.6	33.8
Received remittances via a money transfer operator (% recipients)	6.5	22.1	14.8
Savings in the Past Year (% age 15+)			
Saved at a financial institution	25.5	15.9	9.9
Saved at a financial institution, 2011	17.8	14.3	11.5
Saved using a savings club or person outside the family	24.1	23.9	16.3
Saved any money	55.2	59.6	46.5
Saved for old age	4.9	9.8	8.3
Saved for a farm or business	21.3	22.7	16.7
Saved for education or school fees	13.2	22.9	16.6
Credit in the Past Year (% age 15+)			
Borrowed from a financial institution	8.2	6.3	8.6
Borrowed from a financial institution, 2011	8.4	4.8	11.7
Borrowed from family or friends	36.6	41.9	34.9
Borrowed from a private informal lender	1.9	4.7	6.5
Borrowed any money	51.3	54.5	52.5
Borrowed for a farm or business	12.8	12.8	12.2
Borrowed for education or school fees	5.1	12.3	10.9
Outstanding mortgage at a financial institution	6.0	5.2	4.1

Saudi Arabia

			High income
Population, age 15+ (millions)	**20.5**	GNI per capita ($)	**26,260**

	Country data	High income: OECD
Account (% age 15+)		
All adults	69.4	94.0
Women	61.1	93.8
Adults belonging to the poorest 40%	63.5	90.6
Young adults (% ages 15–24)	64.5	84.1
Adults living in rural areas	71.6	93.8
Financial Institution Account (% age 15+)		
All adults	69.4	94.0
All adults, 2011	46.4	90.0
Mobile Account (% age 15+)		
All adults	..	..
Access to Financial Institution Account (% age 15+)		
Has debit card	63.6	79.7
Has debit card, 2011	42.3	61.9
ATM is the main mode of withdrawal (% with an account)	..	..
ATM is the main mode of withdrawal (% with an account), 2011	89.5	68.5
Use of Account in the Past Year (% age 15+)		
Used an account to receive wages	9.7	44.3
Used an account to receive government transfers	6.1	17.2
Used a financial institution account to pay utility bills	23.1	61.1
Other Digital Payments in the Past Year (% age 15+)		
Used a debit card to make payments	34.8	65.3
Used a credit card to make payments	8.1	46.7
Used the Internet to pay bills or make purchases	16.2	54.1
Domestic Remittances in the Past Year (% age 15+)		
Sent remittances	..	..
Sent remittances via a financial institution (% senders)	..	..
Sent remittances via a mobile phone (% senders)	..	..
Sent remittances via a money transfer operator (% senders)	..	..
Received remittances	..	..
Received remittances via a financial institution (% recipients)	..	..
Received remittances via a mobile phone (% recipients)	..	..
Received remittances via a money transfer operator (% recipients)	..	..
Savings in the Past Year (% age 15+)		
Saved at a financial institution	15.5	51.6
Saved at a financial institution, 2011	17.2	45.3
Saved using a savings club or person outside the family	..	..
Saved any money	45.4	70.8
Saved for old age	9.0	39.7
Saved for a farm or business	13.5	9.0
Saved for education or school fees	13.9	25.0
Credit in the Past Year (% age 15+)		
Borrowed from a financial institution	12.2	18.4
Borrowed from a financial institution, 2011	2.1	14.2
Borrowed from family or friends	37.3	14.9
Borrowed from a private informal lender	18.3	0.9
Borrowed any money	53.5	39.8
Borrowed for a farm or business	5.6	2.6
Borrowed for education or school fees	7.3	5.6
Outstanding mortgage at a financial institution	14.1	26.1

Senegal

Sub-Saharan Africa		Lower middle income

Population, age 15+ (millions)	8.0	GNI per capita ($)	1,050

	Country data	Sub-Saharan Africa	Lower middle income
Account (% age 15+)			
All adults	15.4	34.2	42.7
Women	11.4	29.9	36.3
Adults belonging to the poorest 40%	4.9	24.6	33.2
Young adults (% ages 15–24)	6.8	25.9	34.7
Adults living in rural areas	9.4	29.2	40.0
Financial Institution Account (% age 15+)			
All adults	11.9	28.9	41.8
All adults, 2011	5.8	23.9	28.7
Mobile Account (% age 15+)			
All adults	6.2	11.5	2.5
Access to Financial Institution Account (% age 15+)			
Has debit card	5.9	17.9	21.2
Has debit card, 2011	1.8	15.0	10.1
ATM is the main mode of withdrawal (% with an account)	23.2	53.8	42.4
ATM is the main mode of withdrawal (% with an account), 2011	..	51.7	28.1
Use of Account in the Past Year (% age 15+)			
Used an account to receive wages	4.1	7.3	5.6
Used an account to receive government transfers	1.0	3.8	3.3
Used a financial institution account to pay utility bills	0.4	2.8	3.1
Other Digital Payments in the Past Year (% age 15+)			
Used a debit card to make payments	1.6	8.7	9.6
Used a credit card to make payments	0.9	1.9	2.8
Used the Internet to pay bills or make purchases	1.0	2.4	2.6
Domestic Remittances in the Past Year (% age 15+)			
Sent remittances	25.4	28.7	14.2
Sent remittances via a financial institution (% senders)	11.6	31.0	30.9
Sent remittances via a mobile phone (% senders)	11.7	30.8	7.7
Sent remittances via a money transfer operator (% senders)	57.5	21.0	18.3
Received remittances	48.4	37.2	17.8
Received remittances via a financial institution (% recipients)	4.0	26.6	26.0
Received remittances via a mobile phone (% recipients)	10.2	27.6	5.7
Received remittances via a money transfer operator (% recipients)	44.3	22.1	16.6
Savings in the Past Year (% age 15+)			
Saved at a financial institution	6.6	15.9	14.8
Saved at a financial institution, 2011	3.7	14.3	11.1
Saved using a savings club or person outside the family	28.6	23.9	12.4
Saved any money	59.0	59.6	45.6
Saved for old age	8.6	9.8	12.6
Saved for a farm or business	23.8	22.7	11.8
Saved for education or school fees	10.3	22.9	20.0
Credit in the Past Year (% age 15+)			
Borrowed from a financial institution	3.5	6.3	7.5
Borrowed from a financial institution, 2011	3.5	4.8	7.3
Borrowed from family or friends	41.4	41.9	33.1
Borrowed from a private informal lender	2.5	4.7	8.5
Borrowed any money	56.6	54.5	47.4
Borrowed for a farm or business	15.3	12.8	9.2
Borrowed for education or school fees	6.1	12.3	10.1
Outstanding mortgage at a financial institution	3.9	5.2	4.7

Serbia

Europe & Central Asia   **Upper middle income**

Population, age 15+ (millions)	**6.0**	GNI per capita ($)		**6,050**

	Country data	Europe & Central Asia	Upper middle income
Account (% age 15+)			
All adults	83.1	51.4	70.5
Women	83.0	47.4	67.3
Adults belonging to the poorest 40%	79.1	44.2	62.7
Young adults (% ages 15–24)	77.8	35.6	58.1
Adults living in rural areas	79.4	45.7	68.8
Financial Institution Account (% age 15+)			
All adults	83.1	51.4	70.4
All adults, 2011	62.2	43.3	57.4
Mobile Account (% age 15+)			
All adults	..	0.3	0.7
Access to Financial Institution Account (% age 15+)			
Has debit card	57.8	36.9	45.9
Has debit card, 2011	43.1	36.4	38.5
ATM is the main mode of withdrawal (% with an account)	38.1	66.7	55.7
ATM is the main mode of withdrawal (% with an account), 2011	36.7	72.5	42.8
Use of Account in the Past Year (% age 15+)			
Used an account to receive wages	31.5	22.5	18.1
Used an account to receive government transfers	5.9	7.3	9.6
Used a financial institution account to pay utility bills	6.2	12.5	12.3
Other Digital Payments in the Past Year (% age 15+)			
Used a debit card to make payments	38.0	22.9	19.9
Used a credit card to make payments	12.0	14.9	14.4
Used the Internet to pay bills or make purchases	9.7	11.9	15.3
Domestic Remittances in the Past Year (% age 15+)			
Sent remittances	13.2	12.9	15.4
Sent remittances via a financial institution (% senders)	24.2	31.5	37.2
Sent remittances via a mobile phone (% senders)	8.5	2.5	8.8
Sent remittances via a money transfer operator (% senders)	19.8	11.8	19.7
Received remittances	12.0	15.5	17.8
Received remittances via a financial institution (% recipients)	17.2	22.1	29.8
Received remittances via a mobile phone (% recipients)	2.3	1.0	5.6
Received remittances via a money transfer operator (% recipients)	21.2	15.6	17.9
Savings in the Past Year (% age 15+)			
Saved at a financial institution	8.7	8.4	32.2
Saved at a financial institution, 2011	3.2	4.9	25.1
Saved using a savings club or person outside the family	2.2	6.6	4.9
Saved any money	27.7	38.5	62.7
Saved for old age	12.0	11.8	30.6
Saved for a farm or business	3.8	5.1	17.6
Saved for education or school fees	6.9	12.1	25.4
Credit in the Past Year (% age 15+)			
Borrowed from a financial institution	8.9	12.4	10.4
Borrowed from a financial institution, 2011	12.3	7.8	7.9
Borrowed from family or friends	18.0	23.6	24.0
Borrowed from a private informal lender	0.0	2.1	2.6
Borrowed any money	32.1	39.5	37.7
Borrowed for a farm or business	2.3	2.8	6.6
Borrowed for education or school fees	2.6	6.2	6.1
Outstanding mortgage at a financial institution	8.5	10.2	9.1

Sierra Leone

Population, age 15+ (millions)	3.6	GNI per capita ($)	660

	Country data	Sub-Saharan Africa	Low income
Account (% age 15+)			
All adults	15.6	34.2	27.5
Women	12.5	29.9	23.9
Adults belonging to the poorest 40%	7.0	24.6	19.4
Young adults (% ages 15–24)	6.4	25.9	20.2
Adults living in rural areas	11.7	29.2	24.8
Financial Institution Account (% age 15+)			
All adults	14.1	28.9	22.3
All adults, 2011	15.3	23.9	21.1
Mobile Account (% age 15+)			
All adults	4.5	11.5	10.0
Access to Financial Institution Account (% age 15+)			
Has debit card	5.2	17.9	6.6
Has debit card, 2011	4.0	15.0	6.3
ATM is the main mode of withdrawal (% with an account)	10.5	53.8	20.2
ATM is the main mode of withdrawal (% with an account), 2011	16.4	51.7	19.7
Use of Account in the Past Year (% age 15+)			
Used an account to receive wages	4.2	7.3	3.2
Used an account to receive government transfers	2.0	3.8	1.0
Used a financial institution account to pay utility bills	0.2	2.8	0.9
Other Digital Payments in the Past Year (% age 15+)			
Used a debit card to make payments	0.0	8.7	2.1
Used a credit card to make payments	0.5	1.9	0.6
Used the Internet to pay bills or make purchases	1.8	2.4	1.2
Domestic Remittances in the Past Year (% age 15+)			
Sent remittances	35.8	28.7	18.3
Sent remittances via a financial institution (% senders)	16.6	31.0	15.4
Sent remittances via a mobile phone (% senders)	5.0	30.8	42.8
Sent remittances via a money transfer operator (% senders)	7.1	21.0	14.1
Received remittances	47.2	37.2	25.6
Received remittances via a financial institution (% recipients)	11.2	26.6	13.0
Received remittances via a mobile phone (% recipients)	2.4	27.6	33.8
Received remittances via a money transfer operator (% recipients)	4.3	22.1	14.8
Savings in the Past Year (% age 15+)			
Saved at a financial institution	10.9	15.9	9.9
Saved at a financial institution, 2011	14.5	14.3	11.5
Saved using a savings club or person outside the family	39.3	23.9	16.3
Saved any money	65.4	59.6	46.5
Saved for old age	19.9	9.8	8.3
Saved for a farm or business	25.6	22.7	16.7
Saved for education or school fees	34.2	22.9	16.6
Credit in the Past Year (% age 15+)			
Borrowed from a financial institution	4.0	6.3	8.6
Borrowed from a financial institution, 2011	6.1	4.8	11.7
Borrowed from family or friends	42.8	41.9	34.9
Borrowed from a private informal lender	6.5	4.7	6.5
Borrowed any money	57.5	54.5	52.5
Borrowed for a farm or business	16.3	12.8	12.2
Borrowed for education or school fees	24.0	12.3	10.9
Outstanding mortgage at a financial institution	9.3	5.2	4.1

Singapore

Population, age 15+ (millions)	**4.5**	GNI per capita ($)	**54,040**

	Country data	High income: OECD
Account (% age 15+)		
All adults	96.4	94.0
Women	96.1	93.8
Adults belonging to the poorest 40%	96.2	90.6
Young adults (% ages 15–24)	92.9	84.1
Adults living in rural areas	..	93.8
Financial Institution Account (% age 15+)		
All adults	96.4	94.0
All adults, 2011	98.2	90.0
Mobile Account (% age 15+)		
All adults	6.1	..
Access to Financial Institution Account (% age 15+)		
Has debit card	89.4	79.7
Has debit card, 2011	28.6	61.9
ATM is the main mode of withdrawal (% with an account)	88.5	..
ATM is the main mode of withdrawal (% with an account), 2011	90.8	68.5
Use of Account in the Past Year (% age 15+)		
Used an account to receive wages	39.7	44.3
Used an account to receive government transfers	25.7	17.2
Used a financial institution account to pay utility bills	37.9	61.1
Other Digital Payments in the Past Year (% age 15+)		
Used a debit card to make payments	78.2	65.3
Used a credit card to make payments	31.3	46.7
Used the Internet to pay bills or make purchases	27.6	54.1
Domestic Remittances in the Past Year (% age 15+)		
Sent remittances	18.0	..
Sent remittances via a financial institution (% senders)	41.4	..
Sent remittances via a mobile phone (% senders)	9.9	..
Sent remittances via a money transfer operator (% senders)	14.8	..
Received remittances	16.8	..
Received remittances via a financial institution (% recipients)	43.4	..
Received remittances via a mobile phone (% recipients)	8.9	..
Received remittances via a money transfer operator (% recipients)	9.1	..
Savings in the Past Year (% age 15+)		
Saved at a financial institution	46.2	51.6
Saved at a financial institution, 2011	58.4	45.3
Saved using a savings club or person outside the family	4.5	..
Saved any money	73.4	70.8
Saved for old age	50.4	39.7
Saved for a farm or business	10.3	9.0
Saved for education or school fees	30.7	25.0
Credit in the Past Year (% age 15+)		
Borrowed from a financial institution	14.2	18.4
Borrowed from a financial institution, 2011	10.0	14.2
Borrowed from family or friends	4.4	14.9
Borrowed from a private informal lender	1.0	0.9
Borrowed any money	20.6	39.8
Borrowed for a farm or business	1.7	2.6
Borrowed for education or school fees	3.5	5.6
Outstanding mortgage at a financial institution	31.5	26.1

Slovak Republic

High income: OECD   **High income**

Population, age 15+ (millions)	4.6	GNI per capita ($)	17,810

	Country data	High income: OECD
Account (% age 15+)		
All adults	77.2	94.0
Women	80.0	93.8
Adults belonging to the poorest 40%	68.2	90.6
Young adults (% ages 15–24)	37.6	84.1
Adults living in rural areas	76.9	93.8
Financial Institution Account (% age 15+)		
All adults	77.2	94.0
All adults, 2011	79.6	90.0
Mobile Account (% age 15+)		
All adults	..	..
Access to Financial Institution Account (% age 15+)		
Has debit card	70.5	79.7
Has debit card, 2011	68.3	61.9
ATM is the main mode of withdrawal (% with an account)	88.3	..
ATM is the main mode of withdrawal (% with an account), 2011	84.5	68.5
Use of Account in the Past Year (% age 15+)		
Used an account to receive wages	43.4	44.3
Used an account to receive government transfers	22.6	17.2
Used a financial institution account to pay utility bills	41.2	61.1
Other Digital Payments in the Past Year (% age 15+)		
Used a debit card to make payments	63.5	65.3
Used a credit card to make payments	13.6	46.7
Used the Internet to pay bills or make purchases	36.7	54.1
Domestic Remittances in the Past Year (% age 15+)		
Sent remittances	9.9	..
Sent remittances via a financial institution (% senders)	..	..
Sent remittances via a mobile phone (% senders)	..	..
Sent remittances via a money transfer operator (% senders)	..	..
Received remittances	13.6	..
Received remittances via a financial institution (% recipients)	22.5	..
Received remittances via a mobile phone (% recipients)	0.0	..
Received remittances via a money transfer operator (% recipients)	6.8	..
Savings in the Past Year (% age 15+)		
Saved at a financial institution	44.0	51.6
Saved at a financial institution, 2011	36.8	45.3
Saved using a savings club or person outside the family	2.5	..
Saved any money	62.5	70.8
Saved for old age	34.6	39.7
Saved for a farm or business	4.7	9.0
Saved for education or school fees	15.4	25.0
Credit in the Past Year (% age 15+)		
Borrowed from a financial institution	17.7	18.4
Borrowed from a financial institution, 2011	11.4	14.2
Borrowed from family or friends	13.4	14.9
Borrowed from a private informal lender	1.5	0.9
Borrowed any money	35.0	39.8
Borrowed for a farm or business	1.7	2.6
Borrowed for education or school fees	2.0	5.6
Outstanding mortgage at a financial institution	25.4	26.1

Slovenia

Population, age 15+ (millions)	**1.8**	GNI per capita ($)	**23,220**

	Country data	High income: OECD
Account (% age 15+)		
All adults	97.2	94.0
Women	97.0	93.8
Adults belonging to the poorest 40%	96.5	90.6
Young adults (% ages 15–24)	91.5	84.1
Adults living in rural areas	96.8	93.8
Financial Institution Account (% age 15+)		
All adults	97.2	94.0
All adults, 2011	97.1	90.0
Mobile Account (% age 15+)		
All adults	..	..
Access to Financial Institution Account (% age 15+)		
Has debit card	91.3	79.7
Has debit card, 2011	91.9	61.9
ATM is the main mode of withdrawal (% with an account)	..	..
ATM is the main mode of withdrawal (% with an account), 2011	78.1	68.5
Use of Account in the Past Year (% age 15+)		
Used an account to receive wages	46.1	44.3
Used an account to receive government transfers	16.8	17.2
Used a financial institution account to pay utility bills	48.4	61.1
Other Digital Payments in the Past Year (% age 15+)		
Used a debit card to make payments	65.8	65.3
Used a credit card to make payments	29.9	46.7
Used the Internet to pay bills or make purchases	35.9	54.1
Domestic Remittances in the Past Year (% age 15+)		
Sent remittances	..	..
Sent remittances via a financial institution (% senders)	..	..
Sent remittances via a mobile phone (% senders)	..	..
Sent remittances via a money transfer operator (% senders)	..	..
Received remittances	..	..
Received remittances via a financial institution (% recipients)	..	..
Received remittances via a mobile phone (% recipients)	..	..
Received remittances via a money transfer operator (% recipients)	..	..
Savings in the Past Year (% age 15+)		
Saved at a financial institution	32.5	51.6
Saved at a financial institution, 2011	28.9	45.3
Saved using a savings club or person outside the family	..	..
Saved any money	65.7	70.8
Saved for old age	32.0	39.7
Saved for a farm or business	10.0	9.0
Saved for education or school fees	21.1	25.0
Credit in the Past Year (% age 15+)		
Borrowed from a financial institution	13.2	18.4
Borrowed from a financial institution, 2011	12.8	14.2
Borrowed from family or friends	16.9	14.9
Borrowed from a private informal lender	1.2	0.9
Borrowed any money	39.4	39.8
Borrowed for a farm or business	3.6	2.6
Borrowed for education or school fees	4.2	5.6
Outstanding mortgage at a financial institution	17.6	26.1

Somalia

Population, age 15+ (millions)	5.5	GNI per capita ($)	..

	Country data	Sub-Saharan Africa	Low income
Account (% age 15+)			
All adults	38.7	34.2	27.5
Women	33.7	29.9	23.9
Adults belonging to the poorest 40%	27.0	24.6	19.4
Young adults (% ages 15–24)	42.7	25.9	20.2
Adults living in rural areas	32.0	29.2	24.8
Financial Institution Account (% age 15+)			
All adults	7.9	28.9	22.3
All adults, 2011	..	23.9	21.1
Mobile Account (% age 15+)			
All adults	37.1	11.5	10.0
Access to Financial Institution Account (% age 15+)			
Has debit card	2.4	17.9	6.6
Has debit card, 2011	..	15.0	6.3
ATM is the main mode of withdrawal (% with an account)	..	53.8	20.2
ATM is the main mode of withdrawal (% with an account), 2011	..	51.7	19.7
Use of Account in the Past Year (% age 15+)			
Used an account to receive wages	5.4	7.3	3.2
Used an account to receive government transfers	2.0	3.8	1.0
Used a financial institution account to pay utility bills	1.6	2.8	0.9
Other Digital Payments in the Past Year (% age 15+)			
Used a debit card to make payments	0.7	8.7	2.1
Used a credit card to make payments	0.2	1.9	0.6
Used the Internet to pay bills or make purchases	2.9	2.4	1.2
Domestic Remittances in the Past Year (% age 15+)			
Sent remittances	20.7	28.7	18.3
Sent remittances via a financial institution (% senders)	4.4	31.0	15.4
Sent remittances via a mobile phone (% senders)	66.5	30.8	42.8
Sent remittances via a money transfer operator (% senders)	35.2	21.0	14.1
Received remittances	23.0	37.2	25.6
Received remittances via a financial institution (% recipients)	4.7	26.6	13.0
Received remittances via a mobile phone (% recipients)	55.1	27.6	33.8
Received remittances via a money transfer operator (% recipients)	54.3	22.1	14.8
Savings in the Past Year (% age 15+)			
Saved at a financial institution	2.8	15.9	9.9
Saved at a financial institution, 2011	..	14.3	11.5
Saved using a savings club or person outside the family	15.1	23.9	16.3
Saved any money	37.2	59.6	46.5
Saved for old age	2.5	9.8	8.3
Saved for a farm or business	15.2	22.7	16.7
Saved for education or school fees	14.6	22.9	16.6
Credit in the Past Year (% age 15+)			
Borrowed from a financial institution	2.0	6.3	8.6
Borrowed from a financial institution, 2011	..	4.8	11.7
Borrowed from family or friends	40.7	41.9	34.9
Borrowed from a private informal lender	9.3	4.7	6.5
Borrowed any money	57.0	54.5	52.5
Borrowed for a farm or business	13.9	12.8	12.2
Borrowed for education or school fees	10.8	12.3	10.9
Outstanding mortgage at a financial institution	2.4	5.2	4.1

South Africa

Sub-Saharan Africa		**Upper middle income**
Population, age 15+ (millions)	37.5	GNI per capita ($)	7,410

	Country data	Sub-Saharan Africa	Upper middle income
Account (% age 15+)			
All adults	70.3	34.2	70.5
Women	70.4	29.9	67.3
Adults belonging to the poorest 40%	57.8	24.6	62.7
Young adults (% ages 15–24)	53.5	25.9	58.1
Adults living in rural areas	70.0	29.2	68.8
Financial Institution Account (% age 15+)			
All adults	68.8	28.9	70.4
All adults, 2011	53.6	23.9	57.4
Mobile Account (% age 15+)			
All adults	14.4	11.5	0.7
Access to Financial Institution Account (% age 15+)			
Has debit card	54.9	17.9	45.9
Has debit card, 2011	45.3	15.0	38.5
ATM is the main mode of withdrawal (% with an account)	81.8	53.8	55.7
ATM is the main mode of withdrawal (% with an account), 2011	88.9	51.7	42.8
Use of Account in the Past Year (% age 15+)			
Used an account to receive wages	26.8	7.3	18.1
Used an account to receive government transfers	28.2	3.8	9.6
Used a financial institution account to pay utility bills	12.2	2.8	12.3
Other Digital Payments in the Past Year (% age 15+)			
Used a debit card to make payments	40.8	8.7	19.9
Used a credit card to make payments	10.8	1.9	14.4
Used the Internet to pay bills or make purchases	7.6	2.4	15.3
Domestic Remittances in the Past Year (% age 15+)			
Sent remittances	41.5	28.7	15.4
Sent remittances via a financial institution (% senders)	63.0	31.0	37.2
Sent remittances via a mobile phone (% senders)	17.6	30.8	8.8
Sent remittances via a money transfer operator (% senders)	56.6	21.0	19.7
Received remittances	54.2	37.2	17.8
Received remittances via a financial institution (% recipients)	54.9	26.6	29.8
Received remittances via a mobile phone (% recipients)	16.0	27.6	5.6
Received remittances via a money transfer operator (% recipients)	61.3	22.1	17.9
Savings in the Past Year (% age 15+)			
Saved at a financial institution	32.7	15.9	32.2
Saved at a financial institution, 2011	22.1	14.3	25.1
Saved using a savings club or person outside the family	30.6	23.9	4.9
Saved any money	66.4	59.6	62.7
Saved for old age	15.9	9.8	30.6
Saved for a farm or business	11.0	22.7	17.6
Saved for education or school fees	23.8	22.9	25.4
Credit in the Past Year (% age 15+)			
Borrowed from a financial institution	12.1	6.3	10.4
Borrowed from a financial institution, 2011	8.9	4.8	7.9
Borrowed from family or friends	71.2	41.9	24.0
Borrowed from a private informal lender	18.4	4.7	2.6
Borrowed any money	85.6	54.5	37.7
Borrowed for a farm or business	7.5	12.8	6.6
Borrowed for education or school fees	18.0	12.3	6.1
Outstanding mortgage at a financial institution	9.2	5.2	9.1

Spain

High income: OECD		High income
Population, age 15+ (millions)	**39.5**	GNI per capita ($) **29,940**

	Country data	High income: OECD
Account (% age 15+)		
All adults	97.6	94.0
Women	97.6	93.8
Adults belonging to the poorest 40%	96.6	90.6
Young adults (% ages 15–24)	84.7	84.1
Adults living in rural areas	97.7	93.8
Financial Institution Account (% age 15+)		
All adults	97.6	94.0
All adults, 2011	93.3	90.0
Mobile Account (% age 15+)		
All adults	..	..
Access to Financial Institution Account (% age 15+)		
Has debit card	82.6	79.7
Has debit card, 2011	62.2	61.9
ATM is the main mode of withdrawal (% with an account)	..	..
ATM is the main mode of withdrawal (% with an account), 2011	64.2	68.5
Use of Account in the Past Year (% age 15+)		
Used an account to receive wages	41.9	44.3
Used an account to receive government transfers	20.7	17.2
Used a financial institution account to pay utility bills	62.8	61.1
Other Digital Payments in the Past Year (% age 15+)		
Used a debit card to make payments	73.9	65.3
Used a credit card to make payments	45.0	46.7
Used the Internet to pay bills or make purchases	57.4	54.1
Domestic Remittances in the Past Year (% age 15+)		
Sent remittances	..	..
Sent remittances via a financial institution (% senders)	..	..
Sent remittances via a mobile phone (% senders)	..	..
Sent remittances via a money transfer operator (% senders)	..	..
Received remittances	..	..
Received remittances via a financial institution (% recipients)	..	..
Received remittances via a mobile phone (% recipients)	..	..
Received remittances via a money transfer operator (% recipients)	..	..
Savings in the Past Year (% age 15+)		
Saved at a financial institution	48.1	51.6
Saved at a financial institution, 2011	35.0	45.3
Saved using a savings club or person outside the family	..	..
Saved any money	67.2	70.8
Saved for old age	26.8	39.7
Saved for a farm or business	14.0	9.0
Saved for education or school fees	26.7	25.0
Credit in the Past Year (% age 15+)		
Borrowed from a financial institution	18.0	18.4
Borrowed from a financial institution, 2011	11.4	14.2
Borrowed from family or friends	22.0	14.9
Borrowed from a private informal lender	1.0	0.9
Borrowed any money	47.1	39.8
Borrowed for a farm or business	6.1	2.6
Borrowed for education or school fees	6.3	5.6
Outstanding mortgage at a financial institution	36.0	26.1

Sri Lanka

South Asia			Lower middle income

Population, age 15+ (millions)	**15.3**	GNI per capita ($)	**3,170**

	Country data	South Asia	Lower middle income
Account (% age 15+)			
All adults	82.7	46.4	42.7
Women	83.1	37.4	36.3
Adults belonging to the poorest 40%	79.8	38.1	33.2
Young adults (% ages 15-24)	85.2	36.7	34.7
Adults living in rural areas	83.4	43.5	40.0
Financial Institution Account (% age 15+)			
All adults	82.7	45.5	41.8
All adults, 2011	68.5	32.3	28.7
Mobile Account (% age 15+)			
All adults	0.1	2.6	2.5
Access to Financial Institution Account (% age 15+)			
Has debit card	24.9	18.0	21.2
Has debit card, 2011	10.0	7.2	10.1
ATM is the main mode of withdrawal (% with an account)	24.3	31.1	42.4
ATM is the main mode of withdrawal (% with an account), 2011	15.4	16.9	28.1
Use of Account in the Past Year (% age 15+)			
Used an account to receive wages	7.1	3.5	5.6
Used an account to receive government transfers	5.3	3.1	3.3
Used a financial institution account to pay utility bills	1.1	2.7	3.1
Other Digital Payments in the Past Year (% age 15+)			
Used a debit card to make payments	10.4	8.5	9.6
Used a credit card to make payments	2.8	2.6	2.8
Used the Internet to pay bills or make purchases	1.6	1.2	2.6
Domestic Remittances in the Past Year (% age 15+)			
Sent remittances	10.2	10.7	14.2
Sent remittances via a financial institution (% senders)	28.8	20.1	30.9
Sent remittances via a mobile phone (% senders)	0.0	7.7	7.7
Sent remittances via a money transfer operator (% senders)	3.5	13.7	18.3
Received remittances	16.2	12.2	17.8
Received remittances via a financial institution (% recipients)	30.2	15.8	26.0
Received remittances via a mobile phone (% recipients)	0.0	4.7	5.7
Received remittances via a money transfer operator (% recipients)	0.5	9.8	16.6
Savings in the Past Year (% age 15+)			
Saved at a financial institution	30.9	12.7	14.8
Saved at a financial institution, 2011	28.1	11.1	11.1
Saved using a savings club or person outside the family	10.4	8.8	12.4
Saved any money	45.2	36.2	45.6
Saved for old age	13.8	9.1	12.6
Saved for a farm or business	7.2	7.3	11.8
Saved for education or school fees	12.6	14.6	20.0
Credit in the Past Year (% age 15+)			
Borrowed from a financial institution	17.9	6.4	7.5
Borrowed from a financial institution, 2011	17.7	8.7	7.3
Borrowed from family or friends	9.0	31.4	33.1
Borrowed from a private informal lender	2.4	10.9	8.5
Borrowed any money	29.1	46.7	47.4
Borrowed for a farm or business	3.1	8.6	9.2
Borrowed for education or school fees	4.4	8.9	10.1
Outstanding mortgage at a financial institution	7.7	3.8	4.7

Sudan

Sub-Saharan Africa			Lower middle income
Population, age 15+ (millions)	**22.3**	GNI per capita ($)	**1,550**

	Country data	Sub-Saharan Africa	Lower middle income
Account (% age 15+)			
All adults	15.3	34.2	42.7
Women	10.0	29.9	36.3
Adults belonging to the poorest 40%	9.3	24.6	33.2
Young adults (% ages 15–24)	10.1	25.9	34.7
Adults living in rural areas	13.1	29.2	40.0
Financial Institution Account (% age 15+)			
All adults	15.3	28.9	41.8
All adults, 2011	6.9	23.9	28.7
Mobile Account (% age 15+)			
All adults	..	11.5	2.5
Access to Financial Institution Account (% age 15+)			
Has debit card	10.3	17.9	21.2
Has debit card, 2011	3.3	15.0	10.1
ATM is the main mode of withdrawal (% with an account)	61.4	53.8	42.4
ATM is the main mode of withdrawal (% with an account), 2011	..	51.7	28.1
Use of Account in the Past Year (% age 15+)			
Used an account to receive wages	3.0	7.3	5.6
Used an account to receive government transfers	0.5	3.8	3.3
Used a financial institution account to pay utility bills	0.5	2.8	3.1
Other Digital Payments in the Past Year (% age 15+)			
Used a debit card to make payments	8.3	8.7	9.6
Used a credit card to make payments	0.0	1.9	2.8
Used the Internet to pay bills or make purchases	1.0	2.4	2.6
Domestic Remittances in the Past Year (% age 15+)			
Sent remittances	20.2	28.7	14.2
Sent remittances via a financial institution (% senders)	26.8	31.0	30.9
Sent remittances via a mobile phone (% senders)	50.4	30.8	7.7
Sent remittances via a money transfer operator (% senders)	12.2	21.0	18.3
Received remittances	21.3	37.2	17.8
Received remittances via a financial institution (% recipients)	21.5	26.6	26.0
Received remittances via a mobile phone (% recipients)	48.8	27.6	5.7
Received remittances via a money transfer operator (% recipients)	17.2	22.1	16.6
Savings in the Past Year (% age 15+)			
Saved at a financial institution	7.5	15.9	14.8
Saved at a financial institution, 2011	3.4	14.3	11.1
Saved using a savings club or person outside the family	21.9	23.9	12.4
Saved any money	41.3	59.6	45.6
Saved for old age	2.4	9.8	12.6
Saved for a farm or business	13.0	22.7	11.8
Saved for education or school fees	15.0	22.9	20.0
Credit in the Past Year (% age 15+)			
Borrowed from a financial institution	4.2	6.3	7.5
Borrowed from a financial institution, 2011	1.8	4.8	7.3
Borrowed from family or friends	38.0	41.9	33.1
Borrowed from a private informal lender	1.6	4.7	8.5
Borrowed any money	45.5	54.5	47.4
Borrowed for a farm or business	6.7	12.8	9.2
Borrowed for education or school fees	10.2	12.3	10.1
Outstanding mortgage at a financial institution	2.4	5.2	4.7

Sweden

High income: OECD   High income

Population, age 15+ (millions)	**8.0**	GNI per capita ($) **61,710**

	Country data	High income: OECD
Account (% age 15+)		
All adults	99.7	94.0
Women	99.8	93.8
Adults belonging to the poorest 40%	99.3	90.6
Young adults (% ages 15–24)	98.6	84.1
Adults living in rural areas	99.7	93.8
Financial Institution Account (% age 15+)		
All adults	99.7	94.0
All adults, 2011	99.0	90.0
Mobile Account (% age 15+)		
All adults	..	..
Access to Financial Institution Account (% age 15+)		
Has debit card	97.6	79.7
Has debit card, 2011	95.5	61.9
ATM is the main mode of withdrawal (% with an account)	..	..
ATM is the main mode of withdrawal (% with an account), 2011	75.8	68.5
Use of Account in the Past Year (% age 15+)		
Used an account to receive wages	66.5	44.3
Used an account to receive government transfers	33.5	17.2
Used a financial institution account to pay utility bills	68.3	61.1
Other Digital Payments in the Past Year (% age 15+)		
Used a debit card to make payments	92.7	65.3
Used a credit card to make payments	35.7	46.7
Used the Internet to pay bills or make purchases	74.6	54.1
Domestic Remittances in the Past Year (% age 15+)		
Sent remittances	..	..
Sent remittances via a financial institution (% senders)	..	..
Sent remittances via a mobile phone (% senders)	..	..
Sent remittances via a money transfer operator (% senders)	..	..
Received remittances	..	..
Received remittances via a financial institution (% recipients)	..	..
Received remittances via a mobile phone (% recipients)	..	..
Received remittances via a money transfer operator (% recipients)	..	..
Savings in the Past Year (% age 15+)		
Saved at a financial institution	75.1	51.6
Saved at a financial institution, 2011	63.6	45.3
Saved using a savings club or person outside the family	..	..
Saved any money	84.5	70.8
Saved for old age	50.9	39.7
Saved for a farm or business	5.8	9.0
Saved for education or school fees	13.7	25.0
Credit in the Past Year (% age 15+)		
Borrowed from a financial institution	27.7	18.4
Borrowed from a financial institution, 2011	23.4	14.2
Borrowed from family or friends	17.2	14.9
Borrowed from a private informal lender	0.4	0.9
Borrowed any money	49.8	39.8
Borrowed for a farm or business	2.0	2.6
Borrowed for education or school fees	4.8	5.6
Outstanding mortgage at a financial institution	41.7	26.1

Switzerland

High income: OECD   **High income**

		Country data	High income: OECD
Population, age 15+ (millions)	6.9	GNI per capita ($)	90,680

	Country data	High income: OECD
Account (% age 15+)		
All adults	98.0	94.0
Women	96.7	93.8
Adults belonging to the poorest 40%	96.7	90.6
Young adults (% ages 15–24)	94.0	84.1
Adults living in rural areas	98.3	93.8
Financial Institution Account (% age 15+)		
All adults	98.0	94.0
All adults, 2011	..	90.0
Mobile Account (% age 15+)		
All adults	..	..
Access to Financial Institution Account (% age 15+)		
Has debit card	84.1	79.7
Has debit card, 2011	..	61.9
ATM is the main mode of withdrawal (% with an account)	..	..
ATM is the main mode of withdrawal (% with an account), 2011	..	68.5
Use of Account in the Past Year (% age 15+)		
Used an account to receive wages	57.3	44.3
Used an account to receive government transfers	14.0	17.2
Used a financial institution account to pay utility bills	59.2	61.1
Other Digital Payments in the Past Year (% age 15+)		
Used a debit card to make payments	74.1	65.3
Used a credit card to make payments	48.2	46.7
Used the Internet to pay bills or make purchases	53.5	54.1
Domestic Remittances in the Past Year (% age 15+)		
Sent remittances	..	..
Sent remittances via a financial institution (% senders)	..	..
Sent remittances via a mobile phone (% senders)	..	..
Sent remittances via a money transfer operator (% senders)	..	..
Received remittances	..	..
Received remittances via a financial institution (% recipients)	..	..
Received remittances via a mobile phone (% recipients)	..	..
Received remittances via a money transfer operator (% recipients)	..	..
Savings in the Past Year (% age 15+)		
Saved at a financial institution	55.4	51.6
Saved at a financial institution, 2011	..	45.3
Saved using a savings club or person outside the family	..	..
Saved any money	76.0	70.8
Saved for old age	47.1	39.7
Saved for a farm or business	5.3	9.0
Saved for education or school fees	20.2	25.0
Credit in the Past Year (% age 15+)		
Borrowed from a financial institution	8.4	18.4
Borrowed from a financial institution, 2011	..	14.2
Borrowed from family or friends	11.1	14.9
Borrowed from a private informal lender	0.6	0.9
Borrowed any money	26.2	39.8
Borrowed for a farm or business	1.1	2.6
Borrowed for education or school fees	2.7	5.6
Outstanding mortgage at a financial institution	33.6	26.1

Taiwan, China

		High income
Population, age 15+ (millions)	**19.9**	GNI per capita ($) **21,620**

	Country data	High income: OECD
Account (% age 15+)		
All adults	91.4	94.0
Women	90.5	93.8
Adults belonging to the poorest 40%	87.0	90.6
Young adults (% ages 15–24)	77.3	84.1
Adults living in rural areas	90.3	93.8
Financial Institution Account (% age 15+)		
All adults	91.4	94.0
All adults, 2011	87.3	90.0
Mobile Account (% age 15+)		
All adults	..	..
Access to Financial Institution Account (% age 15+)		
Has debit card	70.5	79.7
Has debit card, 2011	37.0	61.9
ATM is the main mode of withdrawal (% with an account)	..	..
ATM is the main mode of withdrawal (% with an account), 2011	67.8	68.5
Use of Account in the Past Year (% age 15+)		
Used an account to receive wages	34.5	44.3
Used an account to receive government transfers	8.0	17.2
Used a financial institution account to pay utility bills	37.6	61.1
Other Digital Payments in the Past Year (% age 15+)		
Used a debit card to make payments	45.5	65.3
Used a credit card to make payments	51.4	46.7
Used the Internet to pay bills or make purchases	36.0	54.1
Domestic Remittances in the Past Year (% age 15+)		
Sent remittances	..	..
Sent remittances via a financial institution (% senders)	..	..
Sent remittances via a mobile phone (% senders)	..	..
Sent remittances via a money transfer operator (% senders)	..	..
Received remittances	..	..
Received remittances via a financial institution (% recipients)	..	..
Received remittances via a mobile phone (% recipients)	..	..
Received remittances via a money transfer operator (% recipients)	..	..
Savings in the Past Year (% age 15+)		
Saved at a financial institution	39.3	51.6
Saved at a financial institution, 2011	45.7	45.3
Saved using a savings club or person outside the family	..	..
Saved any money	71.2	70.8
Saved for old age	43.3	39.7
Saved for a farm or business	18.9	9.0
Saved for education or school fees	35.1	25.0
Credit in the Past Year (% age 15+)		
Borrowed from a financial institution	13.9	18.4
Borrowed from a financial institution, 2011	9.6	14.2
Borrowed from family or friends	10.0	14.9
Borrowed from a private informal lender	0.3	0.9
Borrowed any money	28.8	39.8
Borrowed for a farm or business	2.1	2.6
Borrowed for education or school fees	6.2	5.6
Outstanding mortgage at a financial institution	19.6	26.1

Tajikistan

Europe & Central Asia   **Low income**

Population, age 15+ (millions)   **5.3**   GNI per capita ($)   **990**

	Country data	Europe & Central Asia	Low income
Account (% age 15+)			
All adults	11.5	51.4	27.5
Women	9.1	47.4	23.9
Adults belonging to the poorest 40%	4.3	44.2	19.4
Young adults (% ages 15–24)	4.5	35.6	20.2
Adults living in rural areas	9.3	45.7	24.8
Financial Institution Account (% age 15+)			
All adults	11.5	51.4	22.3
All adults, 2011	2.5	43.3	21.1
Mobile Account (% age 15+)			
All adults	0.0	0.3	10.0
Access to Financial Institution Account (% age 15+)			
Has debit card	4.2	36.9	6.6
Has debit card, 2011	1.8	36.4	6.3
ATM is the main mode of withdrawal (% with an account)	..	66.7	20.2
ATM is the main mode of withdrawal (% with an account), 2011	..	72.5	19.7
Use of Account in the Past Year (% age 15+)			
Used an account to receive wages	4.1	22.5	3.2
Used an account to receive government transfers	0.7	7.3	1.0
Used a financial institution account to pay utility bills	2.6	12.5	0.9
Other Digital Payments in the Past Year (% age 15+)			
Used a debit card to make payments	1.5	22.9	2.1
Used a credit card to make payments	0.6	14.9	0.6
Used the Internet to pay bills or make purchases	0.9	11.9	1.2
Domestic Remittances in the Past Year (% age 15+)			
Sent remittances	6.0	12.9	18.3
Sent remittances via a financial institution (% senders)	..	31.5	15.4
Sent remittances via a mobile phone (% senders)	..	2.5	42.8
Sent remittances via a money transfer operator (% senders)	..	11.8	14.1
Received remittances	14.9	15.5	25.6
Received remittances via a financial institution (% recipients)	18.4	22.1	13.0
Received remittances via a mobile phone (% recipients)	3.4	1.0	33.8
Received remittances via a money transfer operator (% recipients)	38.0	15.6	14.8
Savings in the Past Year (% age 15+)			
Saved at a financial institution	1.5	8.4	9.9
Saved at a financial institution, 2011	0.3	4.9	11.5
Saved using a savings club or person outside the family	3.5	6.6	16.3
Saved any money	31.3	38.5	46.5
Saved for old age	7.0	11.8	8.3
Saved for a farm or business	3.7	5.1	16.7
Saved for education or school fees	9.8	12.1	16.6
Credit in the Past Year (% age 15+)			
Borrowed from a financial institution	3.8	12.4	8.6
Borrowed from a financial institution, 2011	4.8	7.8	11.7
Borrowed from family or friends	12.2	23.6	34.9
Borrowed from a private informal lender	1.9	2.1	6.5
Borrowed any money	24.8	39.5	52.5
Borrowed for a farm or business	3.0	2.8	12.2
Borrowed for education or school fees	6.2	6.2	10.9
Outstanding mortgage at a financial institution	3.7	10.2	4.1

Tanzania

Population, age 15+ (millions)	**27.2**	GNI per capita ($)	**860**

	Country data	Sub-Saharan Africa	Low income
Account (% age 15+)			
All adults	39.8	34.2	27.5
Women	34.3	29.9	23.9
Adults belonging to the poorest 40%	24.0	24.6	19.4
Young adults (% ages 15–24)	31.9	25.9	20.2
Adults living in rural areas	33.2	29.2	24.8
Financial Institution Account (% age 15+)			
All adults	19.0	28.9	22.3
All adults, 2011	17.3	23.9	21.1
Mobile Account (% age 15+)			
All adults	32.4	11.5	10.0
Access to Financial Institution Account (% age 15+)			
Has debit card	11.5	17.9	6.6
Has debit card, 2011	12.0	15.0	6.3
ATM is the main mode of withdrawal (% with an account)	62.0	53.8	20.2
ATM is the main mode of withdrawal (% with an account), 2011	69.9	51.7	19.7
Use of Account in the Past Year (% age 15+)			
Used an account to receive wages	5.2	7.3	3.2
Used an account to receive government transfers	1.2	3.8	1.0
Used a financial institution account to pay utility bills	0.5	2.8	0.9
Other Digital Payments in the Past Year (% age 15+)			
Used a debit card to make payments	4.3	8.7	2.1
Used a credit card to make payments	0.4	1.9	0.6
Used the Internet to pay bills or make purchases	1.4	2.4	1.2
Domestic Remittances in the Past Year (% age 15+)			
Sent remittances	35.9	28.7	18.3
Sent remittances via a financial institution (% senders)	10.7	31.0	15.4
Sent remittances via a mobile phone (% senders)	71.5	30.8	42.8
Sent remittances via a money transfer operator (% senders)	10.4	21.0	14.1
Received remittances	47.1	37.2	25.6
Received remittances via a financial institution (% recipients)	10.1	26.6	13.0
Received remittances via a mobile phone (% recipients)	62.8	27.6	33.8
Received remittances via a money transfer operator (% recipients)	7.3	22.1	14.8
Savings in the Past Year (% age 15+)			
Saved at a financial institution	9.0	15.9	9.9
Saved at a financial institution, 2011	11.9	14.3	11.5
Saved using a savings club or person outside the family	13.1	23.9	16.3
Saved any money	59.2	59.6	46.5
Saved for old age	7.2	9.8	8.3
Saved for a farm or business	32.8	22.7	16.7
Saved for education or school fees	22.9	22.9	16.6
Credit in the Past Year (% age 15+)			
Borrowed from a financial institution	6.5	6.3	8.6
Borrowed from a financial institution, 2011	6.6	4.8	11.7
Borrowed from family or friends	39.9	41.9	34.9
Borrowed from a private informal lender	6.6	4.7	6.5
Borrowed any money	55.6	54.5	52.5
Borrowed for a farm or business	22.3	12.8	12.2
Borrowed for education or school fees	17.2	12.3	10.9
Outstanding mortgage at a financial institution	4.5	5.2	4.1

Thailand

Population, age 15+ (millions)	**54.8**	GNI per capita ($)	**5,340**

	Country data	East Asia & Pacific	Upper middle income
Account (% age 15+)			
All adults	78.1	69.0	70.5
Women	75.4	67.0	67.3
Adults belonging to the poorest 40%	72.0	60.9	62.7
Young adults (% ages 15–24)	70.6	60.7	58.1
Adults living in rural areas	78.2	64.5	68.8
Financial Institution Account (% age 15+)			
All adults	78.1	68.8	70.4
All adults, 2011	72.7	55.1	57.4
Mobile Account (% age 15+)			
All adults	1.3	0.4	0.7
Access to Financial Institution Account (% age 15+)			
Has debit card	54.8	42.9	45.9
Has debit card, 2011	43.1	34.7	38.5
ATM is the main mode of withdrawal (% with an account)	62.3	53.3	55.7
ATM is the main mode of withdrawal (% with an account), 2011	59.3	37.0	42.8
Use of Account in the Past Year (% age 15+)			
Used an account to receive wages	8.3	15.1	18.1
Used an account to receive government transfers	9.0	8.1	9.6
Used a financial institution account to pay utility bills	1.7	11.8	12.3
Other Digital Payments in the Past Year (% age 15+)			
Used a debit card to make payments	7.9	14.8	19.9
Used a credit card to make payments	3.7	10.8	14.4
Used the Internet to pay bills or make purchases	4.4	15.6	15.3
Domestic Remittances in the Past Year (% age 15+)			
Sent remittances	36.7	16.6	15.4
Sent remittances via a financial institution (% senders)	35.6	36.9	37.2
Sent remittances via a mobile phone (% senders)	2.0	8.7	8.8
Sent remittances via a money transfer operator (% senders)	25.3	18.5	19.7
Received remittances	46.4	20.6	17.8
Received remittances via a financial institution (% recipients)	28.6	29.0	29.8
Received remittances via a mobile phone (% recipients)	1.2	4.9	5.6
Received remittances via a money transfer operator (% recipients)	19.9	15.8	17.9
Savings in the Past Year (% age 15+)			
Saved at a financial institution	40.6	36.5	32.2
Saved at a financial institution, 2011	42.8	28.5	25.1
Saved using a savings club or person outside the family	8.4	6.0	4.9
Saved any money	80.5	71.0	62.7
Saved for old age	59.2	36.5	30.6
Saved for a farm or business	16.4	21.3	17.6
Saved for education or school fees	24.1	30.7	25.4
Credit in the Past Year (% age 15+)			
Borrowed from a financial institution	15.4	11.0	10.4
Borrowed from a financial institution, 2011	19.4	8.6	7.9
Borrowed from family or friends	31.1	28.3	24.0
Borrowed from a private informal lender	9.1	2.5	2.6
Borrowed any money	50.3	41.2	37.7
Borrowed for a farm or business	12.8	8.3	6.6
Borrowed for education or school fees	7.6	7.1	6.1
Outstanding mortgage at a financial institution	10.9	8.0	9.1

Togo

Population, age 15+ (millions)	4.0	GNI per capita ($)	530

	Country data	Sub-Saharan Africa	Low income
Account (% age 15+)			
All adults	18.3	34.2	27.5
Women	15.1	29.9	23.9
Adults belonging to the poorest 40%	11.6	24.6	19.4
Young adults (% ages 15–24)	12.3	25.9	20.2
Adults living in rural areas	14.3	29.2	24.8
Financial Institution Account (% age 15+)			
All adults	17.6	28.9	22.3
All adults, 2011	10.2	23.9	21.1
Mobile Account (% age 15+)			
All adults	1.4	11.5	10.0
Access to Financial Institution Account (% age 15+)			
Has debit card	2.3	17.9	6.6
Has debit card, 2011	1.2	15.0	6.3
ATM is the main mode of withdrawal (% with an account)	7.8	53.8	20.2
ATM is the main mode of withdrawal (% with an account), 2011	4.9	51.7	19.7
Use of Account in the Past Year (% age 15+)			
Used an account to receive wages	2.3	7.3	3.2
Used an account to receive government transfers	0.6	3.8	1.0
Used a financial institution account to pay utility bills	0.5	2.8	0.9
Other Digital Payments in the Past Year (% age 15+)			
Used a debit card to make payments	0.4	8.7	2.1
Used a credit card to make payments	0.3	1.9	0.6
Used the Internet to pay bills or make purchases	0.9	2.4	1.2
Domestic Remittances in the Past Year (% age 15+)			
Sent remittances	12.5	28.7	18.3
Sent remittances via a financial institution (% senders)	17.2	31.0	15.4
Sent remittances via a mobile phone (% senders)	7.6	30.8	42.8
Sent remittances via a money transfer operator (% senders)	14.9	21.0	14.1
Received remittances	19.6	37.2	25.6
Received remittances via a financial institution (% recipients)	15.6	26.6	13.0
Received remittances via a mobile phone (% recipients)	4.5	27.6	33.8
Received remittances via a money transfer operator (% recipients)	17.4	22.1	14.8
Savings in the Past Year (% age 15+)			
Saved at a financial institution	6.7	15.9	9.9
Saved at a financial institution, 2011	3.6	14.3	11.5
Saved using a savings club or person outside the family	18.7	23.9	16.3
Saved any money	37.5	59.6	46.5
Saved for old age	5.0	9.8	8.3
Saved for a farm or business	8.8	22.7	16.7
Saved for education or school fees	14.5	22.9	16.6
Credit in the Past Year (% age 15+)			
Borrowed from a financial institution	3.7	6.3	8.6
Borrowed from a financial institution, 2011	3.8	4.8	11.7
Borrowed from family or friends	17.1	41.9	34.9
Borrowed from a private informal lender	2.2	4.7	6.5
Borrowed any money	28.6	54.5	52.5
Borrowed for a farm or business	5.4	12.8	12.2
Borrowed for education or school fees	5.6	12.3	10.9
Outstanding mortgage at a financial institution	2.2	5.2	4.1

Tunisia

Upper middle income

Population, age 15+ (millions)	**8.4**	GNI per capita ($)	**4,200**

	Country data	Upper middle income
Account (% age 15+)		
All adults	27.4	70.5
Women	20.7	67.3
Adults belonging to the poorest 40%	17.2	62.7
Young adults (% ages 15–24)	18.8	58.1
Adults living in rural areas	22.4	68.8
Financial Institution Account (% age 15+)		
All adults	27.3	70.4
All adults, 2011	..	57.4
Mobile Account (% age 15+)		
All adults	0.6	0.7
Access to Financial Institution Account (% age 15+)		
Has debit card	12.3	45.9
Has debit card, 2011	..	38.5
ATM is the main mode of withdrawal (% with an account)	29.0	55.7
ATM is the main mode of withdrawal (% with an account), 2011	..	42.8
Use of Account in the Past Year (% age 15+)		
Used an account to receive wages	4.3	18.1
Used an account to receive government transfers	1.1	9.6
Used a financial institution account to pay utility bills	2.1	12.3
Other Digital Payments in the Past Year (% age 15+)		
Used a debit card to make payments	7.7	19.9
Used a credit card to make payments	6.3	14.4
Used the Internet to pay bills or make purchases	4.4	15.3
Domestic Remittances in the Past Year (% age 15+)		
Sent remittances	7.8	15.4
Sent remittances via a financial institution (% senders)	..	37.2
Sent remittances via a mobile phone (% senders)	..	8.8
Sent remittances via a money transfer operator (% senders)	..	19.7
Received remittances	14.7	17.8
Received remittances via a financial institution (% recipients)	27.3	29.8
Received remittances via a mobile phone (% recipients)	5.2	5.6
Received remittances via a money transfer operator (% recipients)	11.1	17.9
Savings in the Past Year (% age 15+)		
Saved at a financial institution	10.3	32.2
Saved at a financial institution, 2011	..	25.1
Saved using a savings club or person outside the family	1.3	4.9
Saved any money	38.0	62.7
Saved for old age	8.5	30.6
Saved for a farm or business	6.5	17.6
Saved for education or school fees	7.2	25.4
Credit in the Past Year (% age 15+)		
Borrowed from a financial institution	8.0	10.4
Borrowed from a financial institution, 2011	..	7.9
Borrowed from family or friends	16.1	24.0
Borrowed from a private informal lender	3.3	2.6
Borrowed any money	34.1	37.7
Borrowed for a farm or business	4.6	6.6
Borrowed for education or school fees	4.8	6.1
Outstanding mortgage at a financial institution	10.7	9.1

Turkey

Population, age 15+ (millions)	**55.7**	GNI per capita ($)	**10,970**

	Country data	Europe & Central Asia	Upper middle income
Account (% age 15+)			
All adults	56.7	51.4	70.5
Women	44.5	47.4	67.3
Adults belonging to the poorest 40%	50.9	44.2	62.7
Young adults (% ages 15–24)	41.6	35.6	58.1
Adults living in rural areas	54.1	45.7	68.8
Financial Institution Account (% age 15+)			
All adults	56.5	51.4	70.4
All adults, 2011	57.6	43.3	57.4
Mobile Account (% age 15+)			
All adults	0.8	0.3	0.7
Access to Financial Institution Account (% age 15+)			
Has debit card	43.3	36.9	45.9
Has debit card, 2011	56.6	36.4	38.5
ATM is the main mode of withdrawal (% with an account)	69.6	66.7	55.7
ATM is the main mode of withdrawal (% with an account), 2011	89.1	72.5	42.8
Use of Account in the Past Year (% age 15+)			
Used an account to receive wages	16.6	22.5	18.1
Used an account to receive government transfers	5.5	7.3	9.6
Used a financial institution account to pay utility bills	18.4	12.5	12.3
Other Digital Payments in the Past Year (% age 15+)			
Used a debit card to make payments	23.9	22.9	19.9
Used a credit card to make payments	29.1	14.9	14.4
Used the Internet to pay bills or make purchases	18.7	11.9	15.3
Domestic Remittances in the Past Year (% age 15+)			
Sent remittances	17.3	12.9	15.4
Sent remittances via a financial institution (% senders)	48.3	31.5	37.2
Sent remittances via a mobile phone (% senders)	3.1	2.5	8.8
Sent remittances via a money transfer operator (% senders)	4.6	11.8	19.7
Received remittances	21.8	15.5	17.8
Received remittances via a financial institution (% recipients)	24.1	22.1	29.8
Received remittances via a mobile phone (% recipients)	1.2	1.0	5.6
Received remittances via a money transfer operator (% recipients)	2.0	15.6	17.9
Savings in the Past Year (% age 15+)			
Saved at a financial institution	9.1	8.4	32.2
Saved at a financial institution, 2011	4.2	4.9	25.1
Saved using a savings club or person outside the family	11.6	6.6	4.9
Saved any money	41.1	38.5	62.7
Saved for old age	10.3	11.8	30.6
Saved for a farm or business	5.3	5.1	17.6
Saved for education or school fees	20.8	12.1	25.4
Credit in the Past Year (% age 15+)			
Borrowed from a financial institution	20.0	12.4	10.4
Borrowed from a financial institution, 2011	4.6	7.8	7.9
Borrowed from family or friends	29.0	23.6	24.0
Borrowed from a private informal lender	2.4	2.1	2.6
Borrowed any money	50.4	39.5	37.7
Borrowed for a farm or business	3.7	2.8	6.6
Borrowed for education or school fees	13.2	6.2	6.1
Outstanding mortgage at a financial institution	10.7	10.2	9.1

Turkmenistan

Europe & Central Asia			Upper middle income

Population, age 15+ (millions)	**3.7**	GNI per capita ($)	**6,880**

	Country data	Europe & Central Asia	Upper middle income
Account (% age 15+)			
All adults	1.8	51.4	70.5
Women	1.6	47.4	67.3
Adults belonging to the poorest 40%	1.2	44.2	62.7
Young adults (% ages 15-24)	0.6	35.6	58.1
Adults living in rural areas	0.7	45.7	68.8
Financial Institution Account (% age 15+)			
All adults	1.8	51.4	70.4
All adults, 2011	0.4	43.3	57.4
Mobile Account (% age 15+)			
All adults	..	0.3	0.7
Access to Financial Institution Account (% age 15+)			
Has debit card	1.2	36.9	45.9
Has debit card, 2011	0.3	36.4	38.5
ATM is the main mode of withdrawal (% with an account)	..	66.7	55.7
ATM is the main mode of withdrawal (% with an account), 2011	..	72.5	42.8
Use of Account in the Past Year (% age 15+)			
Used an account to receive wages	0.7	22.5	18.1
Used an account to receive government transfers	0.0	7.3	9.6
Used a financial institution account to pay utility bills	0.0	12.5	12.3
Other Digital Payments in the Past Year (% age 15+)			
Used a debit card to make payments	0.7	22.9	19.9
Used a credit card to make payments	0.0	14.9	14.4
Used the Internet to pay bills or make purchases	0.1	11.9	15.3
Domestic Remittances in the Past Year (% age 15+)			
Sent remittances	21.4	12.9	15.4
Sent remittances via a financial institution (% senders)	0.5	31.5	37.2
Sent remittances via a mobile phone (% senders)	0.0	2.5	8.8
Sent remittances via a money transfer operator (% senders)	1.6	11.8	19.7
Received remittances	25.8	15.5	17.8
Received remittances via a financial institution (% recipients)	0.8	22.1	29.8
Received remittances via a mobile phone (% recipients)	0.0	1.0	5.6
Received remittances via a money transfer operator (% recipients)	4.7	15.6	17.9
Savings in the Past Year (% age 15+)			
Saved at a financial institution	0.7	8.4	32.2
Saved at a financial institution, 2011	0.1	4.9	25.1
Saved using a savings club or person outside the family	2.5	6.6	4.9
Saved any money	57.1	38.5	62.7
Saved for old age	26.2	11.8	30.6
Saved for a farm or business	11.6	5.1	17.6
Saved for education or school fees	11.8	12.1	25.4
Credit in the Past Year (% age 15+)			
Borrowed from a financial institution	2.2	12.4	10.4
Borrowed from a financial institution, 2011	0.8	7.8	7.9
Borrowed from family or friends	32.7	23.6	24.0
Borrowed from a private informal lender	2.4	2.1	2.6
Borrowed any money	55.8	39.5	37.7
Borrowed for a farm or business	1.7	2.8	6.6
Borrowed for education or school fees	2.7	6.2	6.1
Outstanding mortgage at a financial institution	6.1	10.2	9.1

Uganda

Sub-Saharan Africa **Low income**

Population, age 15+ (millions)	19.4	GNI per capita ($)	600

	Country data	Sub-Saharan Africa	Low income
Account (% age 15+)			
All adults	44.4	34.2	27.5
Women	36.6	29.9	23.9
Adults belonging to the poorest 40%	27.2	24.6	19.4
Young adults (% ages 15–24)	35.0	25.9	20.2
Adults living in rural areas	45.7	29.2	24.8
Financial Institution Account (% age 15+)			
All adults	27.8	28.9	22.3
All adults, 2011	20.5	23.9	21.1
Mobile Account (% age 15+)			
All adults	35.1	11.5	10.0
Access to Financial Institution Account (% age 15+)			
Has debit card	17.8	17.9	6.6
Has debit card, 2011	10.3	6.3	6.3
ATM is the main mode of withdrawal (% with an account)	60.3	53.8	20.2
ATM is the main mode of withdrawal (% with an account), 2011	41.7	51.7	19.7
Use of Account in the Past Year (% age 15+)			
Used an account to receive wages	6.4	7.3	3.2
Used an account to receive government transfers	1.0	3.8	1.0
Used a financial institution account to pay utility bills	2.6	2.8	0.9
Other Digital Payments in the Past Year (% age 15+)			
Used a debit card to make payments	6.6	8.7	2.1
Used a credit card to make payments	0.9	1.9	0.6
Used the Internet to pay bills or make purchases	1.7	2.4	1.2
Domestic Remittances in the Past Year (% age 15+)			
Sent remittances	46.9	28.7	18.3
Sent remittances via a financial institution (% senders)	11.7	31.0	15.4
Sent remittances via a mobile phone (% senders)	69.4	30.8	42.8
Sent remittances via a money transfer operator (% senders)	3.6	21.0	14.1
Received remittances	56.5	37.2	25.6
Received remittances via a financial institution (% recipients)	12.7	26.6	13.0
Received remittances via a mobile phone (% recipients)	66.0	27.6	33.8
Received remittances via a money transfer operator (% recipients)	2.2	22.1	14.8
Savings in the Past Year (% age 15+)			
Saved at a financial institution	16.8	15.9	9.9
Saved at a financial institution, 2011	16.3	14.3	11.5
Saved using a savings club or person outside the family	36.7	23.9	16.3
Saved any money	75.2	59.6	46.5
Saved for old age	9.5	9.8	8.3
Saved for a farm or business	34.3	22.7	16.7
Saved for education or school fees	41.8	22.9	16.6
Credit in the Past Year (% age 15+)			
Borrowed from a financial institution	15.7	6.3	8.6
Borrowed from a financial institution, 2011	8.9	4.8	11.7
Borrowed from family or friends	69.4	41.9	34.9
Borrowed from a private informal lender	6.3	4.7	6.5
Borrowed any money	79.0	54.5	52.5
Borrowed for a farm or business	22.3	12.8	12.2
Borrowed for education or school fees	39.1	12.3	10.9
Outstanding mortgage at a financial institution	9.8	5.2	4.1

Ukraine

	Country data	Europe & Central Asia	Lower middle income
Lower middle income			

Population, age 15+ (millions)	**38.9**	GNI per capita ($)	**3,960**

	Country data	Europe & Central Asia	Lower middle income
Account (% age 15+)			
All adults	52.7	51.4	42.7
Women	51.7	47.4	36.3
Adults belonging to the poorest 40%	44.3	44.2	33.2
Young adults (% ages 15–24)	55.9	35.6	34.7
Adults living in rural areas	47.2	45.7	40.0
Financial Institution Account (% age 15+)			
All adults	52.7	51.4	41.8
All adults, 2011	41.3	43.3	28.7
Mobile Account (% age 15+)			
All adults	..	0.3	2.5
Access to Financial Institution Account (% age 15+)			
Has debit card	39.7	36.9	21.2
Has debit card, 2011	33.6	36.4	10.1
ATM is the main mode of withdrawal (% with an account)	83.1	66.7	42.4
ATM is the main mode of withdrawal (% with an account), 2011	75.2	72.5	28.1
Use of Account in the Past Year (% age 15+)			
Used an account to receive wages	30.0	22.5	5.6
Used an account to receive government transfers	12.6	7.3	3.3
Used a financial institution account to pay utility bills	5.6	12.5	3.1
Other Digital Payments in the Past Year (% age 15+)			
Used a debit card to make payments	27.1	22.9	9.6
Used a credit card to make payments	19.5	14.9	2.8
Used the Internet to pay bills or make purchases	13.3	11.9	2.6
Domestic Remittances in the Past Year (% age 15+)			
Sent remittances	10.5	12.9	14.2
Sent remittances via a financial institution (% senders)	29.0	31.5	30.9
Sent remittances via a mobile phone (% senders)	4.2	2.5	7.7
Sent remittances via a money transfer operator (% senders)	15.5	11.8	18.3
Received remittances	10.0	15.5	17.8
Received remittances via a financial institution (% recipients)	30.1	22.1	26.0
Received remittances via a mobile phone (% recipients)	2.9	1.0	5.7
Received remittances via a money transfer operator (% recipients)	21.0	15.6	16.6
Savings in the Past Year (% age 15+)			
Saved at a financial institution	7.8	8.4	14.8
Saved at a financial institution, 2011	5.4	4.9	11.1
Saved using a savings club or person outside the family	2.9	6.6	12.4
Saved any money	40.1	38.5	45.6
Saved for old age	14.4	11.8	12.6
Saved for a farm or business	3.1	5.1	11.8
Saved for education or school fees	7.7	12.1	20.0
Credit in the Past Year (% age 15+)			
Borrowed from a financial institution	8.3	12.4	7.5
Borrowed from a financial institution, 2011	8.1	7.8	7.3
Borrowed from family or friends	22.1	23.6	33.1
Borrowed from a private informal lender	2.3	2.1	8.5
Borrowed any money	35.7	39.5	47.4
Borrowed for a farm or business	2.5	2.8	9.2
Borrowed for education or school fees	2.9	6.2	10.1
Outstanding mortgage at a financial institution	10.3	10.2	4.7

United Arab Emirates

Population, age 15+ (millions)	7.9	GNI per capita ($)	38,360

	Country data	High income: OECD
Account (% age 15+)		
All adults	83.7	94.0
Women	67.7	93.8
Adults belonging to the poorest 40%	79.0	90.6
Young adults (% ages 15–24)	66.7	84.1
Adults living in rural areas	89.7	93.8
Financial Institution Account (% age 15+)		
All adults	83.2	94.0
All adults, 2011	59.7	90.0
Mobile Account (% age 15+)		
All adults	11.5	..
Access to Financial Institution Account (% age 15+)		
Has debit card	76.9	79.7
Has debit card, 2011	55.4	61.9
ATM is the main mode of withdrawal (% with an account)	..	..
ATM is the main mode of withdrawal (% with an account), 2011	86.2	68.5
Use of Account in the Past Year (% age 15+)		
Used an account to receive wages	41.8	44.3
Used an account to receive government transfers	3.1	17.2
Used a financial institution account to pay utility bills	21.3	61.1
Other Digital Payments in the Past Year (% age 15+)		
Used a debit card to make payments	59.3	65.3
Used a credit card to make payments	33.4	46.7
Used the Internet to pay bills or make purchases	33.6	54.1
Domestic Remittances in the Past Year (% age 15+)		
Sent remittances	..	..
Sent remittances via a financial institution (% senders)	..	..
Sent remittances via a mobile phone (% senders)	..	..
Sent remittances via a money transfer operator (% senders)	..	..
Received remittances	..	..
Received remittances via a financial institution (% recipients)	..	..
Received remittances via a mobile phone (% recipients)	..	..
Received remittances via a money transfer operator (% recipients)	..	..
Savings in the Past Year (% age 15+)		
Saved at a financial institution	32.1	51.6
Saved at a financial institution, 2011	19.2	45.3
Saved using a savings club or person outside the family	..	..
Saved any money	66.6	70.8
Saved for old age	24.5	39.7
Saved for a farm or business	18.6	9.0
Saved for education or school fees	29.8	25.0
Credit in the Past Year (% age 15+)		
Borrowed from a financial institution	15.4	18.4
Borrowed from a financial institution, 2011	10.8	14.2
Borrowed from family or friends	28.5	14.9
Borrowed from a private informal lender	5.9	0.9
Borrowed any money	50.1	39.8
Borrowed for a farm or business	6.1	2.6
Borrowed for education or school fees	9.9	5.6
Outstanding mortgage at a financial institution	16.4	26.1

United Kingdom

Population, age 15+ (millions)	**52.8**	GNI per capita ($) **41,680**

	Country data	High income: OECD
Account (% age 15+)		
All adults	98.9	94.0
Women	98.7	93.8
Adults belonging to the poorest 40%	98.3	90.6
Young adults (% ages 15–24)	90.8	84.1
Adults living in rural areas	99.4	93.8
Financial Institution Account (% age 15+)		
All adults	98.9	94.0
All adults, 2011	97.2	90.0
Mobile Account (% age 15+)		
All adults	..	..
Access to Financial Institution Account (% age 15+)		
Has debit card	96.4	79.7
Has debit card, 2011	87.6	61.9
ATM is the main mode of withdrawal (% with an account)	..	..
ATM is the main mode of withdrawal (% with an account), 2011	70.1	68.5
Use of Account in the Past Year (% age 15+)		
Used an account to receive wages	51.5	44.3
Used an account to receive government transfers	18.7	17.2
Used a financial institution account to pay utility bills	71.6	61.1
Other Digital Payments in the Past Year (% age 15+)		
Used a debit card to make payments	91.8	65.3
Used a credit card to make payments	55.3	46.7
Used the Internet to pay bills or make purchases	72.8	54.1
Domestic Remittances in the Past Year (% age 15+)		
Sent remittances	..	..
Sent remittances via a financial institution (% senders)	..	..
Sent remittances via a mobile phone (% senders)	..	..
Sent remittances via a money transfer operator (% senders)	..	..
Received remittances	..	..
Received remittances via a financial institution (% recipients)	..	..
Received remittances via a mobile phone (% recipients)	..	..
Received remittances via a money transfer operator (% recipients)	..	..
Savings in the Past Year (% age 15+)		
Saved at a financial institution	52.3	51.6
Saved at a financial institution, 2011	43.8	45.3
Saved using a savings club or person outside the family	..	..
Saved any money	71.3	70.8
Saved for old age	40.6	39.7
Saved for a farm or business	10.2	9.0
Saved for education or school fees	13.4	25.0
Credit in the Past Year (% age 15+)		
Borrowed from a financial institution	21.1	18.4
Borrowed from a financial institution, 2011	11.8	14.2
Borrowed from family or friends	12.6	14.9
Borrowed from a private informal lender	2.6	0.9
Borrowed any money	39.1	39.8
Borrowed for a farm or business	3.5	2.6
Borrowed for education or school fees	3.3	5.6
Outstanding mortgage at a financial institution	29.0	26.1

United States

High income: OECD   **High income**

Population, age 15+ (millions)	**254.3**	GNI per capita ($)	**53,470**

	Country data	High income: OECD
Account (% age 15+)		
All adults	93.6	94.0
Women	94.8	93.8
Adults belonging to the poorest 40%	87.1	90.6
Young adults (% ages 15–24)	87.6	84.1
Adults living in rural areas	93.2	93.8
Financial Institution Account (% age 15+)		
All adults	93.6	94.0
All adults, 2011	88.0	90.0
Mobile Account (% age 15+)		
All adults	..	..
Access to Financial Institution Account (% age 15+)		
Has debit card	76.2	79.7
Has debit card, 2011	71.8	61.9
ATM is the main mode of withdrawal (% with an account)	..	..
ATM is the main mode of withdrawal (% with an account), 2011	55.0	68.5
Use of Account in the Past Year (% age 15+)		
Used an account to receive wages	43.3	44.3
Used an account to receive government transfers	18.1	17.2
Used a financial institution account to pay utility bills	63.2	61.1
Other Digital Payments in the Past Year (% age 15+)		
Used a debit card to make payments	67.1	65.3
Used a credit card to make payments	57.1	46.7
Used the Internet to pay bills or make purchases	64.7	54.1
Domestic Remittances in the Past Year (% age 15+)		
Sent remittances	..	..
Sent remittances via a financial institution (% senders)	..	..
Sent remittances via a mobile phone (% senders)	..	..
Sent remittances via a money transfer operator (% senders)	..	..
Received remittances	..	..
Received remittances via a financial institution (% recipients)	..	..
Received remittances via a mobile phone (% recipients)	..	..
Received remittances via a money transfer operator (% recipients)	..	..
Savings in the Past Year (% age 15+)		
Saved at a financial institution	54.1	51.6
Saved at a financial institution, 2011	50.4	45.3
Saved using a savings club or person outside the family	..	..
Saved any money	75.6	70.8
Saved for old age	45.1	39.7
Saved for a farm or business	9.5	9.0
Saved for education or school fees	32.7	25.0
Credit in the Past Year (% age 15+)		
Borrowed from a financial institution	23.3	18.4
Borrowed from a financial institution, 2011	20.1	14.2
Borrowed from family or friends	19.8	14.9
Borrowed from a private informal lender	1.4	0.9
Borrowed any money	51.4	39.8
Borrowed for a farm or business	2.5	2.6
Borrowed for education or school fees	9.5	5.6
Outstanding mortgage at a financial institution	31.8	26.1

Uruguay

Population, age 15+ (millions)	**2.7**	GNI per capita ($)	**15,180**

	Country data	High income: OECD
Account (% age 15+)		
All adults	45.6	94.0
Women	41.3	93.8
Adults belonging to the poorest 40%	35.0	90.6
Young adults (% ages 15–24)	29.5	84.1
Adults living in rural areas	42.7	93.8
Financial Institution Account (% age 15+)		
All adults	45.4	94.0
All adults, 2011	23.5	90.0
Mobile Account (% age 15+)		
All adults	1.2	..
Access to Financial Institution Account (% age 15+)		
Has debit card	37.7	79.7
Has debit card, 2011	16.4	61.9
ATM is the main mode of withdrawal (% with an account)	84.9	..
ATM is the main mode of withdrawal (% with an account), 2011	66.3	68.5
Use of Account in the Past Year (% age 15+)		
Used an account to receive wages	16.3	44.3
Used an account to receive government transfers	6.0	17.2
Used a financial institution account to pay utility bills	6.3	61.1
Other Digital Payments in the Past Year (% age 15+)		
Used a debit card to make payments	22.2	65.3
Used a credit card to make payments	36.0	46.7
Used the Internet to pay bills or make purchases	13.4	54.1
Domestic Remittances in the Past Year (% age 15+)		
Sent remittances	17.0	..
Sent remittances via a financial institution (% senders)	15.2	..
Sent remittances via a mobile phone (% senders)	0.0	..
Sent remittances via a money transfer operator (% senders)	50.0	..
Received remittances	14.2	..
Received remittances via a financial institution (% recipients)	9.2	..
Received remittances via a mobile phone (% recipients)	5.2	..
Received remittances via a money transfer operator (% recipients)	43.7	..
Savings in the Past Year (% age 15+)		
Saved at a financial institution	12.5	51.6
Saved at a financial institution, 2011	5.7	45.3
Saved using a savings club or person outside the family	2.2	..
Saved any money	38.5	70.8
Saved for old age	8.5	39.7
Saved for a farm or business	6.0	9.0
Saved for education or school fees	9.4	25.0
Credit in the Past Year (% age 15+)		
Borrowed from a financial institution	21.0	18.4
Borrowed from a financial institution, 2011	14.8	14.2
Borrowed from family or friends	8.0	14.9
Borrowed from a private informal lender	0.9	0.9
Borrowed any money	39.4	39.8
Borrowed for a farm or business	2.8	2.6
Borrowed for education or school fees	3.2	5.6
Outstanding mortgage at a financial institution	14.7	26.1

Uzbekistan

Europe & Central Asia			**Lower middle income**
Population, age 15+ (millions)	**21.6**	GNI per capita ($)	**1,880**

	Country data	Europe & Central Asia	Lower middle income
Account (% age 15+)			
All adults	40.7	51.4	42.7
Women	39.3	47.4	36.3
Adults belonging to the poorest 40%	34.1	44.2	33.2
Young adults (% ages 15–24)	24.9	35.6	34.7
Adults living in rural areas	41.8	45.7	40.0
Financial Institution Account (% age 15+)			
All adults	40.7	51.4	41.8
All adults, 2011	22.5	43.3	28.7
Mobile Account (% age 15+)			
All adults	..	0.3	2.5
Access to Financial Institution Account (% age 15+)			
Has debit card	24.6	36.9	21.2
Has debit card, 2011	20.4	36.4	10.1
ATM is the main mode of withdrawal (% with an account)	4.6	66.7	42.4
ATM is the main mode of withdrawal (% with an account), 2011	14.9	72.5	28.1
Use of Account in the Past Year (% age 15+)			
Used an account to receive wages	17.8	22.5	5.6
Used an account to receive government transfers	5.1	7.3	3.3
Used a financial institution account to pay utility bills	30.0	12.5	3.1
Other Digital Payments in the Past Year (% age 15+)			
Used a debit card to make payments	23.1	22.9	9.6
Used a credit card to make payments	1.0	14.9	2.8
Used the Internet to pay bills or make purchases	0.6	11.9	2.6
Domestic Remittances in the Past Year (% age 15+)			
Sent remittances	5.2	12.9	14.2
Sent remittances via a financial institution (% senders)	..	31.5	30.9
Sent remittances via a mobile phone (% senders)	..	2.5	7.7
Sent remittances via a money transfer operator (% senders)	..	11.8	18.3
Received remittances	8.0	15.5	17.8
Received remittances via a financial institution (% recipients)	..	22.1	26.0
Received remittances via a mobile phone (% recipients)	..	1.0	5.7
Received remittances via a money transfer operator (% recipients)	..	15.6	16.6
Savings in the Past Year (% age 15+)			
Saved at a financial institution	1.8	8.4	14.8
Saved at a financial institution, 2011	0.8	4.9	11.1
Saved using a savings club or person outside the family	14.4	6.6	12.4
Saved any money	43.5	38.5	45.6
Saved for old age	9.1	11.8	12.6
Saved for a farm or business	7.5	5.1	11.8
Saved for education or school fees	11.5	12.1	20.0
Credit in the Past Year (% age 15+)			
Borrowed from a financial institution	1.3	12.4	7.5
Borrowed from a financial institution, 2011	1.5	7.8	7.3
Borrowed from family or friends	11.1	23.6	33.1
Borrowed from a private informal lender	1.5	2.1	8.5
Borrowed any money	16.6	39.5	47.4
Borrowed for a farm or business	1.1	2.8	9.2
Borrowed for education or school fees	2.0	6.2	10.1
Outstanding mortgage at a financial institution	1.2	10.2	4.7

Venezuela, RB

Latin America & Caribbean			Upper middle income

Population, age 15+ (millions)	**21.7**	GNI per capita ($)	**12,550**

	Country data	Latin America & the Carib.	Upper middle income
Account (% age 15+)			
All adults	57.0	51.4	70.5
Women	53.3	48.6	67.3
Adults belonging to the poorest 40%	48.0	41.2	62.7
Young adults (% ages 15–24)	27.6	37.4	58.1
Adults living in rural areas	52.4	46.0	68.8
Financial Institution Account (% age 15+)			
All adults	56.9	51.1	70.4
All adults, 2011	44.1	39.3	57.4
Mobile Account (% age 15+)			
All adults	3.0	1.7	0.7
Access to Financial Institution Account (% age 15+)			
Has debit card	49.6	40.4	45.9
Has debit card, 2011	35.1	28.9	38.5
ATM is the main mode of withdrawal (% with an account)	78.9	71.1	55.7
ATM is the main mode of withdrawal (% with an account), 2011	63.6	57.0	42.8
Use of Account in the Past Year (% age 15+)			
Used an account to receive wages	16.1	18.0	18.1
Used an account to receive government transfers	2.0	9.0	9.6
Used a financial institution account to pay utility bills	10.3	6.3	12.3
Other Digital Payments in the Past Year (% age 15+)			
Used a debit card to make payments	46.1	27.7	19.9
Used a credit card to make payments	19.2	18.0	14.4
Used the Internet to pay bills or make purchases	9.9	6.9	15.3
Domestic Remittances in the Past Year (% age 15+)			
Sent remittances	7.3	9.5	15.4
Sent remittances via a financial institution (% senders)	..	..	37.2
Sent remittances via a mobile phone (% senders)	..	..	8.8
Sent remittances via a money transfer operator (% senders)	..	..	19.7
Received remittances	10.1	11.3	17.8
Received remittances via a financial institution (% recipients)	34.8	34.2	29.8
Received remittances via a mobile phone (% recipients)	5.0	4.3	5.6
Received remittances via a money transfer operator (% recipients)	19.7	28.4	17.9
Savings in the Past Year (% age 15+)			
Saved at a financial institution	22.8	13.5	32.2
Saved at a financial institution, 2011	13.6	9.6	25.1
Saved using a savings club or person outside the family	10.5	7.9	4.9
Saved any money	47.2	40.6	62.7
Saved for old age	15.7	10.6	30.6
Saved for a farm or business	10.5	10.6	17.6
Saved for education or school fees	20.4	17.2	25.4
Credit in the Past Year (% age 15+)			
Borrowed from a financial institution	2.0	11.3	10.4
Borrowed from a financial institution, 2011	1.7	7.9	7.9
Borrowed from family or friends	15.7	13.5	24.0
Borrowed from a private informal lender	4.1	4.7	2.6
Borrowed any money	26.0	32.7	37.7
Borrowed for a farm or business	3.1	6.1	6.6
Borrowed for education or school fees	7.6	8.3	6.1
Outstanding mortgage at a financial institution	5.7	9.6	9.1

Vietnam

Lower middle income

Population, age 15+ (millions)	**69.3**	GNI per capita ($)	**1,740**

	Country data	East Asia & Pacific	Lower middle income
Account (% age 15+)			
All adults	31.0	69.0	42.7
Women	32.0	67.0	36.3
Adults belonging to the poorest 40%	18.9	60.9	33.2
Young adults (% ages 15–24)	37.4	60.7	34.7
Adults living in rural areas	27.0	64.5	40.0
Financial Institution Account (% age 15+)			
All adults	30.9	68.8	41.8
All adults, 2011	21.4	55.1	28.7
Mobile Account (% age 15+)			
All adults	0.5	0.4	2.5
Access to Financial Institution Account (% age 15+)			
Has debit card	26.5	42.9	21.2
Has debit card, 2011	14.6	34.7	10.1
ATM is the main mode of withdrawal (% with an account)	73.4	53.3	42.4
ATM is the main mode of withdrawal (% with an account), 2011	50.8	37.0	28.1
Use of Account in the Past Year (% age 15+)			
Used an account to receive wages	7.8	15.1	5.6
Used an account to receive government transfers	1.6	8.1	3.3
Used a financial institution account to pay utility bills	0.5	11.8	3.1
Other Digital Payments in the Past Year (% age 15+)			
Used a debit card to make payments	3.1	14.8	9.6
Used a credit card to make payments	1.2	10.8	2.8
Used the Internet to pay bills or make purchases	9.1	15.6	2.6
Domestic Remittances in the Past Year (% age 15+)			
Sent remittances	15.1	16.6	14.2
Sent remittances via a financial institution (% senders)	42.1	36.9	30.9
Sent remittances via a mobile phone (% senders)	0.7	8.7	7.7
Sent remittances via a money transfer operator (% senders)	13.6	18.5	18.3
Received remittances	17.3	20.6	17.8
Received remittances via a financial institution (% recipients)	39.0	29.0	26.0
Received remittances via a mobile phone (% recipients)	0.7	4.9	5.7
Received remittances via a money transfer operator (% recipients)	18.1	15.8	16.6
Savings in the Past Year (% age 15+)			
Saved at a financial institution	14.6	36.5	14.8
Saved at a financial institution, 2011	7.7	28.5	11.1
Saved using a savings club or person outside the family	11.6	6.0	12.4
Saved any money	63.3	71.0	45.6
Saved for old age	22.9	36.5	12.6
Saved for a farm or business	12.6	21.3	11.8
Saved for education or school fees	34.2	30.7	20.0
Credit in the Past Year (% age 15+)			
Borrowed from a financial institution	18.4	11.0	7.5
Borrowed from a financial institution, 2011	16.2	8.6	7.3
Borrowed from family or friends	29.9	28.3	33.1
Borrowed from a private informal lender	1.8	2.5	8.5
Borrowed any money	46.8	41.2	47.4
Borrowed for a farm or business	7.1	8.3	9.2
Borrowed for education or school fees	10.2	7.1	10.1
Outstanding mortgage at a financial institution	6.6	8.0	4.7

West Bank and Gaza

Middle East			**Lower middle income**
Population, age 15+ (millions)	**2.5**	GNI per capita ($)	**3,070**

	Country data	Middle East	Lower middle income
Account (% age 15+)			
All adults	24.2	14.2	42.7
Women	21.2	9.2	36.3
Adults belonging to the poorest 40%	16.0	7.3	33.2
Young adults (% ages 15–24)	10.6	7.6	34.7
Adults living in rural areas	15.2	10.7	40.0
Financial Institution Account (% age 15+)			
All adults	24.2	14.0	41.8
All adults, 2011	19.4	10.9	28.7
Mobile Account (% age 15+)			
All adults	..	0.7	2.5
Access to Financial Institution Account (% age 15+)			
Has debit card	10.6	8.5	21.2
Has debit card, 2011	10.7	5.5	10.1
ATM is the main mode of withdrawal (% with an account)	32.2	44.9	42.4
ATM is the main mode of withdrawal (% with an account), 2011	41.0	42.4	28.1
Use of Account in the Past Year (% age 15+)			
Used an account to receive wages	6.6	3.3	5.6
Used an account to receive government transfers	2.4	0.9	3.3
Used a financial institution account to pay utility bills	3.0	0.2	3.1
Other Digital Payments in the Past Year (% age 15+)			
Used a debit card to make payments	3.3	3.3	9.6
Used a credit card to make payments	1.0	1.5	2.8
Used the Internet to pay bills or make purchases	1.6	2.1	2.6
Domestic Remittances in the Past Year (% age 15+)			
Sent remittances	4.6	9.3	14.2
Sent remittances via a financial institution (% senders)	..	..	30.9
Sent remittances via a mobile phone (% senders)	..	..	7.7
Sent remittances via a money transfer operator (% senders)	..	..	18.3
Received remittances	8.2	11.3	17.8
Received remittances via a financial institution (% recipients)	..	9.8	26.0
Received remittances via a mobile phone (% recipients)	..	0.2	5.7
Received remittances via a money transfer operator (% recipients)	..	15.6	16.6
Savings in the Past Year (% age 15+)			
Saved at a financial institution	5.1	4.0	14.8
Saved at a financial institution, 2011	5.5	2.7	11.1
Saved using a savings club or person outside the family	7.2	11.5	12.4
Saved any money	22.9	30.5	45.6
Saved for old age	3.8	5.0	12.6
Saved for a farm or business	3.2	5.1	11.8
Saved for education or school fees	7.4	9.1	20.0
Credit in the Past Year (% age 15+)			
Borrowed from a financial institution	4.2	5.6	7.5
Borrowed from a financial institution, 2011	4.1	4.4	7.3
Borrowed from family or friends	25.7	30.7	33.1
Borrowed from a private informal lender	8.5	7.9	8.5
Borrowed any money	38.9	45.7	47.4
Borrowed for a farm or business	2.4	4.2	9.2
Borrowed for education or school fees	5.9	8.2	10.1
Outstanding mortgage at a financial institution	4.7	6.2	4.7

Yemen, Rep.

Middle East			**Lower middle income**
Population, age 15+ (millions)	**14.6**	GNI per capita ($)	**1,330**

	Country data	Middle East	Lower middle income
Account (% age 15+)			
All adults	6.4	14.2	42.7
Women	1.7	9.2	36.3
Adults belonging to the poorest 40%	4.0	7.3	33.2
Young adults (% ages 15–24)	1.7	7.6	34.7
Adults living in rural areas	5.9	10.7	40.0
Financial Institution Account (% age 15+)			
All adults	6.4	14.0	41.8
All adults, 2011	3.7	10.9	28.7
Mobile Account (% age 15+)			
All adults	..	0.7	2.5
Access to Financial Institution Account (% age 15+)			
Has debit card	1.9	8.5	21.2
Has debit card, 2011	2.2	5.5	10.1
ATM is the main mode of withdrawal (% with an account)	..	44.9	42.4
ATM is the main mode of withdrawal (% with an account), 2011	..	42.4	28.1
Use of Account in the Past Year (% age 15+)			
Used an account to receive wages	2.3	3.3	5.6
Used an account to receive government transfers	1.7	0.9	3.3
Used a financial institution account to pay utility bills	0.0	0.2	3.1
Other Digital Payments in the Past Year (% age 15+)			
Used a debit card to make payments	0.1	3.3	9.6
Used a credit card to make payments	0.2	1.5	2.8
Used the Internet to pay bills or make purchases	0.7	2.1	2.6
Domestic Remittances in the Past Year (% age 15+)			
Sent remittances	8.1	9.3	14.2
Sent remittances via a financial institution (% senders)	..	..	30.9
Sent remittances via a mobile phone (% senders)	..	..	7.7
Sent remittances via a money transfer operator (% senders)	..	..	18.3
Received remittances	18.3	11.3	17.8
Received remittances via a financial institution (% recipients)	2.0	9.8	26.0
Received remittances via a mobile phone (% recipients)	0.0	0.2	5.7
Received remittances via a money transfer operator (% recipients)	31.1	15.6	16.6
Savings in the Past Year (% age 15+)			
Saved at a financial institution	0.9	4.0	14.8
Saved at a financial institution, 2011	1.1	2.7	11.1
Saved using a savings club or person outside the family	4.5	11.5	12.4
Saved any money	20.6	30.5	45.6
Saved for old age	1.4	5.0	12.6
Saved for a farm or business	3.6	5.1	11.8
Saved for education or school fees	3.7	9.1	20.0
Credit in the Past Year (% age 15+)			
Borrowed from a financial institution	0.4	5.6	7.5
Borrowed from a financial institution, 2011	0.9	4.4	7.3
Borrowed from family or friends	51.7	30.7	33.1
Borrowed from a private informal lender	15.0	7.9	8.5
Borrowed any money	65.9	45.7	47.4
Borrowed for a farm or business	3.9	4.2	9.2
Borrowed for education or school fees	3.7	8.2	10.1
Outstanding mortgage at a financial institution	0.6	6.2	4.7

Zambia

Lower middle income

	Country data	Sub-Saharan Africa	Lower middle income
Population, age 15+ (millions)	**7.8**	GNI per capita ($)	**1,810**

	Country data	Sub-Saharan Africa	Lower middle income
Account (% age 15+)			
All adults	35.6	34.2	42.7
Women	33.2	29.9	36.3
Adults belonging to the poorest 40%	20.9	24.6	33.2
Young adults (% ages 15–24)	28.8	25.9	34.7
Adults living in rural areas	34.8	29.2	40.0
Financial Institution Account (% age 15+)			
All adults	31.3	28.9	41.8
All adults, 2011	21.4	23.9	28.7
Mobile Account (% age 15+)			
All adults	12.1	11.5	2.5
Access to Financial Institution Account (% age 15+)			
Has debit card	18.7	17.9	21.2
Has debit card, 2011	15.7	15.0	10.1
ATM is the main mode of withdrawal (% with an account)	68.5	53.8	42.4
ATM is the main mode of withdrawal (% with an account), 2011	74.4	51.7	28.1
Use of Account in the Past Year (% age 15+)			
Used an account to receive wages	7.6	7.3	5.6
Used an account to receive government transfers	1.5	3.8	3.3
Used a financial institution account to pay utility bills	1.9	2.8	3.1
Other Digital Payments in the Past Year (% age 15+)			
Used a debit card to make payments	7.3	8.7	9.6
Used a credit card to make payments	1.1	1.9	2.8
Used the Internet to pay bills or make purchases	2.5	2.4	2.6
Domestic Remittances in the Past Year (% age 15+)			
Sent remittances	29.0	28.7	14.2
Sent remittances via a financial institution (% senders)	27.0	31.0	30.9
Sent remittances via a mobile phone (% senders)	22.6	30.8	7.7
Sent remittances via a money transfer operator (% senders)	51.7	21.0	18.3
Received remittances	35.8	37.2	17.8
Received remittances via a financial institution (% recipients)	26.7	26.6	26.0
Received remittances via a mobile phone (% recipients)	20.2	27.6	5.7
Received remittances via a money transfer operator (% recipients)	53.2	22.1	16.6
Savings in the Past Year (% age 15+)			
Saved at a financial institution	16.8	15.9	14.8
Saved at a financial institution, 2011	11.8	14.3	11.1
Saved using a savings club or person outside the family	24.3	23.9	12.4
Saved any money	70.1	59.6	45.6
Saved for old age	3.8	9.8	12.6
Saved for a farm or business	30.7	22.7	11.8
Saved for education or school fees	32.3	22.9	20.0
Credit in the Past Year (% age 15+)			
Borrowed from a financial institution	4.8	6.3	7.5
Borrowed from a financial institution, 2011	6.1	4.8	7.3
Borrowed from family or friends	53.3	41.9	33.1
Borrowed from a private informal lender	6.3	4.7	8.5
Borrowed any money	68.0	54.5	47.4
Borrowed for a farm or business	20.8	12.8	9.2
Borrowed for education or school fees	20.8	12.3	10.1
Outstanding mortgage at a financial institution	4.6	5.2	4.7

Zimbabwe

Sub-Saharan Africa   **Low income**

	Population, age 15+ (millions)	**8.6**	GNI per capita ($)	**860**

	Country data	Sub-Saharan Africa	Low income
Account (% age 15+)			
All adults	32.4	34.2	27.5
Women	29.0	29.9	23.9
Adults belonging to the poorest 40%	17.2	24.6	19.4
Young adults (% ages 15–24)	24.0	25.9	20.2
Adults living in rural areas	26.8	29.2	24.8
Financial Institution Account (% age 15+)			
All adults	17.2	28.9	22.3
All adults, 2011	39.7	23.9	21.1
Mobile Account (% age 15+)			
All adults	21.6	11.5	10.0
Access to Financial Institution Account (% age 15+)			
Has debit card	13.8	17.9	6.6
Has debit card, 2011	28.3	15.0	6.3
ATM is the main mode of withdrawal (% with an account)	46.8	53.8	20.2
ATM is the main mode of withdrawal (% with an account), 2011	28.3	51.7	19.7
Use of Account in the Past Year (% age 15+)			
Used an account to receive wages	5.5	7.3	3.2
Used an account to receive government transfers	0.6	3.8	1.0
Used a financial institution account to pay utility bills	0.5	2.8	0.9
Other Digital Payments in the Past Year (% age 15+)			
Used a debit card to make payments	7.7	8.7	2.1
Used a credit card to make payments	1.0	1.9	0.6
Used the Internet to pay bills or make purchases	1.5	2.4	1.2
Domestic Remittances in the Past Year (% age 15+)			
Sent remittances	31.2	28.7	18.3
Sent remittances via a financial institution (% senders)	10.6	31.0	15.4
Sent remittances via a mobile phone (% senders)	71.8	30.8	42.8
Sent remittances via a money transfer operator (% senders)	8.1	21.0	14.1
Received remittances	42.8	37.2	25.6
Received remittances via a financial institution (% recipients)	9.5	26.6	13.0
Received remittances via a mobile phone (% recipients)	67.6	27.6	33.8
Received remittances via a money transfer operator (% recipients)	9.8	22.1	14.8
Savings in the Past Year (% age 15+)			
Saved at a financial institution	5.2	15.9	9.9
Saved at a financial institution, 2011	17.3	14.3	11.5
Saved using a savings club or person outside the family	17.8	23.9	16.3
Saved any money	52.0	59.6	46.5
Saved for old age	3.2	9.8	8.3
Saved for a farm or business	13.6	22.7	16.7
Saved for education or school fees	22.8	22.9	16.6
Credit in the Past Year (% age 15+)			
Borrowed from a financial institution	4.0	6.3	8.6
Borrowed from a financial institution, 2011	4.9	4.8	11.7
Borrowed from family or friends	55.4	41.9	34.9
Borrowed from a private informal lender	4.8	4.7	6.5
Borrowed any money	62.4	54.5	52.5
Borrowed for a farm or business	7.3	12.8	12.2
Borrowed for education or school fees	22.1	12.3	10.9
Outstanding mortgage at a financial institution	1.5	5.2	4.1

Glossary

Account denotes the percentage of respondents who report having an account (by themselves or together with someone else) at a bank or another type of financial institution (see definition for "financial institution account") or report personally using a mobile money service in the past 12 months (see definition for "mobile account").

ATM is the main mode of withdrawal denotes, among respondents reporting having an account at a bank or another type of financial institution, the percentage who used an automated teller machine (ATM) as their usual mode of access to get cash from their account.

ATM is the main mode of withdrawal, 2011 denotes, among respondents in 2011 who reported having an account at a bank or another type of financial institution, the percentage who used an automated teller machine (ATM) as their usual mode of access to get cash from their account. (Demirguc-Kunt and Klapper 2013)

Borrowed any money denotes the percentage of respondents who report borrowing any money for any reason and from any source in the past 12 months.

Borrowed for a farm or business denotes the percentage of respondents who report borrowing any money in the past 12 months to start, operate, or expand a farm or business.

Borrowed for education or school fees denotes the percentage of respondents who report borrowing any money in the past 12 months for education or school fees.

Borrowed from a financial institution denotes the percentage of respondents who report borrowing any money in the past 12 months from a bank or another type of financial institution.

Borrowed from a financial institution, 2011 denotes the percentage of respondents in 2011 who reported borrowing any money in the past 12 months from a bank or another type of financial institution. (Demirguc-Kunt and Klapper 2013)

Borrowed from a private informal lender denotes the percentage of respondents who report borrowing any money in the past 12 months from a private informal lender.

Borrowed from family or friends denotes the percentage of respondents who report borrowing any money in the past 12 months from family, relatives, or friends.

Financial institution account denotes the percentage of respondents who report having an account (by themselves or together with someone else) at a bank or another type of financial institution.[1]

Financial institution account, 2011 denotes the percentage of respondents in 2011 who reported having an account (by themselves or together with

Glossary

someone else) at a bank or another type of financial institution. (Demirguc-Kunt and Klapper 2013)

GNI per capita ($) is gross national income (GNI) converted to U.S. dollars using the World Bank Atlas method divided by total midyear population. GNI is the sum of value added by all resident producers plus any product taxes (less subsidies) not included in the valuation of output plus net receipts of primary income (compensation of employees and property income) from abroad. GNI, calculated in national currency, is usually converted to U.S. dollars at official exchange rates for comparisons across economies. The World Bank Atlas method is used to smooth fluctuations in prices and exchange rates. It averages the exchange rate for a given year and the two preceding years, adjusted for differences in rates of inflation between the country and the euro area, Japan, the United Kingdom, and the United States. Data are for 2013. Aggregates include economies not shown in this book. (World Bank)

Has debit card denotes the percentage of respondents who report having a debit card.

Has debit card, 2011 denotes the percentage of respondents in 2011 who reported having a debit card. (Demirguc-Kunt and Klapper 2013)

Mobile account denotes the percentage of respondents who report personally using a mobile money service in the past 12 months.[2]

Outstanding mortgage at a financial institution denotes the percentage of respondents who report having an outstanding loan from a bank or another type of financial institution to purchase a home, apartment, or land.

Population, age 15+ is the midyear estimate of all adult residents age 15 and above regardless of legal status or citizenship, except for refugees not permanently settled in the country of asylum who are generally considered part of the population of their country of origin. Data are for 2013. Aggregates include economies not shown in this book. (Eurostat, United Nations Population Division, and World Bank)

Received remittances denotes the percentage of respondents who report personally receiving any money in the past 12 months from a relative or friend living in a different area of their country. This includes any money received in person.

Received remittances via a financial institution denotes, among respondents reporting personally receiving any money in the past 12 months from a relative or friend living in a different area of their country, the percentage who received it through a bank or another type of financial institution. This includes at a branch, at an automated teller machine (ATM), or through direct deposit into an account, using their own account or someone else's.

Received remittances via a mobile phone denotes, among respondents reporting personally receiving any money in the past 12 months from a relative or friend living in a different area of their country, the percentage who received it through a mobile phone, using their own account or someone else's.

Received remittances via a money transfer operator denotes, among respondents reporting personally receiving any money in the past 12 months from a relative or friend living in a different area of their country, the percentage who received it through a money transfer operator.

Saved any money denotes the percentage of respondents who report personally saving or setting aside any money for any reason and using any mode of saving in the past 12 months.

Saved at a financial institution denotes the percentage of respondents who report saving or setting aside any money in the past 12 months by using an account at a bank or another type of financial institution.

Saved at a financial institution, 2011 denotes the percentage of respondents in 2011 who reported saving or setting aside any money in the past 12 months by using an account at a bank or another type of financial institution. (Demirguc-Kunt and Klapper 2013)

Saved for a farm or business denotes the percentage of respondents who report saving or setting aside any money in the past 12 months to start, operate, or expand a farm or business.

Saved for education or school fees denotes the percentage of respondents who report saving or setting aside any money in the past 12 months for education or school fees.

Saved for old age denotes the percentage of respondents who report saving or setting aside any money in the past 12 months for old age.

Saved using a savings club or person outside the family denotes the percentage of respondents who report saving or setting aside any money in the past 12 months by using an informal savings club or a person outside the family.

Sent remittances denotes the percentage of respondents who report personally giving or sending any of their money in the past 12 months to a relative or friend living in a different area of their country. This can be money they brought themselves or sent in some other way.

Sent remittances via a financial institution denotes, among respondents reporting personally giving or sending any of their money in the past 12 months to a relative or friend living in a different area of their country, the percentage who sent it through a bank or another type of financial institution. This includes at a branch, at an ATM, or through direct deposit into an account, using their own account or someone else's.

Sent remittances via a mobile phone denotes, among respondents reporting personally giving or sending any of their money in the past 12 months to a relative or friend living in a different area of their country, the percentage who sent it through a mobile phone, using their own account or someone else's.

Sent remittances via a money transfer operator denotes, among respondents reporting personally giving or sending any of their money in the past 12

Glossary

months to a relative or friend living in a different area of their country, the percentage who sent it through a money transfer operator.

Used a credit card to make payments denotes the percentage of respondents who report using their own credit card in the past 12 months.

Used a debit card to make payments denotes the percentage of respondents who report using their own debit card to directly make a purchase in the past 12 months.

Used a financial institution account to pay utility bills denotes the percentage of respondents who report making a payment in the past 12 months for water, electricity, or trash collection directly from an account at a bank or another type of financial institution.

Used an account to receive government transfers denotes the percentage of respondents who report receiving any financial support from the government directly into an account at a bank or another type of financial institution, into a card, or through a mobile phone in the past 12 months.

Used an account to receive wages denotes the percentage of respondents who report receiving a salary or wages directly into an account at a bank or another type of financial institution, into a card, or through a mobile phone in the past 12 months.

Used the Internet to pay bills or make purchases denotes the percentage of respondents who report paying bills or making purchases online using the Internet in the past 12 months.

Notes

For indicators for which the source of data is other than the 2014 edition of the Global Findex database, the source is given at the end of the definition. The source for 2011 Global Findex data is Asli Demirguc-Kunt and Leora Klapper, "Measuring Financial Inclusion: Explaining Variation in Use of Financial Services across and within Countries," *Brookings Papers on Economic Activity* (Spring 2013).

1. *Financial institution account* includes respondents who report having an account at a bank or at another type of financial institution, such as a credit union, microfinance institution, cooperative, or the post office (if applicable), or having a debit card in their own name. It includes an additional 2.77 percent of respondents who report receiving wages, government transfers, or payments for agricultural products into an account at a financial institution in the past 12 months; paying utility bills or school fees from an account at a financial institution in the past 12 months; or receiving wages or government transfers into a card in the past 12 months.

2. *Mobile account* includes respondents who report personally using GSM Association (GSMA) Mobile Money for the Unbanked (MMU) services in the past 12 months to pay bills or to send or receive money. It includes an additional 0.28 percent of respondents who report receiving wages, government transfers, or payments for agricultural products through a mobile phone in the past 12 months.

Reference

The reference citation for the 2014 Global Findex data provided in this book is as follows:

Demirguc-Kunt, Asli, Leora Klapper, Dorothe Singer, and Peter Van Oudheusden. 2015. "The Global Findex Database 2014: Measuring Financial Inclusion around the World." Policy Research Working Paper 7255, World Bank, Washington, DC.